14th Conference on Computational Natural Language Learning 2010

(CoNLL 2010: Shared Task)

Co-Located with ACL 2010

Uppsala, Sweden
15-16 July 2010

ISBN: 978-1-61738-814-9

Printed from e-media with permission by:

Curran Associates, Inc.
57 Morehouse Lane
Red Hook, NY 12571

Some format issues inherent in the e-media version may also appear in this print version.

Printed by Curran Associates, Inc. (2010)

For permission requests, please contact the Association for Computational Linguistics at the address below.

Association for Computational Linguistics
209 N. Eighth Street
Stroudsburg, Pennsylvania 18360

Phone: 1-570-476-8006
Fax: 1-570-476-0860

acl@aclweb.org

Additional copies of this publication are available from:

Curran Associates, Inc.
57 Morehouse Lane
Red Hook, NY 12571 USA
Phone: 845-758-0400
Fax: 845-758-2634
Email: curran@proceedings.com
Web: www.proceedings.com

Introduction

This volume consists of the descriptions of the CoNLL-2010 Shared Task and the participating systems. The shared task was dedicated to the detection of uncertainty cues and their linguistic scope in natural language text. The motivation behind this task was that distinguishing factual and uncertain information in texts is of essential importance in information extraction.

The shared task addressed the detection of uncertainty in two domains. As uncertainty detection is extremely important for biomedical information extraction and most existing approaches have targeted such applications, participants were asked to develop systems for hedge detection in biological scientific articles. Uncertainty detection is also important, e.g. in encyclopedias, where the goal is to collect reliable world knowledge about real-world concepts and topics.

Two uncertainty detection tasks, sentence classification and in-sentence hedge scope detection were given to the participants. A total of 23 teams participated in the shared task. Those who participated in both tasks were invited to write a paper up to 8 pages. The page limit for those who participated only in the first task was 6 pages.

Although several approaches were introduced by the participants of the shared task and we believe that the ideas described in this proceedings can serve as an excellent starting point for the development of an uncertainty detector, there is a lot of room for improving such systems. The manually annotated datasets and software tools developed for the shared task may act as benchmarks for these future experiments and they are freely available at `http://www.inf.u-szeged.hu/rgai/conll2010st`.

Szeged, May, 2010

Richárd Farkas, for the Shared Task organizers

Organizers:

Richárd Farkas, Human Language Technology Group, University of Szeged
Veronika Vincze, Human Language Technology Group, University of Szeged
György Szarvas, Ubiquitous Knowledge Processing Lab, Technische Universität Darmstadt
György Móra, Human Language Technology Group, University of Szeged
János Csirik, Research Group on Artificial Intelligence, Hungarian Academy of Sciences

Reviewers:

Ekaterina Buyko, University of Jena
Kevin B. Cohen, University of Colorado
Hercules Dalianis, Stockholm University
Maria Georgescul, University of Geneva
Filip Ginter, University of Turku
Henk Harkema, University of Pittsburgh
Shen Jianping, Harbin Institute of Technology
Yoshinobu Kano, University of Tokyo
Jin-Dong Kim, Database Center for Life Science, Japan
Ruy Milidiú, Pontifícia Universidade Católica do Rio de Janeiro
Roser Morante, University of Antwerp
Lilja Øvrelid, University of Potsdam
Arzucan Özgür, University of Michigan
Vinodkumar Prabhakaran, Columbia University
Sampo Pyysalo, University of Tokyo
Marek Rei, Cambridge University
Buzhou Tang, Harbin Institute of Technology
Erik Tjong Kim Sang, University of Groningen
Katrin Tomanek, University of Jena
Erik Velldal, University of Oslo
Andreas Vlachos, University of Wisconsin-Madison
Xinglong Wang, University of Manchester
Torsten Zesch, Technische Universität Darmstadt
Qi Zhao, Harbin Institute of Technology
HuiWei Zhou, Dalian University of Technology

Table of Contents

Conference Program

Thursday, July 15, 2010

Shared Task Session 1: Overview and Oral Presentations (16:00-17:30)

16:00–16:20 *The CoNLL-2010 Shared Task: Learning to Detect Hedges and their Scope in Natural Language Text*
Richárd Farkas, Veronika Vincze, György Móra, János Csirik and György Szarvas

16:20–16:30 *A Cascade Method for Detecting Hedges and their Scope in Natural Language Text*
Buzhou Tang, Xiaolong Wang, Xuan Wang, Bo Yuan and Shixi Fan

16:30–16:40 *Detecting Speculative Language Using Syntactic Dependencies and Logistic Regression*
Andreas Vlachos and Mark Craven

16:40–16:50 *A Hedgehop over a Max-Margin Framework Using Hedge Cues*
Maria Georgescul

16:50–17:00 *Detecting Hedge Cues and their Scopes with Average Perceptron*
Feng Ji, Xipeng Qiu and Xuanjing Huang

17:00–17:10 *Memory-Based Resolution of In-Sentence Scopes of Hedge Cues*
Roser Morante, Vincent Van Asch and Walter Daelemans

17:10–17:20 *Resolving Speculation: MaxEnt Cue Classification and Dependency-Based Scope Rules*
Erik Velldal, Lilja Øvrelid and Stephan Oepen

17:20–17:30 *Combining Manual Rules and Supervised Learning for Hedge Cue and Scope Detection*
Marek Rei and Ted Briscoe

Shared Task Discussion Panel (17:30-18:00)

Friday, July 16, 2010

Shared Task Session 2: Poster Session (11:00-12:30)

(Systems for both Task1 and Task2)

Friday, July 16, 2010 (continued)

(Systems for Task1)

A Lucene and Maximum Entropy Model Based Hedge Detection System
Lin Chen and Barbara Di Eugenio

HedgeHunter: A System for Hedge Detection and Uncertainty Classification
David Clausen

Exploiting CCG Structures with Tree Kernels for Speculation Detection
Liliana Mamani Sánchez, Baoli Li and Carl Vogel

Uncertainty Learning Using SVMs and CRFs
Vinodkumar Prabhakaran

Features for Detecting Hedge Cues
Nobuyuki Shimizu and Hiroshi Nakagawa

A Simple Ensemble Method for Hedge Identification
Ferenc Szidarovszky, Illés Solt and Domonkos Tikk

A Baseline Approach for Detecting Sentences Containing Uncertainty
Erik Tjong Kim Sang

Hedge Classification with Syntactic Dependency Features Based on an Ensemble Classifier
Yi Zheng, Qifeng Dai, Qiming Luo and Enhong Chen

The CoNLL-2010 Shared Task: Learning to Detect Hedges and their Scope in Natural Language Text

Richárd Farkas[1,2], **Veronika Vincze**[1], **György Móra**[1], **János Csirik**[1,2], **György Szarvas**[3]
[1] University of Szeged, Department of Informatics
[2] Hungarian Academy of Sciences, Research Group on Artificial Intelligence
[3] Technische Universität Darmstadt, Ubiquitous Knowledge Processing Lab
{rfarkas,vinczev,gymora,csirik}@inf.u-szeged.hu,
szarvas@tk.informatik.tu-darmstadt.de

Abstract

The CoNLL-2010 Shared Task was dedicated to the detection of uncertainty cues and their linguistic scope in natural language texts. The motivation behind this task was that distinguishing factual and uncertain information in texts is of essential importance in information extraction. This paper provides a general overview of the shared task, including the annotation protocols of the training and evaluation datasets, the exact task definitions, the evaluation metrics employed and the overall results. The paper concludes with an analysis of the prominent approaches and an overview of the systems submitted to the shared task.

1 Introduction

Every year since 1999, the Conference on Computational Natural Language Learning (CoNLL) provides a competitive shared task for the Computational Linguistics community. After a five-year period of multi-language semantic role labeling and syntactic dependency parsing tasks, a new task was introduced in 2010, namely the detection of uncertainty and its linguistic scope in natural language sentences.

In natural language processing (NLP) – and in particular, in information extraction (IE) – many applications seek to extract factual information from text. In order to distinguish facts from unreliable or uncertain information, linguistic devices such as hedges (indicating that authors do not or cannot back up their opinions/statements with facts) have to be identified. Applications should handle detected speculative parts in a different manner. A typical example is protein-protein interaction extraction from biological texts, where the aim is to mine text evidence for biological entities that are in a particular relation with each other. Here, while an uncertain relation might be of some interest for an end-user as well, such information must not be confused with factual textual evidence (reliable information).

Uncertainty detection has two levels. Automatic hedge detectors might attempt to identify sentences which contain uncertain information and handle whole sentences in a different manner or they might attempt to recognize in-sentence spans which are speculative. In-sentence uncertainty detection is a more complicated task compared to the sentence-level one, but it has benefits for NLP applications as there may be spans containing useful factual information in a sentence that otherwise contains uncertain parts. For example, in the following sentence the subordinated clause starting with *although* contains factual information while uncertain information is included in the main clause and the embedded question.

> Although IL-1 has been reported to contribute to Th17 differentiation in mouse and man, it remains to be determined {**whether** therapeutic targeting of IL-1 will substantially affect IL-17 in RA}.

Both tasks were addressed in the CoNLL-2010 Shared Task, in order to provide uniform manually annotated benchmark datasets for both and to compare their difficulties and state-of-the-art solutions for them. The uncertainty detection problem consists of two stages. First, keywords/cues indicating uncertainty should be recognized then either a sentence-level decision is made or the linguistic scope of the cue words has to be identified. The latter task falls within the scope of semantic analysis of sentences exploiting syntactic patterns, as hedge spans can usually be determined on the basis of syntactic patterns dependent on the keyword.

Proceedings of the Fourteenth Conference on Computational Natural Language Learning: Shared Task, pages 1–12,
Uppsala, Sweden, 15-16 July 2010.

2 Related Work

The term *hedging* was originally introduced by Lakoff (1972). However, hedge detection has received considerable interest just recently in the NLP community. Light et al. (2004) used a handcrafted list of hedge cues to identify speculative sentences in MEDLINE abstracts and several biomedical NLP applications incorporate rules for identifying the certainty of extracted information (Friedman et al., 1994; Chapman et al., 2007; Aramaki et al., 2009; Conway et al., 2009).

The most recent approaches to uncertainty detection exploit machine learning models that utilize manually labeled corpora. Medlock and Briscoe (2007) used single words as input features in order to classify sentences from biological articles (FlyBase) as speculative or non-speculative based on semi-automatically collected training examples. Szarvas (2008) extended the methodology of Medlock and Briscoe (2007) to use n-gram features and a semi-supervised selection of the keyword features. Kilicoglu and Bergler (2008) proposed a linguistically motivated approach based on syntactic information to semi-automatically refine a list of hedge cues. Ganter and Strube (2009) proposed an approach for the automatic detection of sentences containing uncertainty based on Wikipedia weasel tags and syntactic patterns.

The BioScope corpus (Vincze et al., 2008) is manually annotated with negation and speculation cues and their linguistic scope. It consists of clinical free-texts, biological texts from full papers and scientific abstracts. Using BioScope for training and evaluation, Morante and Daelemans (2009) developed a scope detector following a supervised sequence labeling approach while Özgür and Radev (2009) developed a rule-based system that exploits syntactic patterns.

Several related works have also been published within the framework of The BioNLP'09 Shared Task on Event Extraction (Kim et al., 2009), where a separate subtask was dedicated to predicting whether the recognized biological events are under negation or speculation, based on the GENIA event corpus annotations (Kilicoglu and Bergler, 2009; Van Landeghem et al., 2009).

3 Uncertainty Annotation Guidelines

The shared task addressed the detection of uncertainty in two domains. As uncertainty detection is extremely important for biomedical information extraction and most existing approaches have targeted such applications, participants were asked to develop systems for hedge detection in biological scientific articles. Uncertainty detection is also important, e.g. in encyclopedias, where the goal is to collect reliable world knowledge about real-world concepts and topics. For example, Wikipedia explicitly declares that statements reflecting author opinions or those not backed up by facts (e.g. references) should be avoided (see 3.2 for details). Thus, the community-edited encyclopedia, Wikipedia became one of the subjects of the shared task as well.

3.1 Hedges in Biological Scientific Articles

In the biomedical domain, sentences were manually annotated for both hedge cues and their linguistic scope. Hedging is typically expressed by using specific linguistic devices (which we refer to as cues in this article) that modify the meaning or reflect the author's attitude towards the content of the text. Typical hedge cues fall into the following categories:

- auxiliaries: *may, might, can, would, should, could*, etc.
- verbs of hedging or verbs with speculative content: *suggest, question, presume, suspect, indicate, suppose, seem, appear, favor*, etc.
- adjectives or adverbs: *probable, likely, possible, unsure*, etc.
- conjunctions: *or, and/or, either . . . or*, etc.

However, there are some cases where a hedge is expressed via a phrase rather than a single word. Complex keywords are phrases that express uncertainty together, but not on their own (either the semantic interpretation or the hedging strength of its subcomponents are significantly different from those of the whole phrase). An instance of a complex keyword can be seen in the following sentence:

> Mild bladder wall thickening {**raises the question of** cystitis}.

The expression *raises the question of* may be substituted by *suggests* and neither the verb *raises* nor the noun *question* convey speculative meaning on their own. However, the whole phrase is speculative therefore it is marked as a hedge cue.

During the annotation process, a min-max strategy for the marking of keywords (min) and their scope (max) was followed. On the one hand, when marking the keywords, the minimal unit that expresses hedging and determines the actual strength of hedging was marked as a keyword. On the other hand, when marking the scopes of speculative keywords, the scope was extended to the largest syntactic unit possible. That is, all constituents that fell within the uncertain interpretation were included in the scope. Our motivation here was that in this way, if we simply disregard the marked text span, the rest of the sentence can usually be used for extracting factual information (if there is any). For instance, in the example above, we can be sure that the symptom *mild bladder wall thickening* is exhibited by the patient but a diagnosis of *cystitis* would be questionable.

The scope of a speculative element can be determined on the basis of syntax. The scopes of the BioScope corpus are regarded as consecutive text spans and their annotation was based on constituency grammar. The scope of verbs, auxiliaries, adjectives and adverbs usually starts right with the keyword. In the case of verbal elements, i.e. verbs and auxiliaries, it ends at the end of the clause or sentence, thus all complements and adjuncts are included. The scope of attributive adjectives generally extends to the following noun phrase, whereas the scope of predicative adjectives includes the whole sentence. Sentential adverbs have a scope over the entire sentence, while the scope of other adverbs usually ends at the end of the clause or sentence. Conjunctions generally have a scope over the syntactic unit whose members they coordinate. Some linguistic phenomena (e.g. passive voice or raising) can change scope boundaries in the sentence, thus they were given special attention during the annotation phase.

3.2 Wikipedia Weasels

The chief editors of Wikipedia have drawn the attention of the public to uncertainty issues they call weasel[1]. A word is considered to be a weasel word if it creates an impression that something important has been said, but what is really communicated is vague, misleading, evasive or ambiguous. Weasel words do not give a neutral account of facts, rather, they offer an opinion without any backup or source. The following sentence does not specify the source of information, it is just the vague term *some people* that refers to the holder of this opinion:

> **Some people** claim that this results in a better taste than that of other diet colas (most of which are sweetened with aspartame alone).

Statements with weasel words usually evoke questions such as *Who says that?*, *Whose opinion is this?* and *How many people think so?*.

Typical instances of weasels can be grouped in the following way (we offer some examples as well):

- Adjectives and adverbs
  - elements referring to uncertainty: *probable, likely, possible, unsure, often, possibly, allegedly, apparently, perhaps*, etc.
  - elements denoting generalization: *widely, traditionally, generally, broadly-accepted, widespread*, etc.
  - qualifiers and superlatives: *global, superior, excellent, immensely, legendary, best, (one of the) largest, most prominent*, etc.
  - elements expressing obviousness: *clearly, obviously, arguably*, etc.
- Auxiliaries
  - *may, might, would, should*, etc.
- Verbs
  - verbs with speculative content and their passive forms: *suggest, question, presume, suspect, indicate, suppose, seem, appear, favor*, etc.
  - passive forms with dummy subjects: *It is claimed that ... It has been mentioned ... It is known ...*
  - *there is / there are* constructions: *There is evidence/concern/indication that...*
- Numerically vague expressions / quantifiers
  - *certain, numerous, many, most, some, much, everyone, few, various, one group of*, etc. *Experts say ... Some people think ... More than 60% percent ...*

[1] http://en.wikipedia.org/wiki/Weasel_word

- Nouns
    - *speculation, proposal, consideration,* etc. *Rumour has it that ... Common sense insists that ...*

However, the use of the above words or grammatical devices does not necessarily entail their being a weasel cue since their use may be justifiable in their contexts.

As the main application goal of weasel detection is to highlight articles which should be improved (by reformulating or adding factual issues), we decided to annotate only weasel cues in Wikipedia articles, but we did not mark their scopes.

During the manual annotation process, the following cue marking principles were employed. Complex verb phrases were annotated as weasel cues since in some cases, both the passive construction and the verb itself are responsible for the weasel. In passive forms with dummy subjects and *there is / there are* constructions, the weasel cue included the grammatical subject (i.e. *it* and *there*) as well. As for numerically vague expressions, the noun phrase containing a quantifier was marked as a weasel cue. If there was no quantifier (in the case of a bare plural), the noun was annotated as a weasel cue. Comparatives and superlatives were annotated together with their article. Anaphoric pronouns referring to a weasel word were also annotated as weasel cues.

4 Task Definitions

Two uncertainty detection tasks (sentence classification and in-sentence hedge scope detection) in two domains (biological publications and Wikipedia articles) with three types of submissions (closed, cross and open) were given to the participants of the CoNLL-2010 Shared Task.

4.1 Detection of Uncertain Sentences

The aim of Task1 was to develop automatic procedures for identifying sentences in texts which contain unreliable or uncertain information. In particular, this task is a binary classification problem, i.e. factual and uncertain sentences have to be distinguished.

As training and evaluation data

- **Task1B**: biological abstracts and full articles (evaluation data contained only full articles) from the BioScope corpus and
- **Task1W**: paragraphs from Wikipedia possibly containing weasel information

were provided. The annotation of weasel/hedge cues was carried out on the phrase level, and sentences containing at least one cue were considered as uncertain, while sentences with no cues were considered as factual. The participating systems had to submit a binary classification (certain vs. uncertain) of the test sentences while marking cues in the submissions was voluntary (but participants were encouraged to do this).

4.2 In-sentence Hedge Scope Resolution

For Task2, in-sentence scope resolvers had to be developed. The training and evaluation data consisted of biological scientific texts, in which instances of speculative spans – that is, keywords and their linguistic scope – were annotated manually. Submissions to Task2 were expected to automatically annotate the cue phrases and the left and right boundaries of their scopes (exactly one scope must be assigned to a cue phrase).

4.3 Evaluation Metrics

The evaluation for Task1 was carried out at the sentence level, i.e. the cue annotations in the sentence were not taken into account. The $F_{\beta=1}$ measure (the harmonic mean of precision and recall) of the uncertain class was employed as the chief evaluation metric.

The Task2 systems were expected to mark cue- and corresponding scope begin/end tags linked together by using some unique IDs. A scope-level $F_{\beta=1}$ measure was used as the chief evaluation metric where true positives were scopes which exactly matched the gold standard cue phrases and gold standard scope boundaries assigned to the cue word. That is, correct scope boundaries with incorrect cue annotation and correct cue words with bad scope boundaries were both treated as errors.

This scope-level metric is very strict. For instance, the requirement of the precise match of the cue phrase is questionable as – from an application point of view – the goal is to find uncertain text spans and the evidence for this is not so important. However, the annotation of cues in datasets is essential for training scope detectors since locating the cues usually precedes the identification of their scope. Hence we decided to incorporate cue matches into the evaluation metric.

Another questionable issue is the strict boundary matching requirement. For example, including or excluding punctuations, citations or some bracketed expressions, like *(see Figure 1)* from a scope is not crucial for an otherwise accurate scope detector. On the other hand, the list of such ignorable phenomena is arguable, especially across domains. Thus, we considered the strict boundary matching to be a straightforward and unambiguous evaluation criterion. Minor issues like those mentioned above could be handled by simple post-processing rules. In conclusion we think that the uncertainty detection community may find more flexible evaluation criteria in the future but the strict scope-level metric is definitely a good starting point for evaluation.

4.4 Closed and Open Challenges

Participants were invited to submit results in different configurations, where systems were allowed to exploit different kinds of annotated resources. The three possible submission categories were:

- **Closed**, where only the labeled and unlabeled data provided for the shared task were allowed, separately for each domain (i.e. biomedical train data for biomedical test set and Wikipedia train data for Wikipedia test set). No further manually crafted resources of uncertainty information (i.e. lists, annotated data, etc.) could be used in any domain. On the other hand, tools exploiting the manual annotation of linguistic phenomena not related to uncertainty (such as POS taggers and parsers trained on labeled corpora) were allowed.

- **Cross**-domain was the same as the closed one but all data provided for the shared task were allowed for both domains (i.e. Wikipedia train data for the biomedical test set, the biomedical train data for Wikipedia test set or a union of Wikipedia and biomedical train data for both test sets).

- **Open**, where any data and/or any additional manually created information and resource (which may be related to uncertainty) were allowed for both domains.

The motivation behind the cross-domain and the open challenges was that in this way, we could assess whether adding extra (i.e. not domain-specific) information to the systems can contribute to the overall performance.

5 Datasets

Training and evaluation corpora were annotated manually for hedge/weasel cues and their scope by two independent linguist annotators. Any differences between the two annotations were later resolved by the chief annotator, who was also responsible for creating the annotation guidelines and training the two annotators. The datasets are freely available[2] for further benchmark experiments at `http://www.inf.u-szeged.hu/rgai/conll2010st`.

Since uncertainty cues play an important role in detecting sentences containing uncertainty, they are tagged in the Task1 datasets as well to enhance training and evaluation of systems.

5.1 Biological Publications

The biological training dataset consisted of the biological part of the BioScope corpus (Vincze et al., 2008), hence it included abstracts from the GENIA corpus, 5 full articles from the functional genomics literature (related to the fruit fly) and 4 articles from the open access BMC Bioinformatics website. The automatic segmentation of the documents was corrected manually and the sentences (14541 in number) were annotated manually for hedge cues and their scopes.

The evaluation dataset was based on 15 biomedical articles downloaded from the publicly available PubMedCentral database, including 5 random articles taken from the *BMC Bioinformatics* journal in October 2009, 5 random articles to which the *drosophila* MeSH term was assigned and 5 random articles having the MeSH terms *human, blood cells* and *transcription factor* (the same terms which were used to create the Genia corpus). These latter ten articles were also published in 2009. The aim of this article selection procedure was to have a theme that was close to the training corpus. The evaluation set contained 5003 sentences, out of which 790 were uncertain. These texts were manually annotated for hedge cues and their scope. To annotate the training and the evaluation datasets, the same annotation principles were applied.

[2]under the Creative Commons Attribute Share Alike license

For both Task1 and Task2, the same dataset was provided, the difference being that for Task1, only hedge cues and sentence-level uncertainty were given, however, for Task2, hedge cues and their scope were marked in the text.

5.2 Wikipedia Datasets

2186 paragraphs collected from Wikipedia archives were also offered as Task1 training data (11111 sentences containing 2484 uncertain ones). The evaluation dataset contained 2346 Wikipedia paragraphs with 9634 sentences, out of which 2234 were uncertain.

For the selection of the Wikipedia paragraphs used to construct the training and evaluation datasets, we exploited the weasel tags added by the editors of the encyclopedia (marking unsupported opinions or expressions of a non-neutral point of view). Each paragraph containing weasel tags (5874 different ones) was extracted from the history dump of English Wikipedia. First, 438 randomly selected paragraphs were manually annotated from this pool then the most frequent cue phrases were collected. Later on, two other sets of Wikipedia paragraphs were gathered on the basis of whether they contained such cue phrases or not. The aim of this sampling procedure was to provide large enough training and evaluation samples containing weasel words and also occurrences of typical weasel words in non-weasel contexts.

Each sentence was annotated manually for weasel cues. Sentences were treated as uncertain if they contained at least one weasel cue, i.e. the scope of weasel words was the entire sentence (which is supposed to be rewritten by Wikipedia editors).

5.3 Unlabeled Data

Unannotated but pre-processed full biological articles (150 articles from the publicly available PubMedCentral database) and 1 million paragraphs from Wikipedia were offered to the participants as well. These datasets did not contain any manual annotation for uncertainty, but their usage permitted data sampling from a large pool of in-domain texts without time-wasting pre-processing tasks (cleaning and sentence splitting).

5.4 Data Format

Both training and evaluation data were released in a custom XML format. For each task, a separate XML file was made available containing the whole document set for the given task. Evaluation datasets were available in the same format as training data without any sentence-level certainty, cue or scope annotations.

The XML format enabled us to provide more detailed information about the documents such as segment boundaries and types (e.g. section titles, figure captions) and it is the straightforward format to represent nested scopes. Nested scopes have overlapping text spans which may contain cues for multiple scopes (there were 1058 occurrences in the training and evaluation datasets together). The XML format utilizes id-references to determine the scope of a given cue. Nested constructions are rather complicated to represent in the standard IOB format, moreover, we did not want to enforce a uniform tokenization.

To support the processing of the data files, reader and writer software modules were developed and offered to the participants for the uCompare (Kano et al., 2009) framework. uCompare provides a universal interface (UIMA) and several text mining and natural language processing tools (tokenizers, POS taggers, syntactic parsers, etc.) for general and biological domains. In this way participants could configure and execute a flexible chain of analyzing tools even with a graphical UI.

6 Submissions and Results

Participants uploaded their results through the shared task website, and the official evaluation was performed centrally. After the evaluation period, the results were published for the participants on the Web. A total of 23 teams participated in the shared task. 22, 16 and 13 teams submitted output for Task1B, Task1W and Task2, respectively.

6.1 Results

Tables 1, 2 and 3 contain the results of the submitted systems for Task1 and Task2. The last name of the first author of the system description paper (published in these proceedings) is used here as a system name[3]. The last column contains the type of submission. The system of Kilicoglu and Bergler (2010) is the only open submission. They adapted their system introduced in Kilicoglu and Bergler (2008) to the datasets of the shared task.

Regarding cross submissions, Zhao et al. (2010) and Ji et al. (2010) managed to achieve a noticeable improvement by exploiting cross-domain

[3]Özgür did not publish a description of her system.

Name	P / R / F	type
Georgescul	72.0 / 51.7 / 60.2	C
Ji	62.7 / 55.3 / 58.7	X
Chen	68.0 / 49.7 / 57.4	C
Morante	80.6 / 44.5 / 57.3	C
Zhang	76.6 / 44.4 / 56.2	C
Zheng	76.3 / 43.6 / 55.5	C
Täckström	78.3 / 42.8 / 55.4	C
Mamani Sánchez	68.3 / 46.2 / 55.1	C
Tang	82.3 / 41.4 / 55.0	C
Kilicoglu	67.9 / 46.0 / 54.9	O
Tjong Kim Sang	74.0 / 43.0 / 54.4	C
Clausen	75.1 / 42.0 / 53.9	C
Özgür	59.4 / 47.9 / 53.1	C
Zhou	85.3 / 36.5 / 51.1	C
Li	88.4 / 31.9 / 46.9	C
Prabhakaran	88.0 / 28.4 / 43.0	C
Ji	94.2 / 6.6 / 12.3	C

Table 1: Task1 Wikipedia results (type ∈ {Closed(C), Cross(X), Open(O)}).

data. Zhao et al. (2010) extended the biological cue word dictionary of their system – using it as a feature for classification – by the frequent cues of the Wikipedia dataset, while Ji et al. (2010) used the union of the two datasets for training (they have reported an improvement from 47.0 to 58.7 on the Wikipedia evaluation set after a post-challenge bugfix).

Name	P / R / F	type
Morante	59.6 / 55.2 / 57.3	C
Rei	56.7 / 54.6 / 55.6	C
Velldal	56.7 / 54.0 / 55.3	C
Kilicoglu	62.5 / 49.5 / 55.2	O
Li	57.4 / 47.9 / 52.2	C
Zhou	45.6 / 43.9 / 44.7	O
Zhou	45.3 / 43.6 / 44.4	C
Zhang	46.0 / 42.9 / 44.4	C
Fernandes	46.0 / 38.0 / 41.6	C
Vlachos	41.2 / 35.9 / 38.4	C
Zhao	34.8 / 41.0 / 37.7	C
Tang	34.5 / 31.8 / 33.1	C
Ji	21.9 / 17.2 / 19.3	C
Täckström	2.3 / 2.0 / 2.1	C

Table 2: Task2 results (type ∈ {Closed(C), Open(O)}).

Each Task2 and Task1W system achieved a

Name	P / R / F	type
Tang	85.0 / 87.7 / 86.4	C
Zhou	86.5 / 85.1 / 85.8	C
Li	90.4 / 81.0 / 85.4	C
Velldal	85.5 / 84.9 / 85.2	C
Vlachos	85.5 / 84.9 / 85.2	C
Täckström	87.1 / 83.4 / 85.2	C
Shimizu	88.1 / 82.3 / 85.1	C
Zhao	83.4 / 84.8 / 84.1	X
Özgür	77.8 / 91.3 / 84.0	C
Rei	83.8 / 84.2 / 84.0	C
Zhang	82.6 / 84.7 / 83.6	C
Kilicoglu	92.1 / 74.9 / 82.6	O
Morante	80.5 / 83.3 / 81.9	X
Morante	81.1 / 82.3 / 81.7	C
Zheng	73.3 / 90.8 / 81.1	C
Tjong Kim Sang	74.3 / 87.1 / 80.2	C
Clausen	79.3 / 80.6 / 80.0	C
Szidarovszky	70.3 / 91.0 / 79.3	C
Georgescul	69.1 / 91.0 / 78.5	C
Zhao	71.0 / 86.6 / 78.0	C
Ji	79.4 / 76.3 / 77.9	C
Chen	74.9 / 79.1 / 76.9	C
Fernandes	70.1 / 71.1 / 70.6	C
Prabhakaran	67.5 / 19.5 / 30.3	X

Table 3: Task1 biological results (type ∈ {Closed(C), Cross(X), Open(O)}).

higher precision than recall. There may be two reasons for this. The systems may have applied only reliable patterns, or patterns occurring in the evaluation set may be imperfectly covered by the training datasets. The most intense participation was on Task1B. Here, participants applied various precision/recall trade-off strategies. For instance, Tang et al. (2010) achieved a balanced precision/recall configuration, while Li et al. (2010) achieved third place thanks to their superior precision.

Tables 4 and 5 show the cue-level performances, i.e. the F-measure of cue phrase matching where true positives were strict matches. Note that it was optional to submit cue annotations for Task1 (if participants submitted systems for both Task2 and Task1B with cue tagging, only the better score of the two was considered).

It is interesting to see that Morante et al. (2010) who obtained the best results on Task2 achieved a medium-ranked F-measure on the cue-level (e.g. their result on the cue-level is lower by 4% compared to Zhou et al. (2010), while on the scope-level the difference is 13% in the reverse direction), which indicates that the real strength of the system of Morante et al. (2010) is the accurate detection of scope boundaries.

Name	P / R / F
Tang	63.0 / 25.7 / 36.5
Li	76.1 / 21.6 / 33.7
Özgür	28.9 / 14.7 / 19.5
Morante	24.6 / 7.3 / 11.3

Table 4: Wikipedia cue-level results.

Name	P / R / F	type
Tang	81.7 / 81.0 / 81.3	C
Zhou	83.1 / 78.8 / 80.9	C
Li	87.4 / 73.4 / 79.8	C
Rei	81.4 / 77.4 / 79.3	C
Velldal	81.2 / 76.3 / 78.7	C
Zhang	82.1 / 75.3 / 78.5	C
Ji	78.7 / 76.2 / 77.4	C
Morante	78.8 / 74.7 / 76.7	C
Kilicoglu	86.5 / 67.7 / 76.0	O
Vlachos	82.0 / 70.6 / 75.9	C
Zhao	76.7 / 73.9 / 75.3	X
Fernandes	79.2 / 64.7 / 71.2	C
Zhao	63.7 / 74.1 / 68.5	C
Täckström	66.9 / 58.6 / 62.5	C
Özgür	49.1 / 57.8 / 53.1	C

Table 5: Biological cue-level results (type $\in$ {Closed(C), Cross(X), Open(O)}).

6.2 Approaches

The approaches to Task1 fall into two major categories. There were six systems which handled the task as a classical sentence classification problem and employed essentially a bag-of-words feature representation (they are marked as BoW in Table 6). The remaining teams focused on the cue phrases and sought to classify every token if it was a part of a cue phrase, then a sentence was predicted as uncertain if it contained at least one recognized cue phrase. Five systems followed a pure token classification approach (TC) for cue detection while others used sequential labeling techniques (usually Conditional Random Fields) to identify cue phrases in sentences (SL).

The feature set employed in Task1 systems typically consisted of the wordform, its lemma or stem, POS and chunk codes and about the half of the participants constructed features from the dependency and/or constituent parse tree of the sentences as well (see Table 6 for details).

It is interesting to see that the top ranked systems of Task1B followed a sequence labeling approach, while the best systems on Task1W applied a bag-of-words sentence classification. This may be due to the fact that biological sentences have relatively simple patterns. Thus the context of the cue words (token classification-based approaches used features derived from a window of the token in question, thus, they exploited the relationship among the tokens and their contexts) can be utilized while Wikipedia weasels have a diverse nature. Another observation is that the top systems in both Task1B and Task1W are the ones which did not derive features from syntactic parsing.

Each Task2 system was built upon a Task1 system, i.e. they attempted to recognize the scopes for the predicted cue phrases (however, Zhang et al. (2010) have argued that the objective functions of Task1 and Task2 cue detection problems are different because of sentences containing multiple hedge spans).

Most systems regarded multiple cues in a sentence to be independent from each other and formed different classification instances from them. There were three systems which incorporated information about other hedge cues (e.g. their distance) of the sentence into the feature space and Zhang et al. (2010) constructed a cascade system which utilized directly the predicted scopes (it processes cue phrases from left to right) during predicting other scopes in the same sentence.

The identification of the scope for a certain cue was typically carried out by classifying each token in the sentence. Task2 systems differ in the number of class labels used as target and in the machine learning approaches applied. Most systems – following Morante and Daelemans (2009) – used three class labels (F)IRST, (L)AST and NONE. Two participants used four classes by adding (I)NSIDE, while three systems followed a binary classification approach (SCOPE versus NONSCOPE). The systems typically included a post-processing procedure to force scopes to be continuous and to include the cue phrase in question. The machine learning methods applied can be again categorized into sequence labeling (SL)

NAME	approach	machine learner	feature selection	features employed							
				dict	ortho	lemma/stem	POS	chunk	dep	docpart	other
Clausen	BoW	MaxEnt				+	+				hedge cue distance
Chen	BoW	MaxEnt	statistical	+		+	+			+	sentencelength
Fernandes	SL	ETL				+	+	+			
Georgescul	BoW	SVM+paramtuning		+							
Ji	TC	ModAvgPerceptron					+				
Kilicoglu	TC	manual		+		+			+		external dict
Li	SL	CRF+postproc	greedy fwd			+	+	+			
Mamani Sánchez	BoW	SVMTreeKernel		+		+	+		+	+	
Morante (wiki)	TC	SVM+postproc	statistical	+		+	+	+	+		
Morante (bio)	SL	KNN	statistical	+		+	+	+	+	+	
Prabhakaran	SL	CRF	greedy fwd	+		+	+		+		LevinClass
Rei	SL	CRF		+		+	+		+		
Shimizu	SL	Bayes Point Machines	GA		+	+	+	+			NEs, unlabeled data
Szidarovszky	SL	CRF	exhaustive	+	+	+					
Täckström	BoW	SVM	greedy fwd			+	+	+	+	+	sentencelength
Tang	SL	CRF,SVMHMM	statistical	+	+	+	+	+			
Tjong Kim Sang	TC	Naive Bayes									
Velldal	TC	MaxEnt	manual	+		+	+		+		
Vlachos	TC	Bayesian LogReg	manual	+		+	+		+		
Zhang	SL	CRF+feature combination	greedy fwd	+		+	+	+	+		NEs
Zhao	SL	CRF	statistical	+		+	+	+			
Zheng	SL	CRF,MaxEnt	manual			+	+	+		+	Constituent Parsing
Zhou	SL	CRF	statistical	+		+	+	+			WordNet

Table 6: System architectures overview for Task1. Approaches: sequence labeling (SL), token classification (TC), bag-of-words model (BoW); Machine learners: Entropy Guided Transformation Learning (ETL), Averaged Perceptron (AP), k-nearest neighbour (KNN); Feature selection: gathering phrases from the training corpus using statistical thresholds (statistical); Features: orthographical information about the token (ortho), lemma or stem of the token (stem), Part-of-Speech codes (POS), syntactic chunk information (chunk), dependency parsing (dep), position inside the document or section information (docpos)

and token classification (TC) approaches (see Table 7). The feature sets used here are the same as for Task1, extended by several features describing the relationship between the cue phrase and the token in question mostly by describing the dependency path between them.

NAME	approach	scope	ML	postproc	tree	dep	multihedge
Fernandes	TC	FL	ETL				
Ji	TC	I	AP			+	
Kilicoglu	HC		manual	+	+	+	
Li	SL	FL	CRF, SVMHMM	+		+	+
Morante	TC	FL	KNN	+		+	
Rei	SL	FIL	manual+CRF	+		+	
Täckström	TC	FI	SVM			+	
Tang	SL	FL	CRF	+	+		+
Velldal	HC		manual			+	
Vlachos	TC	I	Bayesian MaxEnt	+		+	
Zhang	SL	FIL	CRF			+	+
Zhao	SL	FL	CRF	+			
Zhou	SL	FL	CRF	+	+		

Table 7: System architectures overview for Task2. Approaches: sequence labeling (SL), token classification (TC), hand-crafted rules (HC); Machine learners: Entropy Guided Transformation Learning (ETL), Averaged Perceptron (AP), k-nearest neighbour (KNN); The way of identifying scopes: predicting first/last tokens (FL), first/inside/last tokens (FIL), just inside tokens (I); Multiple Hedges: the system applied a mechanism for handling multiple hedges inside a sentence

and token classification (TC) approaches (see Table 7). The feature sets used here are the same as for Task1, extended by several features describing the relationship between the cue phrase and the token in question mostly by describing the dependency path between them.

7 Conclusions

The CoNLL-2010 Shared Task introduced the novel task of uncertainty detection. The challenge consisted of a sentence identification task on uncertainty (Task1) and an in-sentence hedge scope detection task (Task2). In the latter task the goal of automatic systems was to recognize speculative text spans inside sentences.

The relatively high number of participants indicates that the problem is rather interesting for the Natural Language Processing community. We think that this is due to the practical importance of the task for (principally biomedical) applications and because it addresses several open research questions. Although several approaches were introduced by the participants of the shared task and we believe that the ideas described in this proceedings can serve as an excellent starting point for the development of an uncertainty detector, there is a lot of room for improving such systems. The manually annotated datasets and software tools developed for the shared task may act as benchmarks for these future experiments (they are freely available at `http://www.inf.u-szeged.hu/rgai/conll2010st`).

Acknowledgements

The authors would like to thank Joakim Nivre and Lluís Márquez for their useful suggestions, comments and help during the organisation of the shared task.

This work was supported in part by the National Office for Research and Technology (NKTH, `http://www.nkth.gov.hu/`) of the Hungarian government within the framework of the projects TEXTREND, BELAMI and MASZEKER.

References

Eiji Aramaki, Yasuhide Miura, Masatsugu Tonoike, Tomoko Ohkuma, Hiroshi Mashuichi, and Kazuhiko Ohe. 2009. TEXT2TABLE: Medical Text Summarization System Based on Named Entity Recognition and Modality Identification. In *Proceedings of the BioNLP 2009 Workshop*, pages 185–192, Boulder, Colorado, June. Association for Computational Linguistics.

Wendy W. Chapman, David Chu, and John N. Dowling. 2007. ConText: An Algorithm for Identifying Contextual Features from Clinical Text. In *Proceedings of the ACL Workshop on BioNLP 2007*, pages 81–88.

Mike Conway, Son Doan, and Nigel Collier. 2009. Using Hedges to Enhance a Disease Outbreak Report

Text Mining System. In *Proceedings of the BioNLP 2009 Workshop*, pages 142–143, Boulder, Colorado, June. Association for Computational Linguistics.

Carol Friedman, Philip O. Alderson, John H. M. Austin, James J. Cimino, and Stephen B. Johnson. 1994. A General Natural-language Text Processor for Clinical Radiology. *Journal of the American Medical Informatics Association*, 1(2):161–174.

Viola Ganter and Michael Strube. 2009. Finding Hedges by Chasing Weasels: Hedge Detection Using Wikipedia Tags and Shallow Linguistic Features. In *Proceedings of the ACL-IJCNLP 2009 Conference Short Papers*, pages 173–176, Suntec, Singapore, August. Association for Computational Linguistics.

Feng Ji, Xipeng Qiu, and Xuanjing Huang. 2010. Detecting Hedge Cues and their Scopes with Average Perceptron. In *Proceedings of the Fourteenth Conference on Computational Natural Language Learning (CoNLL-2010): Shared Task*, pages 139–146, Uppsala, Sweden, July. Association for Computational Linguistics.

Yoshinobu Kano, William A. Baumgartner, Luke McCrohon, Sophia Ananiadou, Kevin B. Cohen, Lawrence Hunter, and Jun'ichi Tsujii. 2009. U-Compare: Share and Compare Text Mining Tools with UIMA. *Bioinformatics*, 25(15):1997–1998, August.

Halil Kilicoglu and Sabine Bergler. 2008. Recognizing Speculative Language in Biomedical Research Articles: A Linguistically Motivated Perspective. In *Proceedings of the Workshop on Current Trends in Biomedical Natural Language Processing*, pages 46–53, Columbus, Ohio, June. Association for Computational Linguistics.

Halil Kilicoglu and Sabine Bergler. 2009. Syntactic Dependency Based Heuristics for Biological Event Extraction. In *Proceedings of the BioNLP 2009 Workshop Companion Volume for Shared Task*, pages 119–127, Boulder, Colorado, June. Association for Computational Linguistics.

Halil Kilicoglu and Sabine Bergler. 2010. A High-Precision Approach to Detecting Hedges and Their Scopes. In *Proceedings of the Fourteenth Conference on Computational Natural Language Learning (CoNLL-2010): Shared Task*, pages 103–110, Uppsala, Sweden, July. Association for Computational Linguistics.

Jin-Dong Kim, Tomoko Ohta, Sampo Pyysalo, Yoshinobu Kano, and Jun'ichi Tsujii. 2009. Overview of BioNLP'09 Shared Task on Event Extraction. In *Proceedings of the BioNLP 2009 Workshop Companion Volume for Shared Task*, pages 1–9, Boulder, Colorado, June. Association for Computational Linguistics.

George Lakoff. 1972. Linguistics and natural logic. In *The Semantics of Natural Language*, pages 545–665, Dordrecht. Reidel.

Xinxin Li, Jianping Shen, Xiang Gao, and Xuan Wang. 2010. Exploiting Rich Features for Detecting Hedges and Their Scope. In *Proceedings of the Fourteenth Conference on Computational Natural Language Learning (CoNLL-2010): Shared Task*, pages 36–41, Uppsala, Sweden, July. Association for Computational Linguistics.

Marc Light, Xin Ying Qiu, and Padmini Srinivasan. 2004. The Language of Bioscience: Facts, Speculations, and Statements in Between. In *Proceedings of the HLT-NAACL 2004 Workshop: Biolink 2004, Linking Biological Literature, Ontologies and Databases*, pages 17–24.

Ben Medlock and Ted Briscoe. 2007. Weakly Supervised Learning for Hedge Classification in Scientific Literature. In *Proceedings of the ACL*, pages 992–999, Prague, Czech Republic, June.

Roser Morante and Walter Daelemans. 2009. Learning the Scope of Hedge Cues in Biomedical Texts. In *Proceedings of the BioNLP 2009 Workshop*, pages 28–36, Boulder, Colorado, June. Association for Computational Linguistics.

Roser Morante, Vincent Van Asch, and Walter Daelemans. 2010. Memory-based Resolution of In-sentence Scopes of Hedge Cues. In *Proceedings of the Fourteenth Conference on Computational Natural Language Learning (CoNLL-2010): Shared Task*, pages 48–55, Uppsala, Sweden, July. Association for Computational Linguistics.

Arzucan Özgür and Dragomir R. Radev. 2009. Detecting Speculations and their Scopes in Scientific Text. In *Proceedings of the 2009 Conference on Empirical Methods in Natural Language Processing*, pages 1398–1407, Singapore, August. Association for Computational Linguistics.

György Szarvas. 2008. Hedge Classification in Biomedical Texts with a Weakly Supervised Selection of Keywords. In *Proceedings of ACL-08: HLT*, pages 281–289, Columbus, Ohio, June. Association for Computational Linguistics.

Buzhou Tang, Xiaolong Wang, Xuan Wang, Bo Yuan, and Shixi Fan. 2010. A Cascade Method for Detecting Hedges and their Scope in Natural Language Text. In *Proceedings of the Fourteenth Conference on Computational Natural Language Learning (CoNLL-2010): Shared Task*, pages 25–29, Uppsala, Sweden, July. Association for Computational Linguistics.

Sofie Van Landeghem, Yvan Saeys, Bernard De Baets, and Yves Van de Peer. 2009. Analyzing Text in Search of Bio-molecular Events: A High-precision Machine Learning Framework. In *Proceedings of the BioNLP 2009 Workshop Companion Volume for*

Shared Task, pages 128–136, Boulder, Colorado, June. Association for Computational Linguistics.

Veronika Vincze, György Szarvas, Richárd Farkas, György Móra, and János Csirik. 2008. The BioScope Corpus: Biomedical Texts Annotated for Uncertainty, Negation and their Scopes. *BMC Bioinformatics*, 9(Suppl 11):S9.

Shaodian Zhang, Hai Zhao, Guodong Zhou, and Baoliang Lu. 2010. Hedge Detection and Scope Finding by Sequence Labeling with Procedural Feature Selection. In *Proceedings of the Fourteenth Conference on Computational Natural Language Learning (CoNLL-2010): Shared Task*, pages 70–77, Uppsala, Sweden, July. Association for Computational Linguistics.

Qi Zhao, Chengjie Sun, Bingquan Liu, and Yong Cheng. 2010. Learning to Detect Hedges and their Scope Using CRF. In *Proceedings of the Fourteenth Conference on Computational Natural Language Learning (CoNLL-2010): Shared Task*, pages 64–69, Uppsala, Sweden, July. Association for Computational Linguistics.

Huiwei Zhou, Xiaoyan Li, Degen Huang, Zezhong Li, and Yuansheng Yang. 2010. Exploiting Multi-Features to Detect Hedges and Their Scope in Biomedical Texts. In *Proceedings of the Fourteenth Conference on Computational Natural Language Learning (CoNLL-2010): Shared Task*, pages 56–63, Uppsala, Sweden, July. Association for Computational Linguistics.

A Cascade Method for Detecting Hedges and their Scope in Natural Language Text

Buzhou Tang, Xiaolong Wang, Xuan Wang, Bo Yuan, Shixi Fan
Key Laboratory of Network Oriented Intelligent Computation
Harbin Institute of Technology Shenzhen Graduate School
Shenzhen, Guangdong, China
{tangbuzhou,yuanbo.hitsz}@gmail.com
{wangxl,wangxuan,fanshixi}@insun.hit.edu.cn

Abstract

Detecting hedges and their scope in natural language text is very important for information inference. In this paper, we present a system based on a cascade method for the CoNLL-2010 shared task. The system composes of two components: one for detecting hedges and another one for detecting their scope. For detecting hedges, we build a cascade subsystem. Firstly, a conditional random field (CRF) model and a large margin-based model are trained respectively. Then, we train another CRF model using the result of the first phase. For detecting the scope of hedges, a CRF model is trained according to the result of the first subtask. The experiments show that our system achieves 86.36% F-measure on biological corpus and 55.05% F-measure on Wikipedia corpus for hedge detection, and 49.95% F-measure on biological corpus for hedge scope detection. Among them, 86.36% is the best result on biological corpus for hedge detection.

1 Introduction

Hedge cues are very common in natural language text. Vincze et al. (2008) report that 17.70% of the sentences in the abstract section and 19.94% of sentences in the full paper section contain hedges on BioScope corpus. As Vincze et al. (2008) suggest that information that falls in the scope of hedges can not be presented as factual information. Detecting hedges and their scope in natural language text is very important for information inference. Recently, relative research has received considerable interest in the biomedical NLP community, including detecting hedges and their in-sentence scope in biomedical texts (Morante and Daelemans, 2009). The CoNLL-2010 has launched a shared task for exploiting the hedge scope annotated in the BioScope (Vincze et al., 2008) and publicly available Wikipedia (Ganter and Strube, 2009) weasel annotations. The shared task contains two subtasks (Farkas et al., 2010): 1. learning to detect hedges in sentences on BioScope and Wikipedia; 2. learning to detect the in-sentence scope of these hedges on BioScope.

In this paper, we present a system based on a cascade method for the CoNLL-2010 shared task. The system composes of two components: one for detecting hedges and another one for detecting their scope. For detecting hedges, we build a cascade subsystem. Firstly, conditional random field (CRF) model and a large margin-based model are trained respectively. Then, we train another CRF model using the result of the first phase. For detecting the scope of hedges, a CRF model is trained according to the result of the first subtask. The experiments show that our system achieves 86.36% F-measure on biological corpus and 55.05% F-measure on Wikipedia corpus for hedge detection, and 49.95% F-measure on biological corpus for hedge scope detection. Among them, 86.36% is the best result on biological corpus for hedge detection.

2 System Description

As there are two subtasks, we present a system based on a cascade supervised machine learning methods for the CoNLL-2010 shared task. The architecture of our system is shown in Figure 1.

The system composes of two subsystems for two subtasks respectively, and the first subsystem is a two-layer cascaded classifier.

2.1 Hedge Detection

The hedges are represented by indicating whether a token is in a hedge and its position in the CoNLL-2010 shared task. Three tags are used for

Proceedings of the Fourteenth Conference on Computational Natural Language Learning: Shared Task, pages 13–17,
Uppsala, Sweden, 15-16 July 2010. ©2010 Association for Computational Linguistics

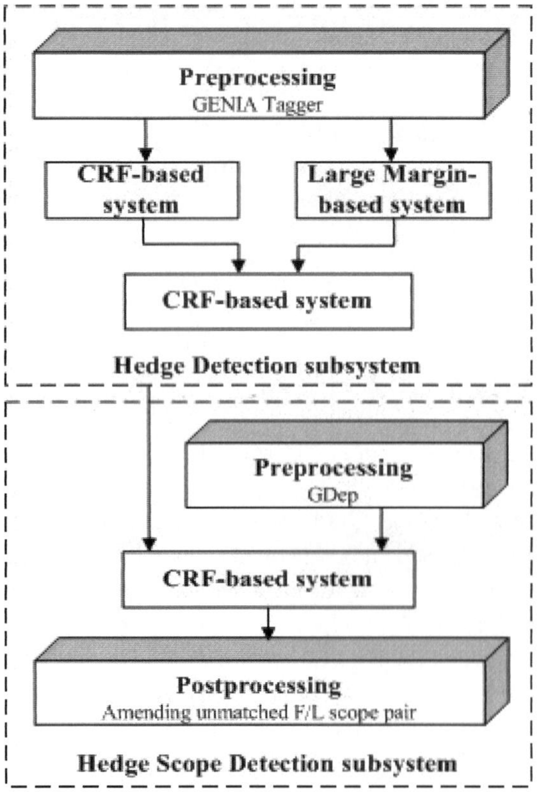

Figure 1: System architecture

this scheme, where O_cue indicates a token outside of a hedge, B_cue indicates a token at the beginning of a hedge and I_cue indicates a token inside of a hedge. In this subsystem, we do preprocessing by GENIA Tagger (version 3.0.1)[1] at first, which does lemma extraction, part-of-speech (POS), chunking and named entity recognition (NER) for feature extraction. For the output of GENIA Tagger, we convert the first char of a lemma into lower case and BIO chunk tag into BIOS chunk tag, where S indicates a token is a chunk, B indicates a token at the beginning of a chunk, I indicates a token inside of a chunk, and O indicates a token outside of a chunk. Then a two-layer cascaded classifier is built for prediction. There are a CRF classifier and a large margin-based classifier in the first layer and a CRF classifier in the second layer.

In the first layer, the following features are used in our system:

- Word and Word Shape of the lemma: we used the similar scheme as shown in (Tsai et al., 2005).
- Prefix and Suffix with length 3-5.
- Context of the lemma, POS and the chunk in the window [-2,2].
- Combined features including L_0C_0, L_iP_0 and L_iC_0, where $-1 \leq i \leq 1$ L denotes the lemma of a word, P denotes a POS and C denotes a chunk tag.
- The type of a chunk; the lemma and POS sequences of it.
- Whether a token is a part of the pairs "neither ... nor" and "either ... or" as both tokens of a pair are always labeled with the same tag.
- Whether a token can possibly be classified into B_cue, I_cue or O_cue; its lemma, POS and chunk tag for each possible case: these features are extracted according to a dictionary extracted from training corpus, which lists all possible hedge tag for each word in the training corpus.

In the second layer, we used some features about the result of the last layer besides those mentioned above. They are listed as follow:

- The lemma and POS sequences of the hedge predicted by each classifier.
- The times of a token classified into B_cue, I_cue and O_cue by the first two classifiers.
- Whether a token is the last token of the hedge predicted by each classifier.

2.2 Hedge Scope Detection

We follow the way of Morante and Daelemans (2009) to represent the scope of a hedge, where F_scope indicates a token at the beginning of a scope sequence, L_scope indicates a token at the last of a scope sequence, and NONE indicates others. In this phase, we do preprocessing by GDep Tagger (version beta1)[2] at first, which does lemma extraction, part-of-speech (POS), chunking, named entity recognition (NER) and dependency parse for feature extraction. For the output of GDep Tagger, we deal with the lemma and chunk tag using the same way mentioned in the last section. Then, a CRF classifier is built for prediction, which uses the following features:

[1]http://www-tsujii.is.s.u-tokyo.ac.jp/GENIA/tagger/

[2]http://www.cs.cmu.edu/ sagae/parser/gdep

- Word.
- Context of the lemma, POS, the chunk, the hedge and the dependency relation in the window [-2,2].
- Combined features including L_0C_0, L_0H_0, L_0D_0, L_iP_0, P_iC_0,P_iH_0, C_iH_0, P_iD_0,C_iD_0, where $-1 \leq i \leq 1$ L denotes the lemma of a word, P denotes a POS, C denotes a chunk tag, H denotes a hedge tag and D denotes a dependency relation tag.
- The type of a chunk; the lemma and POS sequences of it.
- The type of a hedge; the lemma, POS and chunk sequences of it.
- The lemma, POS, chunk, hedge and dependency relation sequences of $1st$ and $2nd$ dependency relation edges; the lemma, POS, chunk, hedge and dependency relation sequences of the path from a token to the root.
- Whether there are hedges in the $1st$, $2nd$ dependency relation edges or path from a token to the root.
- The location of a token relative to the negation signal: previous the first hedge, in the first hedge, between two hedge cues, in the last hedge, post the last hedge.

At last, we provided a postprocessing system for the output of the classifier to build the complete sequence of tokens that constitute the scope. We applied the following postprocessing:

- If a hedge is bracketed by a F_scope and a L_scope, its scope is formed by the tokens between them.
- If a hedge is only bracketed by a F_scope, and there is no L_scope in the sentence, we search the first possible word from the end of the sentence according to a dictionary, which extracted from the training corpus, and assign it as L_scope. The scope of the hedge is formed by the tokens between them.
- If a hedge is only bracketed by a F_scope, and there are at least one L_scope in the sentence, we think the last L_scope is the L_scope of the hedge, and its scope is formed by the tokens between them.
- If a hedge is only bracketed by a L_scope, and there is no F_scope in the sentence, we search the first possible word from the beginning of the sentence to the hedge according to the dictionary, and assign it as F_scope. The scope of the hedge is formed by the tokens between them.
- If a hedge is only bracketed by a L_scope, and there are at least one F_scope in the sentence, we search the first possible word from the hedge to the beginning of the sentence according to the dictionary, and think it as the F_scope of the hedge. The scope of the hedge is formed by the tokens between them.
- If a hedge is bracketed by neither of them, we remove it.

3 Experiments and Results

Two annotated corpus: BioScope and Wikipedia are supplied for the CoNLL-2010 shared task. The BioScope corpus consists of two parts: biological paper abstracts and biological full papers, and it is used for two subtasks. The Wikipedia corpus is only used for hedge detection. The detailed information of these two corpora is shown in Table 1 and Table 2, respectively.

	Abstracts	Papers	Test
#Documents	1273	9	15
#Sentences	11871	2670	5003
%Hedge sent.	17.70	19.44	15.75
#Hedges	2694	682	1043
#AvL. of sent.	30.43	27.95	31.30
#AvL. of scopes	17.27	14.17	17.51

Table 1: The detailed information of BioScope corpus. "AvL." stands for average length.

	Train	Test
#Documents	2186	2737
#Sentences	11111	9634
%Hedge sentences	22.36	23.19
#Hedges	3133	3143
#AvL. of sentences	23.07	20.82

Table 2: The detail information of Wikipedia corpus. "AvL." stands for average length.

In our experiments, CRF++-0.53[3] implemen-

[3] http://crfpp.sourceforge.net/

tation is employed to CRF, and svm_hmm_3.10[4] implementation is employed to the large margin method. All parameters are default except C (the trade-off between training error and margin, C=8000, for selecting C, the training corpus is partitioned into three parts, two of them are used for training and the left one is used as a development dataset) in svm_hmm. Both of them are state-of-the-art toolkits for the sequence labeling problem.

3.1 Hedge Detection

We first compare the performance of each single classifier with the cascaded system on two corpora in domain, respectively. Each model is trained by whole corpus, and the performance of them was evaluated by the official tool of the CoNLL-2010 shared task. There were two kinds of measure: one for sentence-level performance and another one for cue-match performance. Here, we only focused on the first one, and the results shown in Table 3.

Corpus	System	Prec.	Recall	F1
BioScope	CRF	87.12	86.46	86.79
	LM	85.24	87.72	86.46
	CAS	85.03	87.72	86.36
Wikipedia	CRF	86.10	35.77	50.54
	LM	82.28	41.36	55.05
	CAS	82.28	41.36	55.05

Table 3: In-sentence performance of the hedge detection subsystem for in-domain test. "Prec." stands for precision, "LM" stands for large margin, and "CAS" stands for cascaded system.

From Table 3, we can see that the cascaded system is not better than other two single classifiers and the single CRF classifier achieves the best performance with F-measure 86.79%. The reason for selecting this cascaded system for our final submission is that the cascaded system achieved the best performance on the two training corpus when we partition each one into three parts: two of them are used for training and the left one is used for testing.

For cross-domain test, we train a cascaded classifier using BioScope+Wikipedia cropus. Table 4 shows the results.

As shown in Table 5, the performance of cross-domain test is worse than that of in-domain test.

[4]http://www.cs.cornell.edu/People/tj/svm_light/svm-hmm.html

Corpus	Precision	Recall	F1
BioScope	89.91	73.29	80.75
Wikipedia	81.56	40.20	53.85

Table 4: Results of the hedge detection for cross-domain test. "LM" stands for large margin, and "CAS" stands for cascaded system.

3.2 Hedge Scope Detection

For test the affect of postprocessing for hedge scope detection, we test our system using two evaluation tools: one for scope tag and the other one for sentence-level scope (the official tool). In order to evaluate our system comprehensively, four results are used for comparison. The "gold" is the performance using golden hedge tags for test, the "CRF" is the performance using the hedge tags prediction of single CRF for test, the "LM" is the performance using the hedge tag prediction of single large margin for test, and "CAS" is the performance of using the hedge tag prediction of cascaded subsystem for test. The results of scope tag and scope sentence-level are listed in Table 5 and Table 6, respectively. Here, we should notice that the result listed here is different with that submitted to the CoNLL-2010 shared task because some errors for feature extraction in the previous system are revised here.

HD	tag	Precision	Recall	F1
gold	F_scope	92.06	78.83	84.94
	L_scope	80.56	68.67	74.14
	NONE	99.68	99.86	99.77
CRF	F_scope	78.83	66.89	72.37
	L_scope	72.52	60.50	65.97
	NONE	99.56	99.75	99.65
LM	F_scope	77.25	67.57	72.09
	L_scope	72.33	61.41	66.42
	NONE	99.56	99.73	99.31
CAS	F_scope	77.32	67.86	72.29
	L_scope	72.00	61.29	66.22
	NONE	99.57	99.73	99.65

Table 5: Results of the hedge scope tag. "HD" stands for hedge detection subsystem we used, "LM" stands for large margin, and "CAS" stands for cascaded system.

As shown in Table 5, the performance of L_scope is much lower than that of F_scope. Therefore, the first problem we should solve is

HD subsystem	Precision	Recall	F1
gold	57.92	55.95	56.92
CRF	52.36	48.40	50.30
LM	51.06	48.89	49.95
CAS	50.96	48.98	49.95

Table 6: Results of the hedge scope in-sentence. "HD" stands for hedge detection subsystem we used, "LM" stands for large margin, and "CAS" stands for cascaded system.

how to improve the prediction performance of L_scope. Moreover, compared the performance shown in Table 5 and 6, about 15% (F1 of L_scope in Table 5 - F1 in Table 6) scope labels are mismatched. An efficient postprocessing is needed to do F-L scope pair match.

As "CRF" hedge detection subsystem is better than the other two subsystems, our system achieves the best performance with F-measure 50.30% when using the "CRF" subsystem.

4 Conclusions

This paper presents a cascaded system for the CoNLL-2010 shared task, which contains two subsystems: one for detecting hedges and another one for detecting their scope. Although the best performance of hedge detection subsystem achieves F-measure 86.79%, the best performance of the whole system only achieves F-measure 50.30%. How to improve it, we think some complex features such as context free grammar may be effective for detecting hedge scope. In addition, the postprocessing can be further improved.

Acknowledgments

We wish to thank the organizers of the CoNLL-2010 shared task for preparing the datasets and organizing the challenge shared tasks. We also wish to thank all authors supplying the toolkits used in this paper. This research has been partially supported by the National Natural Science Foundation of China (No.60435020 and No.90612005), National 863 Program of China (No.2007AA01Z194) and the Goal-oriented Lessons from the National 863 Program of China (No.2006AA01Z197).

References

Richárd Farkas, Veronika Vincze, György Móra, János Csirik, György Szarvas. 2010. The CoNLL-2010 Shared Task: Learning to Detect Hedges and their Scope in Natural Language Text. In *Proceedings of the Fourteenth Conference on Computational Natural Language Learning (CoNLL-2010): Shared Task*, pages 1–12, Uppsala, Sweden, July. Association for Computational Linguistics.

Viola Ganter and Michael Strube. 2009. Finding hedges by chasing weasels: Hedge detection using wikipedia tags and shallow linguistic features. In *Proceedings of the ACL-IJCNLP 2009 Conference Short Papers*, pages 173–176, Suntec, Singapore, August. Association for Computational Linguistics.

Roser Morante and Walter Daelemans. 2009. Learning the scope of hedge cues in biomedical texts. In *Proceedings of the BioNLP 2009 Workshop*, pages 28–36, Boulder, Colorado, June. Association for Computational Linguistics.

Tzong-Han Tsai, Chia-Wei Wu, and Wen-Lian Hsu. 2005. Using Maximum Entropy to Extract Biomedical Named Entities without Dictionaries. In *Second International Joint Conference on Natural Language Processing*, pages 268–273.

Veronika Vincze, György Szarvas, Richárd Farkas, György Móra, and János Csirik. 2008. The BioScope corpus: biomedical texts annotated for uncertainty, negation and their scopes. *BMC Bioinformatics*, 9(Suppl 11):S9.

Detecting Speculative Language Using Syntactic Dependencies and Logistic Regression

Andreas Vlachos and **Mark Craven**
Department of Biostatistics and Medical Informatics
University of Wisconsin-Madison
{vlachos,craven}@biostat.wisc.edu

Abstract

In this paper we describe our approach to the CoNLL-2010 shared task on detecting speculative language in biomedical text. We treat the detection of sentences containing uncertain information (Task1) as a token classification task since the existence or absence of *cues* determines the sentence label. We distinguish words that have speculative and non-speculative meaning by employing syntactic features as a proxy for their semantic content. In order to identify the *scope* of each cue (Task2), we learn a classifier that predicts whether each token of a sentence belongs to the scope of a given cue. The features in the classifier are based on the syntactic dependency path between the cue and the token. In both tasks, we use a Bayesian logistic regression classifier incorporating a sparsity-enforcing Laplace prior. Overall, the performance achieved is 85.21% F-score and 44.11% F-score in Task1 and Task2, respectively.

1 Introduction

The term *speculative language*, also known as *hedging*, refers to expressions of uncertainty over statements. Recognition of such statements is important for higher-level applications. For example, a multi-document summarization system can assign different weights to speculative and non-speculative statements when aggregating information on a particular issue.

The CoNLL-2010 shared task (Farkas et al., 2010) formulates speculative language detection as two subtasks. In the first subtask (Task1), systems need to determine whether a sentence contains uncertain information or not. In the second subtask (Task2), systems need to identify the hedge *cues* and their *scope* in the sentence. Table 1 provides an example from the training data.

The participants are provided with data from two domains: biomedical scientific literature (both abstracts and full articles) and Wikipedia. We choose to focus on the former. The training data for this domain are nine full articles and 1,273 abstracts from the BioScope corpus (Szarvas et al., 2008) and the test data are 15 full articles.

Our approach to speculative language detection relies on syntactic parsing and machine learning. We give a description of the techniques used in Sections 2 and 3. We treat the detection of sentences containing uncertain information (Task1) as a token classification task in which we learn a classifier to predict whether a token is a *cue* or not. In order to handle words that have speculative and non-speculative meaning (e.g. "indicating" in the example of Table 1), we employ syntactic features as a proxy for their semantic content (Section 4). For *scope* identification (Task2), we learn a classifier that predicts whether each token of the sentence belongs to the scope of a particular cue (Section 6). The features used are based on the syntactic dependency path between the cue and the token. We report results and perform error analysis for both tasks, pointing out annotation issues that could be ameliorated (Sections 5 and 7). Based on our experience we suggest improvements on the task definition taking into account work from the broader field (Section 8).

2 Syntactic parsing for the biomedical domain

The syntactic parser we chose for our experiments is the C&C Combinatory Categorial Grammar (CCG) parser adapted to the biomedical domain (Rimell and Clark, 2009). In this framework, parsing is performed in three stages: part-of-speech (PoS) tagging, CCG supertagging and parse selection. The parse selection module de-

Proceedings of the Fourteenth Conference on Computational Natural Language Learning: Shared Task, pages 18–25,
Uppsala, Sweden, 15-16 July 2010.

The Orthology and Combined modules both have states that achieve likelihood ratios above 400 (as high as 1207 for the Orthology module and 613 for the Combined module), {**indicating that** both these modules {**can**, on their own, predict some interacting protein pairs with a posterior odds ratio above 1}}.

Table 1: Sentence annotated as speculative with two cues (in boldface) and their scopes (in brackets).

rives the actual parse tree using the information from the other two components. The intermediate CCG supertagging stage assigns each token to a lexical category which attempts to capture its syntactic role in the sentence. Lexical categories contain more information than PoS tags (mainly on subcategorization) and they are more numerous, thereby making their assignment a relatively difficult task. Therefore, the parse selection module takes into account multiple predictions per token which allows recovery from supertagging errors while still reducing the ambiguity propagated. An interesting aspect of this three-stage parsing approach is that, if the parse selection module fails to construct a parse tree for the sentence (a common issue when syntactic parsers are ported to new domains), the lexical categories obtained by the supertagger preserve some of the syntactic information that would not be found in PoS tags.

The adaptation to the biomedical domain by Rimell and Clark (2009) involved re-training the PoS tagger and the CCG supertagger using in-domain resources, while the parse selection component was left intact. As recent work in the BioNLP 2009 shared task has shown (Kim et al., 2009), domain-adapted parsing benefits information extraction systems.

The native output of the C&C parser is converted into the Stanford Dependency (SD) collapsed dependency format (de Marneffe and Manning, 2008). These dependencies define binary relations between tokens and the labels of these relations are obtained from a hierarchy. While the conversion is unlikely to be perfect given that the native C&C output follows a different formalism, we made this choice because it allows for the use of different parsers with minimal adaptation.

Finally, an important pre-processing step we take is tokenization of the original text. Since the PoS tagger is trained on the GENIA corpus which follows the Penn TreeBank tokenization scheme, we use the tokenization script provided by the treebank.[1]

[1]http://www.cis.upenn.edu/~treebank/tokenization.html

3 Bayesian logistic regression

In both tasks, we use a Bayesian logistic regression classifier incorporating a sparsity-enforcing Laplace prior (Genkin et al., 2006). Logistic regression models are of the form:

$$p(y = +1|\beta, x) = \frac{exp(x\beta^T)}{1 + exp(x\beta^T)} \quad (1)$$

where $y \in \{+1, -1\}$ is a binary class label, x is the feature vector representation of the instance to be classified and β is the feature weight vector which is learnt from the training data. Since feature interactions are not directly represented, the interactions that are expected to matter for the task considered must be specified as additional features. In Bayesian logistic regression, a prior distribution on β is used which encodes our prior beliefs on the feature weights. In this work, we use the Laplace prior which encourages the feature weight vector to be sparse, reflecting our belief that most features will be irrelevant to the task.

4 Detecting sentences containing speculation

In Task1, systems need to determine whether a sentence contains uncertain information (labeled *uncertain*) or not (labeled *certain*). A sentence is *uncertain* if one or more of its tokens denote uncertainty. Such tokens are labeled as *cues* and they are provided by the organizers for training. If a cue is a present, any other (potentially "unhedging") token becomes irrelevant to the task. Therefore, we cast the task as a binary token classification problem and determine the sentence label from the token-level decisions.

Words used as speculative cues do not always denote speculation. For example, in BioScope "if" and "appear" are annotated as cues 4% and 83% of the times they are encountered. In order to gain better understanding of the task, we build a dictionary-based cue extractor. First we extract all the cues from the training data and use their lemmas, obtained using *morpha* (Minnen et al., 2001), to tag tokens in the test data. We keep only single-token cues in order to avoid non-indicative lem-

token=indicating PoS=VBG	lemma=indicate lemma+PoS=indicate+VBG
CCG=(S[ng]\NP)/S[em] lemma+CCG=indicate+(S[ng]\NP)/S[em]	

Table 2: Features extracted for the token "indicating" from the Example in Table 1. CCG supertag (S[ng]\NP)/S[em] denotes that "indicating" expects an embedded clause (S[em]) to its right (indicated by the forward slash /) and a noun phrase (NP) to its left (indicated by the backward slash \) to form a present participle (S[ng]).

mas entering the dictionary (e.g. "that" in "indicate that"). Since the test data consist of full articles only, we evaluate the performance of the dictionary-based approach using four-fold cross-validation on the nine full articles of the training data with the abstracts added as training data in every fold, but not used as test data. The recall achieved is 98.07%, but F-score is lower (59.53%) demonstrating that the single-token cues in the training data provide adequate coverage, but low precision. The restricted domain helps precision as it precludes some word meanings from appearing. For example "might" is unlikely to be encountered as a noun in the biomedical domain. Nevertheless, in order to achieve better performance it is important to further refine the cue identification procedure.

Determining whether a token is used as a speculative cue or not resembles supervised word sense disambiguation. The main difference is that instead of having an inventory of senses for each word, we have two senses applicable to all words. As in most word sense disambiguation tasks, the classification of a word as cue or not is dependent on the other words in the sentence, which we take into account using syntax. The syntactic context of words is a useful proxy to their semantics, as shown in recent work on verb sense disambiguation (Chen and Palmer, 2009). Furthermore, it is easy to obtain syntactic information automatically using a parser, even though there will be some noise due to parsing errors. Similar intuitions were exploited by Kilicoglu and Bergler (2008) in refining a dictionary of cues with syntactic rules.

In what follows, we present the features extracted for each token for our final system, along with an example of their application in Table 2. Where appropriate we give the relevant labels in the Stanford Dependency (SD) scheme in parentheses for reproducibility:

- We extract the token itself and its lemma as features.
- To handle cases where word senses are identifiable by the PoS of a token ("might result" vs "the might"), we combine the latter with the lemma and add it as a feature.
- We combine the lemma with the CCG supertag and add it as a feature in order to capture cases where the hedging function of a word is determined by its syntactic role in the sentence. For example, "indicating" in the example of Table 1 is followed by a clausal complement (a very reliable predictor of hedging function for epistemic verbs), which is captured by its CCG supertag. As explained in Section 2, this information can be recovered even in sentences where the parser fails to produce a parse.
- Passive voice is commonly employed to limit commitment to the statement made, therefore we add it as a feature combined with the lemma to verbs in that voice (*nsubjpass*).
- Modal auxiliaries are prime hedging devices but they are also among the most ambiguous. For example, "can" is annotated as a cue in 16% of its occurrences and it is the fifth most frequent cue in the full articles. To resolve this ambiguity, we add as features the lemma of the main verb the auxiliary is dependent on (*aux*) as well as the lemmas of any dependents of the main verb. Thus we can capture some stereotypical speculative expressions in scientific articles (e.g "could be due"), while avoiding false positives that are distinguished by the use of first person plural pronoun and/or reference to objective enabling conditions (Kilicoglu and Bergler, 2008).
- Speculation can be expressed via negation of a word expressing certainty (e.g. "we do not know"), therefore we add the lemma of the token prefixed with "not" (*neg*).
- In order to capture stereotypical hedging expressions such as "raises the question" and "on the assumption" we add as features the direct object of verbs combined with the lemma of their object (*dobj*) and the preposition for nouns in a prepositional relation (*prep_**).
- In order to capture the effect of adverbs on the hedging function of verbs (e.g. "theoretically

features	Recall	Precision	F-score
tokens, lemmas	75.92	81.07	78.41
+PoS, CCG	78.23	83.71	80.88
+syntax	81.00	81.31	81.15
+combs	79.58	84.98	82.19

Table 3: Performance of various feature sets on Task1 using cross-validation on full articles.

features	Recall	Precision	F-score
tokens, lemmas	79.19	80.43	79.81
+PoS, CCG	81.12	85.22	83.12
+syntax	83.43	84.57	84.00
+combs	85.16	85.99	85.58

Table 4: Performance of various feature sets on Task1 using cross-validation on full articles incorporating the abstracts as training data.

considered") we add the lemma of the adverb as a feature to the verb (*advmod*).

- To distinguish the probabilistic/numerical sense from the hedging sense of adjectives such as "possible", we add the lemma and the number of the noun they modify as features (*amod*), since plural number tends to be associated with the probabilistic/numerical sense (e.g. "all possible combinations").

Finally, given that this stage is meant to identify cues in order to recover their scopes in Task2, we attempt to resolve multi-token cues in the training data into single-token ones. This agrees with the *minimal* strategy for marking cues stated in the corpus guidelines (Szarvas et al., 2008) and it simplifies scope detection. Therefore, during training multi-token cues are resolved to their syntactic head according to the dependency output, e.g. in Table 1 "indicate that" is restricted to "indicate" only. There were two cases in which this process failed; the cues being "cannot" (S3.167) and "not clear" (S3.269). We argue that the former is inconsistently annotated (the sentence reads "cannot be defined..." and it would have been resolved to "defined"), while the latter is headed syntactically by the verb "be" which is preceding it.

5 Task1 results and error analysis

Initially we experiment using the full-articles part of the training data only divided in four folds. The reason for this choice is that the language of the abstracts is relatively restricted and phenomena that appear only in full papers could be obscured by the abstracts, especially since the latter consist of more sentences in total (11,871 vs. 2,670). Such phenomena include language related to figures and descriptions of probabilistic models.

Each row in Table 3 is produced by adding extra features to the feature set represented on the row directly above it. First we consider using only the tokens and their lemmas as features which amounts to a weighted dictionary but which achieves reasonable performance. The inclusion of PoS tags and CCG supertags improves performance, whereas syntactic context increases recall while decreasing precision slightly. This is due to the fact that logistic regression does not represent feature interactions and the effect of these features varies across words. For example, clausal complements affect epistemic verbs but not other words ("indicate" vs. "state" in the example of Table 1) and negation affects only words expressing certainty. In order to ameliorate this limitation we add the lexicalized features described in Section 4, for example the combination of the lemma with the negation syntactic dependency. These additional features improved precision from 81.31% to 84.98%.

Finally, we add the abstracts to the training data which improves recall but harms precision slightly (Table 4) when only tokens and lemmas are used as features. Nevertheless, we decided to keep them as they have a positive effect for all other feature representations.

A misinterpretation of the BioScope paper (Szarvas et al., 2008) led us to believe that five of the nine full articles in the training data were annotated using the guidelines of Medlock and Briscoe (2007). After the shared task, the organizers clarified to us that all the full articles were annotated using the BioScope guidelines. Due to our misinterpretation, we change our experimental setup to cross-validate on the four full articles annotated in BioScope only, considering the other five full articles and the abstracts only as training data. We keep this setup for the remainder of the paper.

We repeat the cross-validation experiments with the full feature set and this new experimental setup and report the results in Table 5. Using the same feature set, we experiment with the Gaussian prior instead of the sparsity-enforcing Laplace prior which results in decreased precision and F-score,

	Recall	Precision	F-score
cross-Laplace	80.33	84.21	82.23
cross-Gaussian	81.59	80.58	81.08
test	84.94	85.48	85.21

Table 5: Performance of the final system in Task1.

therefore confirming our intuition that most features extracted are irrelevant to the task and should have zero weight. Finally, we report our performance on the test data using the Laplace prior.

6 Detecting the scope of the hedges

In Task2, the systems need to identify speculative cues and their respective scopes. Since our system for Task1 identifies cues, our discussion of Task2 focuses on identifying the scope of a given cue. It is a non-trivial task, since scopes can be nested and can span over a large number of tokens of the sentence.

An initial approach explored was to associate each cue with the token representing the syntactic head of its scope and then to infer the scope using syntactic parsing. In order to achieve this, we resolved the (almost always multi-token) scopes to their syntactic heads and then built a classifier whose features are based on syntactic dependency paths. Multi-token scopes which were not headed syntactically by a single token (according to the parser) were discarded in order to obtain a cleaner dataset for training. This phenomenon occurs rather frequently, therefore reducing the training instances. At testing, the classifier identifies the syntactic head of the scope for each cue and we infer the scope from the syntactic parser's output. If more than one scope head is identified for a particular cue, then the scopes are concatenated.

The performance of this approach turned out to be very low, 10.34% in F-score. We identified two principal reasons for this. First, relying on the syntactic parser's output to infer the scope is unavoidably affected by parsing errors. Second, the scope annotation takes into account semantics instead of syntax. For example bibliographic references are excluded based on their semantics.

In order to handle these issues, we developed an approach that predicts whether each token of the sentence belongs to the scope of a given cue. The overall scope for that cue becomes the string enclosed by the left- and right-most tokens predicted to belong to the scope. The features used by the classifier to predict whether a token belongs to the scope of a particular cue are based on the shortest syntactic dependency path connecting them, which is found using Dijkstra's algorithm. If no such path is found (commonly due to parsing failure), then the token is classified as not belonging to the scope of that cue. The features we use are the following:

- The dependency path between the cue and the token, combined with both their lemmas.
- According to the guidelines, different cues have different preferences in having their scopes extended to their left or to their right. For example modal auxiliaries like "can" in Table 1 extend their scope to their right. Therefore we add the dependency path feature defined above refined by whether the token is on the left or the right of the cue in question.
- We combine the dependency path and the lemmas of the cue and the token with their PoS tags and CCG supertags, since these tags refine the syntactic function of the tokens.

The features defined above are very sparse, especially when longer dependency paths are involved. This can affect performance substantially, as the scopes can be rather long, in many cases spanning over the whole sentence. An unseen dependency path between a cue and a token during testing results in the token being excluded from the scope of that cue. In turn, this causes predicted scopes to be shorter than they should be. We attempt to alleviate this sparsity in two stages. First, we make the following simplifications to the labels of the dependencies:

- Adjectival, noun compound, relative clause and participial modifiers (*amod*, *nn*, *rcmod*, *partmod*) are converted to generic modifiers (*mod*).
- Passive auxiliary (*auxpass*) and copula (*cop*) relations are converted to auxiliary relations (*aux*).
- Clausal complement relations with internal/external subject (*ccomp*/*xcomp*) are converted to complement relations (*comp*).
- All subject relations in passive or active voice (*nsubj*, *nsubjpass*, *csubj*, *csubjpass*) are converted to subjects (*subj*).
- Direct and indirect object relations (*iobj*, *dobj*) are converted to objects (*obj*).

- We de-lexicalize conjunct (*conj_**) and prepositional modifier relations (*prep_**).

Second, we shorten the dependency paths:

- Since the SD collapsed dependencies format treats conjunctions asymmetrically (*conj*), we propagate the subject and object dependencies of the head of the conjunction to the dependent. We process appositional and abbreviation modifiers (*appos*, *abbrev*) in the same way.
- Determiner and predeterminer relations (*det*, *predet*) in the end of the dependency path are removed, since the determiners (e.g. "the") and predeterminers (e.g. "both") are included in/excluded from the scope following their syntactic heads.
- Consecutive modifier and dependent relations (*mod*, *dep*) are replaced by a single relation of the same type.
- Auxiliary relations (*aux*) that are not in the beginning or the end of the path are removed.

Despite these simplifications, it is still possible during testing to encounter dependency paths unseen in the training data. In order to ameliorate this issue, we implement a backoff strategy that progressively shortens the dependency path until it matches a dependency path seen in the training data. For example, if the path from a cue to a token is *subj-mod-mod* and it has not been seen in the training data, we test if *subj-mod* has been seen. If it has, we consider it as the dependency path to define the features described earlier. If not, we test for *subj* in the same way. This strategy relies on the assumption that tokens that are likely to be included in/excluded from the scope following the tokens they are syntactically dependent on. For example, modifiers are likely to follow the token being modified.

7 Task2 results and error analysis

In order to evaluate the performance of our approach, we performed four-fold cross-validation on the four BioScope full articles, using the remaining full articles and the abstracts as training data only. The performance achieved using the features mentioned in Section 6 is 28.62% F-score, while using the simplified dependency paths instead of the path extracted from the parser's output improves it to 34.35% F-score. Applying the back-off strategy for unseen dependency paths to the simplified paths results in 35.37% F-score (Table 6).

features	Recall	Precision	F-score
standard	27.54	29.79	28.62
simplified	33.11	35.69	34.35
+backoff	34.10	36.75	35.37
+post	40.98	44.17	42.52

Table 6: Performance on Task2 using cross-validation on BioScope full articles.

Our system predicts only single token cues. This agrees in spirit with the minimal cue annotation strategy stated in the BioScope guidelines. The guidelines allow for multi-token cues, referred to as *complex keywords*, which are defined as cases where the tokens of a phrase cannot express uncertainty independently. We argue that this definition is rather vague, and combined with the requirement for contiguity, results in cue instances such as "indicating that" (multiple occurrences), "looks as" (S4.232) and "address a number of questions" (S4.36) annotated as cues. It is unclear why "suggesting that" or "appears that" are not annotated as cues as well, or why "that" contributes to the semantic content of "indicate". "that" does help determine the sense of "indicate", but we argue that it should not be part of the cue as it does not contribute to its semantic content. "indicate that" is the only consistent multi-token cue pattern in the training data. Therefore, when our system identifies as a cue a token with the lemma "indicate", if this token is followed by "that", "that" is added to the cue. Given the annotation difficulties multi-token cues present, it would be useful during evaluation to relax cue matching in the same way as in the BioNLP 2009 shared task, i.e. considering as correct those cues predicted within one token of the gold standard annotation.

As explained in Section 6, bibliographic references are excluded from scopes and cannot be recognized by means of syntactic parsing only. Additionally, in some cases the XML formatting does not preserve the parentheses and/or brackets around numerical references. We employ two post-processing steps to deal with these issues. First, if the ultimate token of a scope happens to be the penultimate token of the sentence and a number, then it is removed from the scope. This step can have a negative effect when the last token of the scope and penultimate token of the sen-

		Recall	Precision	F-score
Cues	cross	74.52	81.63	77.91
	test	74.50	81.85	78.00
Task2	cross	40.98	44.17	42.52
	test	42.40	45.96	44.11

Table 7: Performance on cue identification and cue/scope identification in Task2.

tence happens to be a genuine number, as in Figure 1. In our experiments however, this heuristic always increased performance. Second, if a scope contains an opening parenthesis but not its closing one, then the scope is limited to the token immediately before the opening one. Note that the training data annotation allows for partial parenthetical statements to be included in scopes, as a result of terminating scopes at bibliographic references which are not the only tokens in a parentheses. For example, in S7.259: "expressed (ED, unpublished)" the scope is terminated after "ED". These post-processing steps improved the performance substantially to 42.52% F-score (Table 6).

The requirement for contiguous scope spans which include their cue(s) is not treated appropriately by our system, since we predict each token of the scope independently. Combined with the fact that the guidelines frequently define scopes to extend either to the left or to the right of the cue, an approach based on sequential tagging and/or predicting boundaries could perform better. However, as mentioned in the guidelines, the contiguity requirement sometimes forced the inclusion of tokens that should have been excluded given the purpose of the task.

Our final performance on the test data is 44.11% in F-score (Table 7). This is higher than the one reported in the official results (38.37%) because we subsequently increased the coverage of the C&C parser (parse failures resulted in 63 cues not receiving a scope), the addition of the back-off strategy for unseen dependency paths and the clarification on the inclusion of bibliographic references in the scopes which resulted in improving the parentheses post-processing steps.

8 Related work

The shared task uses only full articles for testing while both abstracts and full articles are used for training. We argue that this represents a realistic scenario for system developers since annotated resources consist mainly of abstracts, while most information extraction systems are applied to full articles. Also, the shared task aimed at detecting the scope of speculation, while most previous work (Light et al., 2004; Medlock and Briscoe, 2007; Kilicoglu and Bergler, 2008) considered only classification of sentences, possibly due to the lack of appropriately annotated resources.

The increasing interest in detecting speculative language in scientific text resulted in a number of guidelines. Compared to the most recent previous definition by Medlock and Briscoe (2007), BioScope differs in the following ways:

- BioScope does not annotate anaphoric hedge references.
- BioScope annotates indications of experimentally observed non-universal behaviour.
- BioScope annotates statements of explicitly proposed alternatives.

The first difference is due to the requirement that the scope of the speculation be annotated, which is not possible when it is present in a different sentence. The other two differences follow from the stated purpose which is the detection of sentences containing uncertain information.

In related work, Hyland (1996) associates the use of speculative language in scholarly publications with the purpose for which they are employed by the authors. In particular, he distinguishes content-oriented hedges from reader-oriented ones. The former are used to calibrate the strength of the claims made, while the latter are employed in order to soften anticipated criticism on behalf of the reader. Content-oriented hedges are further distinguished as accuracy-oriented ones, used to express uncertain claims more accurately, and writer-oriented ones, used to limit the commitment of the author(s) to the claims. While the boundaries between these distinctions are not clear-cut and instances of hedging can serve more than one of these purposes simultaneously, it is worth bearing them in mind while approaching the task. With respect to the shared task, taking into account that hedging is used to express statements more accurately can help resolve the ambiguity when annotating certain statements about uncertainty. Such statements, which involve words such as "estimate", "possible", "predict", occur frequently in full articles.

Wilson (2008) analyzes speculation detection

inside a general framework for sentiment analysis centered around the notion of private states (emotions, thoughts, intentions, etc.) that are not open to objective observation or verification. Speculation is annotated with a *spec-span/spec-target* scheme by answering the questions *what the speculation is* and *what the speculation is about.* With respect to the BioScope guidelines, *spec-span* is similar to what *scope* attempts to capture. *spec-span* and *spec-target* do not need to be present at the same time, which could help annotating anaphoric cues.

9 Conclusions

This paper describes our approach to the CoNLL-2010 shared task on speculative language detection using logistic regression and syntactic dependencies. We achieved competitive performance on sentence level uncertainty classification (Task1), but not on scope identification (Task2). Motivated by our error analysis we suggest refinements to the task definition that could improve annotation.

Our approach to detecting speculation cues successfully employed syntax as a proxy for the semantic content of words. In addition, we demonstrated that performance gains can be obtained by choosing an appropriate prior for feature weights in logistic regression. Finally, our performance in scope detection was improved substantially by the simplification scheme used to reduce the sparsity of the dependency paths. It was devised using human judgment, but as information extraction systems become increasingly reliant on syntax and each task is likely to need a different scheme, future work should investigate how this could be achieved using machine learning.

Acknowledgements

We would like to thank the organizers for providing the infrastructure and the data for the shared task, Laura Rimell for her help with the C&C parser and Marina Terkourafi for useful discussions. The authors were funded by NIH/NLM grant R01/LM07050.

References

Jinying Chen and Martha Palmer. 2009. Improving English Verb Sense Disambiguation Performance with Linguistically Motivated Features and Clear Sense Distinction Boundaries. *Language Resources and Evaluation*, 43(2):143–172.

Marie-Catherine de Marneffe and Christopher D. Manning. 2008. The Stanford typed dependencies representation. In *CrossParser '08: Coling 2008: Proceedings of the Workshop on Cross-Framework and Cross-Domain Parser Evaluation*, pages 1–8.

Richárd Farkas, Veronika Vincze, György Móra, János Csirik, and György Szarvas. 2010. The CoNLL-2010 Shared Task: Learning to Detect Hedges and their Scope in Natural Language Text. In *Proceedings of CoNLL-2010 Shared Task*, pages 1–12.

Alexander Genkin, David D. Lewis, and David Madigan. 2006. Large-scale Bayesian Logistic Regression for Text Classification. *Technometrics*, 49(3):291–304.

Ken Hyland. 1996. Writing Without Conviction? Hedging in Science Research Articles. *Applied Linguistics*, 17(4):433–454.

Halil Kilicoglu and Sabine Bergler. 2008. Recognizing speculative language in biomedical research articles: a linguistically motivated perspective. In *BioNLP '08: Proceedings of the Workshop on Current Trends in Biomedical Natural Language Processing*, pages 46–53.

Jin-Dong Kim, Tomoko Ohta, Sampo Pyysalo, Yoshinobu Kano, and Jun'ichi Tsujii. 2009. Overview of BioNLP'09 shared task on event extraction. In *BioNLP '09: Proceedings of the Workshop on BioNLP*, pages 1–9.

Marc Light, Xin Ying Qiu, and Padmini Srinivasan. 2004. The Language of Bioscience: Facts, Speculations, and Statements In Between. In *HLT-NAACL 2004 Workshop: BioLINK 2004, Linking Biological Literature, Ontologies and Databases*, pages 17–24.

Ben Medlock and Ted Briscoe. 2007. Weakly Supervised Learning for Hedge Classification in Scientific Literature. In *Proceedings of the 45th Annual Meeting of the Association of Computational Linguistics*, pages 992–999.

Guido Minnen, John Carroll, and Darren Pearce. 2001. Applied morphological processing of English. *Natural Language Engineering*, 7(3):207–223.

Laura Rimell and Stephen Clark. 2009. Porting a lexicalized-grammar parser to the biomedical domain. *Journal of Biomedical Informatics*, 42(5):852–865.

György Szarvas, Veronika Vincze, Richárd Farkas, and János Csirik. 2008. The BioScope corpus: annotation for negation, uncertainty and their scope in biomedical texts. In *BioNLP '08: Proceedings of the Workshop on Current Trends in Biomedical Natural Language Processing*, pages 38–45.

Theresa Ann Wilson. 2008. *Fine-grained Subjectivity and Sentiment Analysis: Recognizing the Intensity, Polarity, and Attitudes of Private States.* Ph.D. thesis, University of Pittsburgh.

A Hedgehop over a Max-Margin Framework Using Hedge Cues

Maria Georgescul
ISSCO, ETI, University of Geneva
40 bd. du Pont-d'Arve
CH-1211 Geneva 4
maria.georgescul@unige.ch

Abstract

In this paper, we describe the experimental settings we adopted in the context of the 2010 CoNLL shared task for detecting sentences containing uncertainty. The classification results reported on are obtained using discriminative learning with features essentially incorporating lexical information. Hyper-parameters are tuned for each domain: using BioScope training data for the biomedical domain and Wikipedia training data for the Wikipedia test set. By allowing an efficient handling of combinations of large-scale input features, the discriminative approach we adopted showed highly competitive empirical results for hedge detection on the Wikipedia dataset: our system is ranked as the first with an F-score of 60.17%.

1 Introduction and related work

One of the first attempts in exploiting a Support Vector Machine (SVM) classifier to select speculative sentences is described in Light et al. (2004). They adopted a bag-of-words representation of text sentences occurring in MEDLINE abstracts and reported on preliminary results obtained. As a baseline they used an algorithm based on finding speculative sentences by simply checking whether any cue (from a given list of 14 cues) occurs in the sentence to be classified.

Medlock and Briscoe (2007) also used single words as input features in order to classify sentences from scientific articles in biomedical domain as speculative or non-speculative. In a first step they employed a weakly supervised Bayesian learning model in order to derive the probability of each word to represent a hedge cue. In the next step, they perform feature selection based on these probabilities. In the last step a classifier trained on a given number of selected features was applied. Medlock and Briscoe (2007) use a similar baseline as the one adopted by Light et al. (2004), i.e. a naïve algorithm based on substring matching, but with a different list of terms to match against. Their baseline has a recall/precision break-even point of 0.60, while their system improves the accuracy to a recall/precision break-even point of 0.76. However Medlock and Briscoe (2007) note that their model is unsuccessful in identifying assertive statements of knowledge paucity which are generally marked rather syntactically than lexically.

Kilicoglu and Bergler (2008) proposed a semi-automatic approach incorporating syntactic and some semantic information in order to enrich or refine a list of lexical hedging cues that are used as input features for automatic detection of uncertain sentences in the biomedical domain. They also used lexical cues and syntactic patterns that strongly suggest non-speculative contexts ("unhedges"). Then they manually expanded and refined the set of lexical hedging and "unhedging" cues using conceptual semantic and lexical relations extracted from WordNet (Fellbaum, 1998) and the UMLS SPECIALIST Lexicon (McCray et al. 1994). Kilicoglu and Bergler (2008) did experiments on the same dataset as Medlock and Briscoe (2007) and their experimental results proved that the classification accuracy can be improved by approximately 9% (from an F-score of 76% to an F-score of 85%) if syntactic and semantic information are incorporated.

The experiments run by Medlock (2008) on the same dataset as Medlock and Briscoe (2007) show that adding features based on part-of-speech tags to a bag-of-words input representation can slightly improve the accuracy, but the "improvements are marginal and not statistically significant". Their experimental results also show that stemming can slightly

Proceedings of the Fourteenth Conference on Computational Natural Language Learning: Shared Task, pages 26–31,
Uppsala, Sweden, 15-16 July 2010.

Dataset	#sentences	%uncertain sentences	#distinct cues	#ambiguous cues	P	R	F
Wikipedia training	11111	22%	1912	188	0.32	0.96	0.48
Wikipedia test	9634	23%	-		0.45	0.86	0.59
BioScope training	14541	18%	168	96	0.46	0.99	0.63
BioScope test	5003	16%	-		0.42	0.98	0.59

Table 1: The percentage of "uncertain" sentences (% uncertain sentences) given the total number of available sentences (#sentences) together with the number of distinct cues in the training corpus and the performance of the baseline algorithm based on the list of cues extracted from the training corpus.

improve the classification accuracy, while using bigrams brings a statistically significant improvement over a simple bag-of-words representation. However, Medlock (2008) illustrates that "whether a particular term acts as a hedge cue is quite often a rather subtle function of its sense usage, in which case the distinctions may well not be captured by part-of-speech tagging".

Móra et al. (2009) also used a machine learning framework based on lexical input features and part-of-speech tags. Other recent work on hedge detection (Ganter and Strube, 2009; Marco and Mercer, 2004; Mercer et al., 2004; Morante and Daelemans, 2009a; Szarvas, 2008) relied primarily on word frequencies as primary features including various shallow syntactic or semantic information.

The corpora made available in the CoNLL shared task (Farkas et al., 2010; Vincze et al., 2008) contains multi-word expressions that have been annotated by linguists as cue words tending to express hedging. In this paper, we test whether it might suffice to rely on this list of cues alone for automatic hedge detection. The classification results reported on are obtained using support vector machines trained with features essentially incorporating lexical information, i.e. features extracted from the list of hedge cues provided with the training corpus.

In the following, we will first describe some preliminary considerations regarding the results that can be achieved using a naïve baseline algorithm (Section 2). Section 3 summarizes the experimental settings and the input features adopted, as well as the experimental results we obtained on the CoNLL test data. We also report on the intermediate results we obtained when only the CoNLL training dataset was available. In Section 4, we conclude with a brief description of the theoretical and practical advantages of our system. Future research directions are mentioned in Section 5.

2 Preliminary Considerations

2.1 Benchmarking

As a baseline for our experiments, we consider a naive algorithm that classifies as "uncertain" any sentence that contains a hedge cue, i.e. any of the multi-word expressions labeled as hedge cues in the training corpus.

Table 1 shows the results obtained when using the baseline naïve algorithm on the CoNLL datasets provided for training and test purposes[1]. The performance of the baseline algorithm is denoted by Precision (P), Recall (R) and F-score (F) measures. The first three columns of the table show the total number of available sentences together with the percentage of "uncertain" sentences occurring in the dataset. The fourth column of the table shows the total number of distinct hedge cues extracted from the training corpus. Those hedge cues occurring in "certain" sentences are denoted as "ambiguous cues". The fifth column of the table shows the number of distinct ambiguous cues.

As we observe from Table 1, the baseline algorithm has very high values for the recall score on the BioScope corpus (both training and test data). The small percentage of false negatives on the BioScope test data reflects the fact that only a small percentage of "uncertain" sentences in the reference test dataset do not contain a hedge cue that occurs in the training dataset.

The precision of the baseline algorithm has values under 0.5 on all four datasets (i.e. on both BioScope and Wikipedia data). This illustrates that ambiguous hedge cues are frequently used in "certain" sentences. That is, the baseline algorithm has less true positives than false

[1] In Section 3.2, we provide the performance of the baseline algorithm obtained when only the CoNLL training dataset was available. When we tuned our system, we obviously had available only the results provided in Table 2 (Section 3.2).

positives, i.e. more than 50% of the sentences containing a hedge cue are labeled as "certain" in the reference datasets.

2.2 Beyond bag-of-words

In order to verify whether simply the frequencies of all words (except stop-words) occurring in a sentence might suffice to discriminate between "certain" and "uncertain" sentences, we performed preliminary experiments with a SVM bag-of-words model. The accuracy of this system is lower than the baseline accuracy on both datasets (BioScope and Wikipedia). For instance, the classifier based on a bag-of-words representation obtains an F-score of approximately 42% on Wikipedia data, while the baseline has an F-score of 49% on the same dataset. Another disadvantage of using a bag-of-words input representation is obviously the large dimension of the system's input matrix. For instance, the input matrix representation of the Wikipedia training dataset would have approximately 11111 rows and over 150000 columns which would require over 6GB of RAM for a non-sparse matrix representation.

3 System Description

3.1 Experimental Settings

In our work for the CoNLL shared task, we used Support Vector Machine classification (Fan et al., 2005; Vapnik, 1998) based on the Gaussian Radial Basis kernel function (RBF). We tuned the width of the RBF kernel (denoted by *gamma*) and the regularization parameter (denoted by *C*) via grid search over the following range of values: $\{2^{-8}, 2^{-7}, 2^{-6}, \ldots 2^{4}\}$ for *gamma* and {1, 10..200 step 10, 200..500 step 100} for *C*. During parameter tuning, we performed 10-fold cross validation for each possible value of these parameters. Since the training data are unbalanced (e.g. 18% of the total number of sentences in the BioScope training data are labeled as "uncertain"), for SVM training we used the following class weights:

- 0.1801 for the "certain" class and 0.8198 for the "uncertain" class on the BioScope dataset;
- 0.2235 for the "certain" class and 0.7764 for the "uncertain" class on the Wikipedia dataset.

The system was trained on the training set provided by the CoNLL shared task organizers and tested on the test set provided. As input features in our max-margin framework, we simply used the frequency of each hedge cue provided with the training corpus in each sentence. We also used as input features during the tuning phase of our system 2-grams and 3-grams extracted from the list of hedge cues provided with the training corpus.

3.2 Classification results

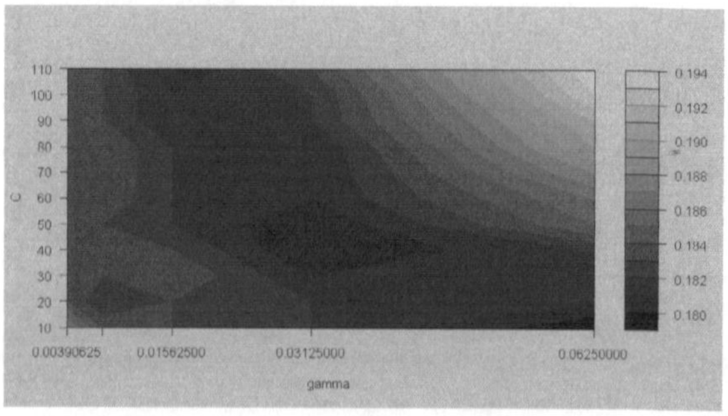

Figure 1: Contour plot of the classification error landscape resulting from a grid search over a range of values of $\{2^{-8}, 2^{-7}, 2^{-6}, 2^{-5}, 2^{-4}\}$ for the *gamma* parameter and a range of values of {10, 20, …, 110} for the *C* parameter on Wikipedia data.

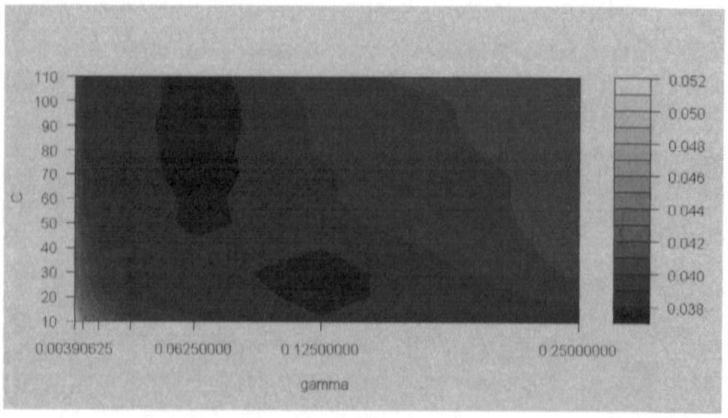

Figure 2: Contour plot of the classification error landscape resulting from a grid search over a range of values of $\{2^{-8}, 2^{-7}, 2^{-6}, \ldots 2^{-2}\}$ for the *gamma* parameter and a range of values of {1, 10, 20, 30, …110} for the *C* parameter on BioScope data.

Figure 1 shows the variability of hedge detection results on Wikipedia training data when changing the RBF-specific kernel parameter and the regularization parameter *C*. The contour plot shows that there are three regions (represented in the figure by the darkest landscape color) for parameter values where the cross validation error is lower than 18.2%. One of these optimal settings for parameter values was used for the results submitted to the CoNLL shared task and we obtained an F-score of 60.17%. When the CoNLL test data containing

Dataset	TP	FP	FN	P	R	F	Run Time
Wikipedia training	1899	1586	585	0.5449	0.7644	0.6362	49.1 seconds
Wikipedia test	1213	471	1021	0.7203	0.5429	0.6191	21.5 seconds
BioScope training	2508	515	112	0.8296	0.9572	0.8888	19.5 seconds
BioScope test	719	322	71	0.6907	0.9101	0.7854	2.6 seconds

Table 2: The performance of our system corresponding to the best parameter values. The performance is denoted in terms of true positives (TP), false positives (FP), false negatives (FN), precision (P), recall (R) and F-score (F)

the reference labels were made available, we also did tests with our system using the other two optimal settings for parameter values.

The optimal classification results on the Wikipedia dataset were obtained for a *gamma* value equal to 0.0625 and for a *C* value equal to 10, corresponding to a cross validation classification error of 17.94%. The model performances corresponding to these best parameter values are provided in Table 2. The P, R, F-score values provided in Table 2 are directly comparable to P, R, F-score values given in Table 1 since exactly the same datasets were used during the evaluation.

The SVM approach we adopted shows highly competitive empirical results for weasel detection on the Wikipedia test dataset in the sense that our system was ranked as the first in the CoNLL shared task. However, the baseline algorithm described in Section 2 proves to be rather difficult to beat given its F-score performance of 59% on the Wikipedia test data. This provides motivation to consider other refinements of our system. In particular, we believe that it might be possible to improve the recall of our system by enriching the list of input features using a lexical ontology in order to extract synonyms for verbs, adjectives and adverbs occurring in the current hedge cue list.

Figure 2 exemplifies the SVM classification results obtained during parameter tuning on BioScope training data. The optimal classification results on the BioScope dataset were obtained for *gamma* equal to 0.0625 and *C* equal to 110, corresponding to a cross validation classification error of 3.73%. The model performance corresponding to the best parameter settings is provided in Table 2. Our system obtained an F-score of 0.78 on the BioScope test dataset while the best ranked system in the CoNLL shared task obtained an F-score of 0.86. In order to identify the weaknesses of our system in this domain, in Subsection 3.2 we will furnish the intermediate results we obtained on the CoNLL training set.

The system is platform independent. We ran the experiments under Windows on a Pentium 4, 3.2GHz with 3GB RAM. The run times necessary for training/testing on the whole training/test dataset are provided in Table 2.

Table 3 shows the approximate intervals of time required for running SVM parameter tuning via grid search on the entire CoNLL training datasets.

Dataset	Range of values	Run time
Wikipedia training data	$\{2^{-8}, 2^{-7}, \ldots 2^{-1}\}$ for *gamma*; {10, 20, …110} for *C*	13 hours
BioScope training data	$\{2^{-8}, 2^{-7}, \ldots 2^{-2}\}$ for *gamma*; {10, 20, …110} for *C*	4 hours

Table 3 : Approximate run times for parameter tuning via 10-fold cross validation

3.3 Intermediate results

In the following we discuss the results obtained when the system was trained on approximately 80% of the CoNLL training corpus and the remaining 20% was used for testing. The 80% of the training corpus was also used to extract the list of hedge cues that were considered as input features for the SVM machine learning system.

The BioScope training corpus provided in CoNLL shared task framework contains 11871 sentences from scientific abstracts and 2670 sentences from scientific full articles.

In a first experiment, we only used sentences from scientific abstracts for training and testing: we randomly selected 9871 sentences for training and the remaining 2000 sentences were used for testing. The results thus obtained are shown in Table 4 on the second line of the table.

Dataset content	#sentences used for training	#sentences used for test	SVM			Baseline		
			P	R	F	P	R	F
Abstracts only	9871	2000	0.85	0.94	0.90	0.49	0.97	0.65
Full articles only	2170	500	0.72	0.87	0.79	0.46	0.91	0.61
Abstracts and full articles	11541	3000	0.81	0.92	0.86	0.47	0.98	0.64

Table 4: Performances when considering separately the dataset containing abstracts only and the dataset containing articles from BioScope corpus. The SVM classifier was trained with gamma = 1 and c=10. Approximately 80% of the CoNLL train corpus was used for training and 20% of the train corpus was held out for testing.

Second, we used only the available 2670 sentences from scientific full articles. We randomly split this small dataset into a training set of 2170 sentences and test set of 500 sentences.

Third, we used the entire set of 14541 sentences (composing scientific abstracts and full articles) for training and testing: we randomly selected 11541 sentences for training and the remaining 3000 sentences were used for testing. The results obtained in this experiment are shown in Table 4 on the fourth line.

We observe from Table 3 a difference of 10% between the F-score obtained on the dataset containing abstracts and the F-score obtained on the dataset containing full articles. This difference in accuracy might simply be due to the fact that the available abstracts training dataset is approximately 5 times larger than the full articles training dataset. In order to check whether this difference in accuracy is only attributable to the small size of the full articles dataset, we further analyze the learning curve of SVM on the abstracts dataset.

To measure the learning curve, we randomly selected from the abstracts dataset 2000 sentences for testing. We divided the remaining sentences into 10 parts, we used two parts for training, then we increased the size of the training dataset by one part incrementally. We show the results obtained in Figure 3. The x-axis shows the number of sentences used for training divided by 1000. We observe that the F-score on the test dataset changed only slightly when more than 4/10 of the training data (i.e. more than 4800 sentences) were used for training. We also observe that using 2 folds for training (i.e. approximately 2000 sentences) gives an F-score of around 87% on the held-out test data. Therefore, using a similar amount of training data for BioScope abstracts as used for BioScope full articles, we still have a difference of 8% between the F-score values obtained. That is, our system is more efficient on abstracts than on full articles.

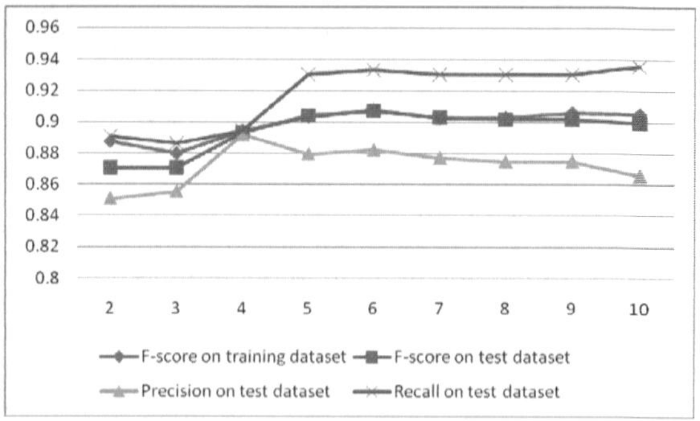

Figure 3: The performance of our system when we used for training various percentages of the BioScope training dataset composed of abstracts only.

4 Conclusions

Our empirical results show that our approach captures informative patterns for hedge detection through the intermedium of a simple low-level feature set.

Our approach has several attractive theoretical and practical properties. Given that the system formulation is based on the max-margin framework underlying SVMs, we can easily incorporate other kernels that induce a feature space that might better separate the data. Furthermore, SVM parameter tuning and the process of building the feature vector matrix, which are the most time and resource consuming, can be easily integrated in a distributed environment considering either cluster-based computing or a GRID technology (Wegener et al., 2007).

From a practical point of view, the key aspects of our proposed system are its simplicity and flexibility. Additional syntactic and semantic based features can easily be added to the SVM input. Also, the simple architecture facilitates the system's integration in an information retrieval system.

5 Future work

The probabilistic discriminative model we have explored appeared to be well suited to tackle the problem of weasel detection. This provides motivation to consider other refinements of our system, by incorporating syntactic or semantic information. In particular, we believe that the recall score of our system can be improved by identifying a list of new potential hedge cues using a lexical ontology.

References

Rong-En Fan, Pai-Hsuen Chen, and Chih-Jen Lin. 2005. Working set selection using the second order information for training SVM. *Journal of Machine Learning Research*, 6: 1889-918.

Richárd Farkas, Veronika Vincze, György Móra, János Csirik, and György Szarvas. 2010. The CoNLL-2010 Shared Task: Learning to Detect Hedges and their Scope in Natural Language Text. In *Proceedings of the Fourteenth Conference on Computational Natural Language Learning (CoNLL-2010): Shared Task*, pages 1–12.

Christiane Fellbaum. 1998. *WordNet: An Electronic Lexical Database*. MIT Press, Cambridge, MA.

Viola Ganter, and Michael Strube. 2009. Finding hedges by chasing weasels: Hedge detection using Wikipedia tags and shallow linguistic features. In *Proceedings of joint conference of the 47th Annual Meeting of the ACL-IJCNLP.*

Halil Kilicoglu, and Sabine Bergler. 2008. Recognizing Speculative Language in Biomedical Research Articles: A Linguistically Motivated Perspective. In *Proceedings of Current Trends in Biomedical Natural Language Processing (BioNLP)*, Columbus, Ohio, USA.

Marc Light, Xin Ying Qiu, and Padmini Srinivasan. 2004. The Language of Bioscience: Facts, Speculations, and Statements in between. In *Proceedings of the HLT BioLINK.*

Chrysanne Di Marco, and Robert E. Mercer. 2004. Hedging in Scientific Articles as a Means of Classifying Citations. In *Proceedings of Working Notes of AAAI Spring Symposium on Exploring Attitude and Affect in Text: Theories and Applications*, Stanford University.

Alexa T. McCray, Suresh Srinivasan, and Allen C. Browne. 1994. Lexical methods for managing variation in biomedical terminologies. In *Proceedings of the 18th Annual Symposium on Computer Applications in Medical Care.*

Ben Medlock. 2008. Exploring hedge identification in biomedical literature. *Journal of Biomedical Informatics*, 41:636-54.

Ben Medlock, and Ted Briscoe. 2007. Weakly Supervised Learning for Hedge Classification in Scientific Literature. In *Proceedings of the 45th Annual Meeting of the Association of Computational Linguistics.*

Robert E.Mercer, Chrysanne Di Marco, and Frederick Kroon. 2004. The frequency of hedging cues in citation contexts in scientific writing. In *Proceedings of the Canadian Society for the Computational Studies of Intelligence (CSCSI)*, London, Ontario.

György Móra, Richárd Farkas, György Szarvas, and Zsolt Molnár. 2009. Exploring ways beyond the simple supervised learning approach for biological event extraction. In *Proceedings of the BioNLP 2009 Workshop Companion Volume for Shared Task.*

Roser Morante, and Walter Daelemans. 2009a. Learning the scope of hedge cues in biomedical texts. In *Proceedings of the BioNLP 2009 Workshop*, Boulder, Colorado. Association for Computational Linguistics.

Roser Morante, and Walter Daelemans. 2009b. Learning the scope of hedge cues in biomedical texts. In *Proceedings of the Workshop on BioNLP.*

György Szarvas. 2008. Hedge classification in biomedical texts with a weakly supervised selection of keywords. In *Proceedings of the ACL-08: HLT.*

Vladimir N. Vapnik. 1998. *Statistical learning theory*. Wiley, New York.

Veronika Vincze, György Szarvas, Richárd Farkas, György Móra, and János Csirik. 2008. The BioScope corpus: biomedical texts annotated for uncertainty, negation and their scopes. *BMC Bioinformatics*, 9.

Dennis Wegener, Thierry Sengstag, Stelios R. Sfakianakis, and Anthony Assi. 2007. GridR: An R-based grid-enabled tool for data analysis in ACGT clinico-genomic trials. In *Proceedings of the 3rd International Conference on e-Science and Grid Computing (eScience 2007).*

Detecting Hedge Cues and their Scopes with Average Perceptron

Feng Ji, Xipeng Qiu, Xuanjing Huang
Fudan University
{fengji,xpqiu,xjhuang}@fudan.edu.cn

Abstract

In this paper, we proposed a hedge detection method with average perceptron, which was used in the closed challenge in CoNLL-2010 Shared Task. There are two subtasks: (1) detecting uncertain sentences and (2) identifying the in-sentence scopes of hedge cues. We use the unified learning algorithm for both subtasks since that the hedge score of sentence can be decomposed into scores of the words, especially the hedge words. On the biomedical corpus, our methods achieved F-measure with 77.86% in detecting in-domain uncertain sentences, 77.44% in recognizing hedge cues, and 19.27% in identifying the scopes.

1 Introduction

Detecting hedged information in biomedical literatures has received considerable interest in the biomedical natural language processing (NLP) community recently. Hedge information indicates that authors do not or cannot back up their opinions or statements with facts (Szarvas et al., 2008), which exists in many natural language texts, such as webpages or blogs, as well as biomedical literatures.

For many NLP applications, such as question answering and information extraction, the information extracted from hedge sentences would be harmful to their final performances. Therefore, the hedge or speculative information should be detected in advance, and dealt with different approaches or discarded directly.

In CoNLL-2010 Shared Task (Farkas et al., 2010), there are two different level subtasks: detecting sentences containing uncertainty and identifying the in-sentence scopes of hedge cues.

For example, in the following sentence:

> These results **suggest** that the IRE motif in the ALAS mRNA is functional and **imply** that translation of the mRNA is controlled by cellular iron availability during erythropoiesis.

The words **suggest** and **imply** indicate that the statements are not supported with facts.

In the first subtask, the sentence is considered as uncertainty.

In the second subtask, **suggest** and **imply** are identified as hedge cues, while the consecutive blocks *suggest that the IRE motif in the ALAS mRNA is functional* and *imply that translation of the mRNA is controlled by cellular iron availability during erythropoiesis* are recognized as their corresponding scopes.

In this paper, we proposed a hedge detection method with average perceptron (Collins, 2002), which was used in the closed challenges in CoNLL-2010 Shared Task (Farkas et al., 2010). Our motivation is to use a unified model to detect two level hedge information (word-level and sentence-level) and the model is easily expanded to joint learning of two subtasks. Since that the hedge score of sentence can be decomposed into scores of the words, especially the hedge words, we chosen linear classifier in our method and used average perceptron as the training algorithm.

The rest of the paper is organized as follows. In Section 2, a brief review of related works is presented. Then, we describe our method in Section 3. Experiments and results are presented in the section 4. Finally, the conclusion will be presented in Section 5.

2 Related works

Although the concept of hedge information has been introduced in linguistic community for a long time, researches on automatic hedge detection emerged from machine learning or compu-

Proceedings of the Fourteenth Conference on Computational Natural Language Learning: Shared Task, pages 32–39,
Uppsala, Sweden, 15-16 July 2010.

tational linguistic perspective in recent years. In this section, we give a brief review on the related works.

For speculative sentences detection, Medlock and Briscoe (2007) report their approach based on weakly supervised learning. In their method, a statistical model is initially derived from a seed corpus, and then iteratively modified by augmenting the training dataset with unlabeled samples according the posterior probability. They only employ bag-of-words features. On the public biomedical dataset[1], their experiments achieve the performance of 0.76 in BEP (break even point). Although they also introduced more linguistic features, such as part-of-speech (POS), lemma and bigram (Medlock, 2008), there are no significant improvements.

In Ganter and Strube (2009), the same task on Wikipedia is presented. In their system, score of a sentence is defined as a normalized tangent value of the sum of scores over all words in the sentence. Shallow linguistic features are introduced in their experiments.

Morante and Daelemans (2009) present their research on identifying hedge cues and their scopes. Their system consists of several classifiers and works in two phases, first identifying the hedge cues in a sentence and secondly finding the full scope for each hedge cue. In the first phase, they use IGTREE algorithm to train a classifier with 3 categories. In the second phase, three different classifiers are trained to find the first token and last token of in-sentence scope and finally combined into a meta classifier. The experiments shown that their system achieves an F1 of nearly 0.85 of identifying hedge cues in the abstracts sub corpus, while nearly 0.79 of finding the scopes with predicted hedge cues. More experiments could be found in their paper (Morante and Daelemans, 2009). They also provide a detail statistics on hedge cues in BioScope corpus[2].

3 Hedge detection with average perceptron

3.1 Detecting uncertain sentences

The first subtask is to identify sentences containing uncertainty information. In particular, this subtask is a binary classification problem at sentence-level.

We define the score of sentence as the confidence that the sentence contains uncertainty information.

The score can be decomposed as the sum of the scores of all words in the sentence,

$$S(\mathbf{x}, y) = \sum_{x_i \in \mathbf{x}} s(x_i, y) = \sum_{x_i \in \mathbf{x}} \mathbf{w}^T \phi(x_i, y)$$

where, $\mathbf{x}$ denotes a sentence and x_i is the i-th word in the sentence $\mathbf{x}$, $\phi(x_i, y)$ is a sparse high-dimensional binary feature vector of word x_i. $y \in \{\textbf{uncertain}, \textbf{certain}\}$ is the category of the sentence. For instance, in the example sentence, if current word is **suggest** while the category of this sentence is uncertain, the following feature is hired,

$$\phi_n(x_i, y) = \begin{cases} 1, & \texttt{if } \substack{x_i=\texttt{``suggest''} \\ y=\texttt{``uncertain''}}, \\ 0, & otherwise \end{cases}$$

where n is feature index.

This representation is commonly used in structured learning algorithms. We can combine the features into a sparse feature vector $\Phi(\mathbf{x}, y) = \sum_i \phi(x_i, y)$.

$$S(\mathbf{x}, y) = \mathbf{w}^T \Phi(x, y) = \sum_{x_i \in \mathbf{x}} \mathbf{w}^T \phi(x_i, y)$$

In the predicting phase, we assign $\mathbf{x}$ to the category with the highest score,

$$y^* = \arg\max_y \mathbf{w}^T \Phi(x, y)$$

We learn the parameters $\mathbf{w}$ with online learning framework. The most common online learner is the perceptron (Duda et al., 2001). It adjusts parameters $\mathbf{w}$ when a misclassification occurs. Although this framework is very simple, it has been shown that the algorithm converges in a finite number of iterations if the data is linearly separable. Moreover, much less training time is required in practice than the batch learning methods, such as support vector machine (SVM) or conditional maximum entropy (CME).

Here we employ a variant perceptron algorithm to train the model, which is commonly named average perceptron since it averages parameters $\mathbf{w}$ across iterations. This algorithm is first proposed in Collins (2002). Many experiments of

[1] http://www.benmedlock.co.uk/hedgeclassif.html

[2] http://www.inf.u-szeged.hu/rgai/bioscope

NLP problems demonstrate better generalization performance than non averaged parameters. More theoretical proofs can be found in Collins (2002). Different from the standard average perceptron algorithm, we slightly modify the average strategy. The reason to this modification is that the original algorithm is slow since parameters accumulate across all iterations. In order to keep fast training speed and avoid overfitting at the same time, we make a slight change of the parameters accumulation strategy, which occurs only after each iteration over the training data finished. Our training algorithm is shown in Algorithm 1.

```
input : training data set:
        (x_n, y_n), n = 1, ··· , N,
        parameters: average number: K,
        maximum iteration number: T.
output: average weight: cw

Initialize: cw ← 0,;
for k = 0 ··· K − 1 do
    w_0 ← 0 ;
    for t = 0 ··· T − 1 do
        receive an example (x_t, y_t);
        predict: ŷ_t = arg max_y w_t^T Φ(x_t, y) ;
        if ŷ_t ≠ y_t then
            w_{t+1} = w_t + Φ(x_t, y_t) − Φ(x_t, ŷ_t)
        end
    end
    cw = cw + w_T ;
end
cw = cw/K ;
```

Algorithm 1: Average Perceptron algorithm

Binary context features are extracted from 6 predefined patterns, which are shown in Figure 1. By using these patterns, we can easily obtain the complicate features. As in the previous example, if the current word is *suggest*, then a new compound feature could be extracted in the form of w_{-1} =*results//*w_0 =*suggest* by employing the pattern $w_{-1}w_0$. // is the separate symbol.

3.2 Identifying hedge cues and their scopes

Our approach for the second subtask consists of two phases: (1) identifying hedge cues in a sentence, then (2) recognizing their corresponding scopes.

3.2.1 Identifying hedge cues

Hedge cues are the most important clues for determining whether a sentence contains uncertain information. Therefore in this phase, we treat the problem of identifying hedge cues as a classification problem. Each word in a sentence would be predicted a category indicating whether this word is a hedge cue word or not. In the previous example, there are two different hedge cues in the sentence (show in bold manner). Words **suggest** and **imply** are assigned with the category *CUE* denoting hedge cue word, while other words are assigned with label *O* denoting non hedge cue word.

In our system, this module is much similar to the module of detecting uncertain sentences. The only difference is that this phase is word level. So that each training sample in this phase is a word, while in detecting speculative sentences training sample is a sentence. The training algorithm is the same as the algorithm shown in Algorithm 1. 12 predefined patterns of context features are shown in Figure 2.

- **unigram**: w_0,p_0
- **bigram**: w_0w_1, w_0p_0, p_0p_1
- **trigram**: $w_{-1}w_0w_1$

Figure 1: Patterns employed in the sentence-level hedge detection. Here w denotes single word, p is part of speech, and the subscript denotes the relative offset compared with current position.

- **unigram**: w_{-2}, w_{-1}, w_0, w_1, w_2, p_0
- **bigram**: $w_{-1}w_0$, w_0w_1, w_0p_0, $p_{-1}p_0$, p_0p_1
- **trigram**: $w_{-1}w_0w_1$

Figure 2: Patterns employed in the word-level hedge detection.

3.2.2 Recognizing in-sentence scopes

After identifying the hedge cues in the first phase, we need to recognize their corresponding in-sentence scopes, which means the boundary of scope should be found within the same sentence.

We consider this problem as a word-cue pair classification problem, where word is any word in a sentence and cue is the identified hedge cue word. Similar to the previous phase, a word-level linear classifier is trained to predict whether each word-cue pair in a sentence is in the scope of the hedge cue.

Besides base context features used in the previous phase, we introduce additional syntactic dependency features. These features are generated by a first-order projective dependency parser (McDonald et al., 2005), and listed in Figure 3.

The scopes of hedge cues are always covering a consecutive block of words including the hedge cue itself. The ideal method should recognize only one consecutive block for each hedge cue. However, our classifier cannot work so well. Therefore, we apply a simple strategy to process the output of the classifier. The simple strategy is to find a maximum consecutive sequence which covers the hedge cue. If a sentence is considered to contain several hedge cues, we simply combine the consecutive sequences, which have at least one common word, to a large block and assign it to the relative hedge cues.

4 Experiments

In this section, we report our experiments on datasets of CoNLL-2010 shared tasks, including the official results and our experimental results when developing the system.

Our system architecture is shown in Figure 4, which consists of the following modules.

1. corpus preprocess module, which employs a tokenizer to normalize the corpus;
2. sentence detection module, which uses a binary sentence-level classifier to determine whether a sentence contains uncertainty information;
3. hedge cues detection module, which identifies which words in a sentence are the hedge cues, we train a binary word-level classifier;
4. cue scope recognition module, which recognizes the corresponding scope for each hedge cue by another word-level classifier.

Our experimental results are obtained on the training datasets by 10-fold cross validation. The maximum iteration number for training the average perceptron is set to 20. Our system is implemented with Java[3].

[3]http://code.google.com/p/fudannlp/

	biomedical	Wikipedia
#sentences	14541	11111
#words	382274	247328
#hedge sentences	2620	2484
%hedge sentences	0.18	0.22
#hedge cues	3378	3133
average number	1.29	1.26
average cue length	1.14	2.45
av. scope length	15.42	-

Table 1: Statistical information on annotated corpus.

4.1 Datasets

In CoNLL-2010 Shared Task, two different datasets are provided to develop the system: (1) biological abstracts and full articles from the BioScope corpus, (2) paragraphs from Wikipedia. Besides manually annotated datasets, three corresponding unlabeled datasets are also allowed for the closed challenges. But we have not employed any unlabeled datasets in our system.

A preliminary statistics can be found in Table 1. We make no distinction between sentences from abstracts or full articles in biomedical dataset. From Table 1, most sentences are certainty while about 18% sentences in biomedical dataset and 22% in Wikipedia dataset are speculative. On the average, there exists nearly 1.29 hedge cues per sentence in biomedical dataset and 1.26 in Wikipedia. The average length of hedge cues varies in these two corpus. In biomedical dataset, hedge cues are nearly one word, but more than two words in Wikipedia. On average, the scope of hedge cue covers 15.42 words.

4.2 Corpus preprocess

The sentence are processed with a maximum-entropy part-of-speech tagger[4] (Toutanova et al., 2003), in which a rule-based tokenzier is used to separate punctuations or other symbols from regular words. Moreover, we train a first-order projective dependency parser with MSTParser[5] (McDonald et al., 2005) on the standard WSJ training corpus, which is converted from constituent trees to dependency trees by several heuristic rules[6].

[4]http://nlp.stanford.edu/software/tagger.shtml

[5]http://www.seas.upenn.edu/~strctlrn/MSTParser/MSTParser.html

[6]http://w3.msi.vxu.se/~nivre/research/Penn2Malt.html

- **word-cue pair**: current word and the hedge cue word pair,
- **word-cue POS pair**: POS pair of current word and the hedge cue word,
- **path of POS**: path of POS from current word to the hedge cue word along dependency tree,
- **path of dependency**: relation path of dependency from current word to the hedge cue word along dependency tree,
- **POS of hedge cue word+direction**: POS of hedge cue word with the direction to the current word. Here direction can be "LEFT" if the hedge cue is on the left to the current word, or "RIGHT" on the right,
- **tree depth**: depth of current in the corresponding dependency tree,
- **surface distance**: surface distance between current word and the hedge cue word. The value of this feature is always 10 in the case of surface distance greater than 10,
- **surface distance+tree depth**: combination of surface distance and tree depth
- **number of punctuations**: number of punctuations between current word and the hedge cue word,
- **number of punctuations + tree depth**: combination of number of punctuations and tree depth

Figure 3: Additional features used in recognizing in-sentence scope

4.3 Uncertain sentences detection

In the first subtask, we carry out the experiments within domain and cross domains. As previously mentioned, we do not use the unlabeled datasets and make no distinction between abstracts and full articles in biomedical dataset. This means we train the models only with the official annotated datasets. The model for cross-domain is trained on the combination of annotated biomedical and Wikipedia datasets.

In this subtask, evaluation is carried out on the sentence level and F-measure of uncertainty sentences is employed as the chief metric.

Table 2 shows the results within domain. After 10-fold cross validation over training dataset, we achieve 84.39% of F1-measure on biomedical while 56.06% on Wikipedia.

We analyzed the low performance of our submission result on Wikipedia. The possible reason is our careless work when dealing with the trained model file. Therefore we retrain a model for Wikipedia and the performance is listed on the bottom line (Wikipedia*) in Table 2.

Dataset	Precision	Recall	F1
10-fold cross validation			
biomedical	91.03	78.66	84.39
Wikipedia	66.54	48.43	56.06
official evaluation			
biomedical	79.45	76.33	77.86
Wikipedia	94.23	6.58	1.23
Wikipedia*	82.19	32.86	46.95

Table 2: Results for in-domain uncertain sentences detection

Table 3 shows the results across domains. We split each annotated dataset into 10 folds. Then training dataset is combined by individually drawing 9 folds out from the split datasets and the rests are used as the test data. On biomedical dataset, F1-measure gets to 79.24% while 56.16% on Wikipedia dataset. Compared with the results within domain, over 5% performance decreases from 84.39% to 79.24% on biomedical, but a slightly increase on Wikipedia.

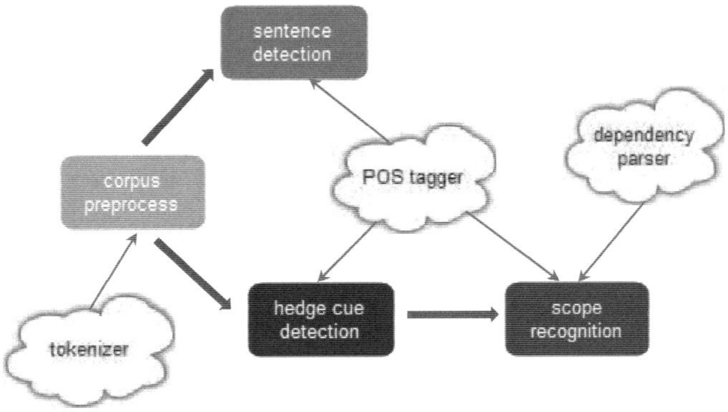

Figure 4: System architecture of our system

Dataset	Precision	Recall	F1
10-fold cross validation			
biomedical	87.86	72.16	79.24
Wikipedia	67.78	47.95	56.16
official evaluation			
biomedical	62.81	79.11	70.03
Wikipedia	62.66	55.28	58.74

Table 3: Results for across-domain uncertain sentences detection

4.3.1 Results analysis

We investigate the weights of internal features and found that the words, which have no uncertainty information, also play the significant roles to predict the uncertainty of the sentence.

Intuitively, the words without uncertainty information should just have negligible effect and the corresponding features should have low weights. However, this ideal case is difficult to reached by learning algorithm due to the sparsity of data.

In Table 4, we list the top 10 words involved in features with the largest weights for each category. These words are ranked by the accumulative scores of their related features.

In Table 5, we list the top 10 POS involved in features with the largest weight for each category.

4.4 Hedge cue identification

Hedge cues identification is one module for the second subtask, we also analyze the performance on this module.

Since we treat this problem as a binary classification problem, we evaluate F-measure of hedge cue words. The results are listed in Table 6.

We have to point out that our evaluation is based on word while official evaluation is based on phrase. That means our results would seem to be higher than the official results, especially on Wikipedia dataset because average length of hedge cues in Wikipedia dataset is more than 2 words.

Dataset	Precision	Recall	F1
10-fold cross validation(word-level)			
biomedical	90.15	84.43	87.19
Wikipedia	57.74	39.81	47.13
official evaluation(phrase-level)			
biomedical	78.7	76.22	77.44

Table 6: Results for in-domain hedge cue identification

4.4.1 Result Analysis

We classify the results into four categories: false negative, false positive, true positive and true negative. We found that most mistakes are made because of polysemy and collocation.

In Table 7, we list top 10 words for each category. For the false results, the words are difficult to distinguish without its context in the corresponding sentence.

4.5 Scopes recognition

For recognizing the in-sentence scopes, F-measure is also used to evaluate the performance of the word-cue pair classifier. The results using gold hedge cues are shown in Table 8. From the results, F-measure achieves respectively 70.44% and 75.94% when individually using the base context features extracted by 12 predefined patterns (see Figure 1) and syntactic dependency features (see Figure 3), while 79.55% when using all features.

The results imply that syntactic dependency

biomedical		Wikipedia		cross domain	
uncertain	certain	uncertain	certain	uncertain	certain
whether	show	probably	the other	suggest	show
may	demonstrate	some	often	whether	used to
suggest	will	many	patients	probably	was
likely	can	one of	another	indicate	CFS
indicate	role	believed	days	appear	demonstrate
possible	found	possibly	CFS	putative	the other
putative	human	considered	are	some	of all
appear	known to	such as	any other	thought	':'
thought	report	several	western	possibly	people
potential	evidence	said to	pop	likely	could not

Table 4: Top 10 significant words in detecting uncertain sentences

biomedical		Wikipedia		cross domain	
uncertain	certain	uncertain	certain	uncertain	certain
MD	SYM	RB	VBZ	JJS	SYM
VBG	PRP	JJS	CD	RBS	':'
VB	NN	RBS	':'	RB	JJR
VBZ	CD	FW	WRB	EX	WDT
IN	WDT	VBP	PRP	CC	CD

Table 5: Top 5 significant POS in detecting uncertain sentences

Dataset	Precision	Recall	F1
base context features			
biomedical	66.04	75.48	70.44
syntactic dependency features			
biomedical	93.77	63.05	75.94
all features			
biomedical	78.72	80.41	79.55

Table 8: Results for scopes recognizing with gold hedge cues (word-level)

features contribute more benefits to recognize scopes than surface context features.

Official results evaluated at block level are also listed in Table 9.

dataset	Precision	Recall	F1
biomedical	21.87	17.23	19.27

Table 9: Official results for scopes recognizing (block level)

From Table 9 and the official result on hedge cue identification in Table 6, we believe that our post-processing strategy would be responsible for the low performance on recognizing scopes. Our strategy is to find a maximum consecutive block covering the corresponding hedge cue. This strategy cannot do well with the complex scope structure. For example, a scope is covered by another scope. Therefore, our system would generate a block covering all hedge cues if there exists more than one hedge cues in a sentence.

5 Conclusion

We present our implemented system for CoNLL-2010 Shared Task in this paper. We introduce syntactic dependency features when recognizing hedge scopes and employ average perceptron algorithm to train the models. On the biomedical corpus, our system achieves F-measure with 77.86% in detecting uncertain sentences, 77.44% in recognizing hedge cues, and 19.27% in identifying the scopes.

Although some results are low and beyond our expectations, we believe that our system can be at least improved within the following fields. Firstly, we would experiment on other kinds of features, such as chunk or named entities in biomedical. Secondly, the unlabeled datasets would be explored in the future.

False Negative	False Positive	True Positive	True Negative
support	considered	suggesting	chemiluminescence
of	potential	may	rhinitis
demonstrate	or	proposal	leukemogenic
a	hope	might	ribosomal
postulate	indicates	indicating	bp
supports	expected	likely	nc82
good	can	appear	intronic/exonic
advocates	should	possible	large
implicated	either	speculate	allele
putative	idea	whether	end

Table 7: Top 10 words with the largest scores for each category in hedge cue identification

Acknowledgments

This work was funded by Chinese NSF (Grant No. 60673038), 973 Program (Grant No. 2010CB327906, and Shanghai Committee of Science and Technology(Grant No. 09511501404).

References

Michael Collins. 2002. Discriminative training methods for hidden markov models: Theory and experiments with perceptron algorithms. In *Proceedings of the ACL-02 conference on Empirical methods in natural language processing*, pages 1–8. Association for Computational Linguistics.

Richard O. Duda, Peter E. Hart, and David G. Stork. 2001. *Pattern classification.* Wiley, New York.

Richárd Farkas, Veronika Vincze, György Móra, János Csirik, and György Szarvas. 2010. The CoNLL-2010 Shared Task: Learning to Detect Hedges and their Scope in Natural Language Text. In *Proceedings of the Fourteenth Conference on Computational Natural Language Learning (CoNLL-2010): Shared Task*, pages 1–12, Uppsala, Sweden, July. Association for Computational Linguistics.

Viola Ganter and Michael Strube. 2009. Finding hedges by chasing weasels: hedge detection using Wikipedia tags and shallow linguistic features. In *Proceedings of the ACL-IJCNLP 2009 Conference Short Papers*, pages 173–176. Association for Computational Linguistics.

Ryan McDonald, Koby Crammer, and Fernando Pereira. 2005. Online large-margin training of dependency parsers. In *Proceedings of the ACL*, pages 91–98. Association for Computational Linguistics.

Ben Medlock and Ted Briscoe. 2007. Weakly supervised learning for hedge classification in scientific literature. In *Proceedings of the 45th Annual Meeting of the Association of Computational Linguistics*, pages 992–999. Association for Computational Linguistics.

Ben Medlock. 2008. Exploring hedge identification in biomedical literature. *Journal of Biomedical Informatics*, 41(4):636–654.

Roser Morante and Walter Daelemans. 2009. Learning the scope of hedge cues in biomedical texts. In *Proceedings of the Workshop on BioNLP*, pages 28–36. Association for Computational Linguistics.

György Szarvas, Veronika Vincze, Richárd Farkas, and János Csirik. 2008. The BioScope corpus: annotation for negation, uncertainty and their scope in biomedical texts. In *Proceedings of the Workshop on Current Trends in Biomedical Natural Language Processing*, pages 38–45. Association for Computational Linguistics.

Kristina Toutanova, Dan Klein, Christopher D. Manning, and Yoram Singer. 2003. Feature-rich part-of-speech tagging with a cyclic dependency network. In *Proceedings of the 2003 Conference of the North American Chapter of the Association for Computational Linguistics on Human Language Technology-Volume 1*, pages 173–180. Association for Computational Linguistics.

Memory-Based Resolution of In-Sentence Scopes of Hedge Cues

Roser Morante, Vincent Van Asch, Walter Daelemans
CLiPS - University of Antwerp
Prinsstraat 13
B-2000 Antwerpen, Belgium
{Roser.Morante,Walter.Daelemans,Vincent.VanAsch}@ua.ac.be

Abstract

In this paper we describe the machine learning systems that we submitted to the CoNLL-2010 Shared Task on Learning to Detect Hedges and Their Scope in Natural Language Text. Task 1 on detecting uncertain information was performed by an SVM-based system to process the Wikipedia data and by a memory-based system to process the biological data. Task 2 on resolving in-sentence scopes of hedge cues, was performed by a memory-based system that relies on information from syntactic dependencies. This system scored the highest F1 (57.32) of Task 2.

1 Introduction

In this paper we describe the machine learning systems that CLiPS[1] submitted to the closed track of the CoNLL-2010 Shared Task on Learning to Detect Hedges and Their Scope in Natural Language Text (Farkas et al., 2010).[2] The task consists of two subtasks: detecting whether a sentence contains uncertain information (Task 1), and resolving in-sentence scopes of hedge cues (Task 2).

To solve Task 1, systems are required to classify sentences into two classes, "Certain" or "Uncertain", depending on whether the sentence contains factual or uncertain information. Three annotated training sets are provided: Wikipedia paragraphs (WIKI), biological abstracts (BIO-ABS) and biological full articles (BIO-ART). The two test sets consist of WIKI and BIO-ART data.

Task 2 requires identifying hedge cues and finding their scope in biomedical texts. Finding the scope of a hedge cue means determining at sentence level which words in the sentence are affected by the hedge cue. For a sentence like the one in (1) extracted from the BIO-ART training corpus, systems have to identify *likely* and *suggested* as hedge cues, and they have to find that *likely* scopes over the full sentence, and that *suggested* scopes over *by the role of murine MIB in TNF*α *signaling*. A scope will be correctly resolved only if both the cue and the scope are correctly identified.

(1) <xcope id=2> The conservation from Drosophila to mammals of these two structurally distinct but functionally similar E3 ubiquitin ligases is <cue ref=2>likely</cue> to reflect a combination of evolutionary advantages associated with: (i) specialized expression pattern, as evidenced by the cell-specific expression of the neur gene in sensory organ precursor cells [52]; (ii) specialized function, as <xcope id=1> <cue ref=1>suggested</cue> by the role of murine MIB in TNFα signaling</xcope> [32]; (iii) regulation of protein stability, localization, and/or activity</xcope>.

Systems are to be trained on BIO-ABS and BIO-ART and tested on BIO-ART. Example (1) shows that sentences in the BIO-ART dataset can be quite complex because of their length, because of their structure - very often they contain enumerations, and because they contain bibliographic references and references to tables and figures. Handling these phenomena is necessary to detect scopes correctly in the setting of this task. Note that the scope of *suggested* above does not include the bibliographic reference [*32*], whereas the scope of *likely* includes all the bibliographic references, and that the scope of *likely* does not include the final punctuation mark.

In the case of the BIO data, we approach Task 1 as a prerequisite for Task 2. Therefore we treat them as two consecutive classification tasks: a first one that consists of classifying the tokens of a sentence as being at the beginning of a hedge signal, inside or outside. This allows the system to find multiword hedge cues. We tag a sentence as uncertain if at least a hedge cue is found in the sentence. The second classification task consists

[1] Web page: http://www.clips.ua.ac.be

[2] Web page: http://www.inf.u-szeged.hu/rgai/conll2010st

Proceedings of the Fourteenth Conference on Computational Natural Language Learning: Shared Task, pages 40–47, Uppsala, Sweden, 15-16 July 2010.

of classifying the tokens of a sentence as being the first element of the scope, the last, or neither. This happens as many times as there are hedge cues in the sentence. The two classification tasks are implemented using memory-based learners. Memory-based language processing (Daelemans and van den Bosch, 2005) is based on the idea that NLP problems can be solved by reuse of solved examples of the problem stored in memory. Given a new problem, the most similar examples are retrieved, and a solution is extrapolated from them.

Section 2 is devoted to related work. In Section 3 we describe how the data have been preprocessed. In Section 4 and Section 5 we present the systems that perform Task 1 and Task 2. Finally, Section 6 puts forward some conclusions.

2 Related work

Hedging has been broadly treated from a theoretical perspective. The term *hedging* is originally due to Lakoff (1972). Palmer (1986) defines a term related to hedging, *epistemic modality*, which expresses the speaker's degree of commitment to the truth of a proposition. Hyland (1998) focuses specifically on scientific texts. He proposes a pragmatic classification of hedge expressions based on an exhaustive analysis of a corpus. The catalogue of hedging cues includes modal auxiliaries, epistemic lexical verbs, epistemic adjectives, adverbs, nouns, and a variety of non–lexical cues. Light et al. (2004) analyse the use of speculative language in MEDLINE abstracts. Some NLP applications incorporate modality information (Friedman et al., 1994; Di Marco and Mercer, 2005). As for annotated corpora, Thompson et al. (2008) report on a list of words and phrases that express modality in biomedical texts and put forward a categorisation scheme. Additionally, the BioScope corpus (Vincze et al., 2008) consists of a collection of clinical free-texts, biological full papers, and biological abstracts annotated with negation and speculation cues and their scope.

Although only a few pieces of research have focused on processing negation, the two tasks of the CoNLL-2010 Shared Task have been addressed previously. As for Task 1, Medlock and Briscoe (2007) provide a definition of what they consider to be hedge instances and define hedge classification as a weakly supervised machine learning task. The method they use to derive a learning model from a seed corpus is based on iteratively predicting labels for unlabeled training samples. They report experiments with SVMs on a dataset that they make publicly available[3]. The experiments achieve a recall/precision break even point (BEP) of 0.76. They apply a bag-of-words approach to sample representation. Medlock (2008) presents an extension of this work by experimenting with more features (part-of-speech, lemmas, and bigrams). With a lemma representation the system achieves a peak performance of 0.80 BEP, and with bigrams of 0.82 BEP. Szarvas (2008) follows Medlock and Briscoe (2007) in classifying sentences as being speculative or non-speculative. Szarvas develops a MaxEnt system that incorporates bigrams and trigrams in the feature representation and performs a complex feature selection procedure in order to reduce the number of keyword candidates. It achieves up to 0.85 BEP and 85.08 F1 by using an external dictionary. Kilicoglu and Bergler (2008) apply a linguistically motivated approach to the same classification task by using knowledge from existing lexical resources and incorporating syntactic patterns. Additionally, hedge cues are weighted by automatically assigning an information gain measure and by assigning weights semi–automatically depending on their types and centrality to hedging. The system achieves results of 0.85 BEP.

As for Task 2, previous work (Morante and Daelemans, 2009; Özgür and Radev, 2009) has focused on finding the scope of hedge cues in the BioScope corpus (Vincze et al., 2008). Both systems approach the task in two steps, identifying the hedge cues and finding their scope. The main difference between the two systems is that Morante and Daelemans (2009) perform the second phase with a machine learner, whereas Özgur and Radev (2009) perform the second phase with a rule-based system that exploits syntactic information.

The approach to resolving the scopes of hedge cues that we present in this paper is similar to the approach followed in Morante and Daelemans (2009) in that the task is modelled in the same way. A difference between the two systems is that this system uses only one classifier to solve Task 2, whereas the system described in Morante and Daelemans (2009) used three classifiers and a met-

[3]Available at http://www.benmedlock.co.uk/hedgeclassif.html.

alearner. Another difference is that the system in Morante and Daelemans (2009) used shallow syntactic features, whereas this system uses features from both shallow and dependency syntax. A third difference is that that system did not use a lexicon of cues, whereas this system uses a lexicon generated from the training data.

3 Preprocessing

As a first step, we preprocess the data in order to extract features for the machine learners. We convert the xml files into a token-per-token representation, following the standard CoNLL format (Buchholz and Marsi, 2006), where sentences are separated by a blank line and fields are separated by a single tab character. A sentence consists of a sequence of tokens, each one starting on a new line.

The WIKI data are processed with the Memory Based Shallow Parser (MBSP) (Daelemans and van den Bosch, 2005) in order to obtain lemmas, part-of-speech (PoS) tags, and syntactic chunks, and with the MaltParser (Nivre, 2006) in order to obtain dependency trees. The BIO data are processed with the GDep parser (Sagae and Tsujii, 2007) in order to get the same information.

#	WORD	LEMMA	PoS	CHUNK	NE	D	LABEL	C	S
1	The	The	DT	B-NP	O	3	NMOD	O	O O
2	structural	structural	JJ	I-NP	O	3	NMOD	O	O O
3	evidence	evidence	NN	I-NP	O	4	SUB	O	O O
4	lends	lend	VBZ	B-VP	O	0	ROOT	B	F O
5	strong	strong	JJ	B-NP	O	6	NMOD	I	O O
6	support	support	NN	I-NP	O	4	OBJ	I	O O
7	to	to	TO	B-PP	O	6	NMOD	O	O O
8	the	the	DT	B-NP	O	11	NMOD	O	O O
9	inferred	inferred	JJ	I-NP	O	11	NMOD	B	O F
10	domain	domain	NN	I-NP	O	11	NMOD	O	O O
11	pair	pair	NN	I-NP	O	7	PMOD	O	L L
12	,	,	,	O	O	4	P	O	O O
13	resulting	result	VBG	B-VP	O	4	VMOD	O	O O
14	in	in	IN	B-PP	O	13	VMOD	O	O O
15	a	a	DT	B-NP	O	18	NMOD	O	O O
16	high	high	JJ	I-NP	O	18	NMOD	O	O O
17	confidence	confidence	NN	I-NP	O	18	NMOD	O	O O
18	set	set	NN	I-NP	O	14	PMOD	O	O O
19	of	of	IN	B-PP	O	18	NMOD	O	O O
20	domain	domain	NN	B-NP	O	21	NMOD	O	O O
21	pairs	pair	NNS	I-NP	O	19	PMOD	O	O O
22	.	.	.	O	O	4	P	O	O O

Table 1: Preprocessed sentence.

Table 1 shows a preprocessed sentence with the following information per token: the token number in the sentence, word, lemma, PoS tag, chunk tag, named entity tag, head of token in the dependency tree, dependency label, cue tag, and scope tags separated by a space, for as many cues as there are in the sentence.

In order to check whether the conversion from the xml format to the CoNLL format is a source of error propagation, we convert the gold CoNLL files into xml format and we run the scorer provided by the task organisers. The results obtained are listed in Table 2.

	Task 1			Task 2	
	WIKI	BIO-ART	BIO-ABS	BIO-ART	BIO-ABS
F1	100.00	100.00	100.00	99.10	99.66

Table 2: Evaluation of the conversion from xml to CoNLL format.

4 Task 1: Detecting uncertain information

In Task 1 sentences have to be classified as containing uncertain or unreliable information or not. The task is performed differently for the WIKI and for the BIO data, since we are interested in finding the hedge cues in the BIO data, as a first step towards Task 2.

4.1 Wikipedia system (WIKI)

In the WIKI data a sentence is marked as uncertain if it contains at least one weasel, or cue for uncertainty. The list of weasels is quite extensive and contains a high number of unique occurrences. For example, the training data contain 3133 weasels and 1984 weasel types, of which 63% are unique. This means that a machine learner will have difficulties in performing the classification task. Even so, some generic structures can be discovered in the list of weasels. For example, the different weasels *A few people* and *A few sprawling grounds* follow a pattern. We manually select the 42 most frequent informative tokens[4] from the list of weasels in the training partition. In the remainder of this section we will refer to these tokens as *weasel cues*.

Because of the wide range of weasels, we opt for predicting the (un)certainty of a sentence, instead of identifying the weasels. The sentence classification is done in three steps: instance creation, SVM classification and sentence labeling.

[4]Weasel cues: *few, number, variety, bit, great, majority, range, variety, all, almost, arguably, certain, commonly, generally, largely, little, many, may, most, much, numerous, often, one, other, others, perhaps, plenty of, popular, possibly, probably, quite, relatively, reportedly, several, some, suggest, there be, the well-known, various, very, wide, widely*.

4.1.1 Instance creation

Although we only want to predict the (un)certainty of a sentence as a whole, we classify every token in the sentence separately. After parsing the data we create one instance per token, with the exception of tokens that have a part-of-speech from the list: #, $, :, LS, RP, UH, WP$, or WRB. The exclusion of these tokens is meant to simplify the classification task.

The features used by the system during classification are the following:

- About the token: word, lemma, PoS tag, chunk tag, dependency head, and dependency label.
- About the token context: lemma, PoS tag, chunk tag and dependency label of the two tokens to the left and right of the token in focus in the string of words of the sentence.
- About the weasel cues: a binary marker that indicates whether the token in focus is a weasel cue or not, and a number defining the number of weasel cues that there are in the entire sentence.

These instances with 24 non-binary features carry the positive class label if the sentence is uncertain. We use a binarization script that rewrites the instance to a format that can be used with a support vector machine and during this process, feature values that occur less than 2 times are omitted.

4.1.2 SVM classification

To label the instances of the unseen data we use SVM^{light} (Joachims, 2002). We performed some experiments with different settings and decided to only change the type of kernel from the default linear kernel to a polynomial kernel. For the Wikipedia training data, the training of the 246,876 instances with 68417 features took approximately 22.5 hours on a 32 bit, 2.2GHz, 2GB RAM Mac OS X machine.

4.1.3 Sentence labeling

In this last step, we collect all instances from the same sentence and inspect the predicted labels for every token. If more than 5% of the instances are marked as uncertain, the whole sentence is marked as uncertain. The idea behind the setup is that many tokens are very ambiguous in respect to uncertainty because they do not carry any information. Fewer tokens are still ambiguous, but contain some information, and a small set of tokens are almost unambiguous. This small set of informative tokens does not have to coincide with weasels nor weasels cues. The result is that we cannot predict the actual weasels in a sentence, but we get an indication of the presence of tokens that are common in uncertain sentences.

4.2 Biological system (BIO)

The system that processes the BIO data is different from the system that processes the WIKI data. The BIO system uses a classifier that predicts whether a token is at the beginning of a hedge signal, inside or outside. So, instances represent tokens. The instance features encode the following information:

- About the token: word, lemma, PoS tag, chunk tag, and dependency label.
- About the context to the left and right in the string of words of the sentence: word of the two previous and three next tokens, lemma and dependency label of previous and next tokens, deplabel, and chunk tag and PoS of next token. A binary feature indicating whether the next token has an SBAR chunk tag.
- About the context in the syntactic dependency tree: chain of PoS tags, chunk tags and dependency label of children of token; word, lemma, PoS tag, chunk tag, and dependency label of father; combined tag with the lemma of the token and the lemma of its father; chain of dependency labels from token to ROOT. Lemma of next token, if next token is syntactic child of token. If token is a verb, lemma of the head of the token that is its subject.
- Dictionary features. We extract a list of hedge cues from the training corpus. Based on this list, two binary features indicate whether token and next token are potential cues.
- Lemmas of the first noun, first verb and first adjective in the sentence.

The classifier is the decision tree IGTree as implemented in TiMBL (version 6.2) [5](Daelemans et al., 2009), a fast heuristic approximation of k-nn, that makes a heuristic approximation of nearest neighbor search by a top down traversal of the tree. It was parameterised by using overlap as the similarity metric and information gain for feature weighting. Running the system on the test data takes 10.44 seconds in a 64 bit 2.8GHz 8GB RAM Intel Xeon machine with 4 cores.

4.3 Results

All the results published in the paper are calculated with the official scorer provided by the task organisers. We provide precision (P), recall (R) and F1. The official results of Task 1 are presented in Table 3. We produce in-domain and

[5]TiMBL: `http://ilk.uvt.nl/timbl`

cross-domain results. The BIO in-domain results have been produced with the BIO system, by training on the training data BIO-ABS+BIO-ART, and testing on the test data BIO-ART. The WIKI in-domain results have been produced by the WIKI system by training on WIKI and testing on WIKI. The BIO cross-domain results have been produced with the BIO system, by training on BIO-ABS+BIO-ART+WIKI and testing on BIO-ART. The WIKI cross-domain results have been produced with the WIKI system by training on BIO-ABS+BIO-ART+WIKI and testing on WIKI. Training the SVM with BIO-ABS+BIO-ART+WIKI augmented the training time exponentially and the system did not finish on time for submission. We report post-evaluation results.

	In-domain			Cross-domain		
	P	R	F1	P	R	F1
WIKI	80.55	44.49	57.32	80.64*	44.94*	57.71*
BIO	81.15	82.28	81.71	80.54	83.29	81.89

Table 3: Uncertainty detection results (Task 1 - closed track). Post-evaluation results are marked with *.

In-domain results confirm that uncertain sentences in Wikipedia text are more difficult to detect than uncertain sentences in biological text. This is caused by a loss in recall of the WIKI system. Compared to results obtained by other systems participating in the CoNLL-2010 Shared Task, the BIO system performs 4.47 F1 lower than the best system, and the WIKI system performs 2.85 F1 lower. This indicates that there is room for improvement. As for cross-domain results, we cannot conclude that the cross-domain data harm the performance of the system, but we cannot state either that the cross-domain data improve the results. Since we performed Task 1 as a step towards Task 2, it is interesting to know what is the performance of the system in identifying hedge cues. Results are shown in Table 4. One of the main sources of errors in detecting the cues are due to the cue *or*. Of the 52 occurrences in the test corpus BIO-ART, the system produces 3 true positives, 8 false positives and 49 false negatives.

	In-domain			Cross-domain		
	P	R	F1	P	R	F1
Bio	78.75	74.69	76.67	78.14	75.45	76.77

Table 4: Cue matching results (Task 1 - closed track).

5 Task 2: Resolution of in-sentence scopes of hedge cues

Task 2 consists of resolving in-sentence scopes of hedge cues in biological texts. The system performs this task in two steps, classification and postprocessing, taking as input the output of the system that finds cues.

5.1 Classification

In the classification step a memory-based classifier classifies tokens as being the first token in the scope sequence, the last, or neither, for as many cues as there are in the sentence. An instance represents a pair of a predicted hedge cue and a token. All tokens in a sentence are paired with all hedge cues that occur in the sentence.

The classifier used is an IB1 memory–based algorithm as implemented in TiMBL (version 6.2)[6] (Daelemans et al., 2009), a memory-based classifier based on the k-nearest neighbor rule (Cover and Hart, 1967). The IB1 algorithm is parameterised by using overlap as the similarity metric, gain ratio for feature weighting, using 7 k-nearest neighbors, and weighting the class vote of neighbors as a function of their inverse linear distance. Running the system on the test data takes 53 minutes in a 64 bit 2.8GHz 8GB RAM Intel Xeon machine with 4 cores.

The features extracted to perform the classification task are listed below. Because, as noted by Özgür and Radev (2009) and stated in the annotation guidelines of the BioScope corpus[7], the scope of a cue can be determined from its lemma, PoS tag, and from the syntactic construction of the clause (passive voice vs. active, coordination, subordination), we use, among others, features that encode information from the dependency tree.

- About the cue: chain of words, PoS label, dependency label, chunk label, chunk type; word, PoS tag, chunk tag, and chunk type of the three previous and next tokens in the string of words in the sentence; first and last word, chain of PoS tags, and chain of words of the chunk where cue is embedded, and the same features for the two previous and two next chunks; binary feature indicating whether cue is the first, last or other token in sentence; binary feature indicating whether cue is in a clause with a copulative construction; PoS tag and dependency label of the head of cue in the dependency tree; binary feature indicating whether cue is located before or after its syntactic head in the string of

[6]TiMBL: http://ilk.uvt.nl/timbl.

[7]Available at: http://www.inf.u-szeged.hu/rgai/project/nlp/bioscope/Annotation%20guidelines2.1.pdf.

words of the sentence; feature indicating whether cue is followed by an S-BAR or a coordinate construction.

- About the token: word, PoS tag, dependency label, chunk tag, chunk type; word, PoS tag, chunk tag, and chunk type of the three previous and three next tokens in the string of words of the sentence; chain of PoS tag and lemmas of two and three tokens to the right of token in the string of words of the sentence; first and last word, chain of PoS tags, and chain of words of the chunk where token is embedded, and the same features for the two previous and two next chunks; PoS tag and deplabel of head of token in the dependency tree; binary feature indicating whether token is part of a cue.

- About the token in relation to cue: binary features indicating whether token is located before or after cue and before or after the syntactic head of cue in the string of words of the sentence; chain of PoS tags between cue and token in the string of words of the sentence; normalised distance between cue and token (number of tokens in between divided by total number of tokens); chain of chunks between cue and token; feature indicating whether token is located before cue, after cue or wihtin cue.

- About the dependency tree: feature indicating who is ancestor (cue, token, other); chain of dependency labels and chain of PoS tags from cue to common ancestor, and from token to common ancestor, if there is a common ancestor; chain of dependency labels and chain of PoS from token to cue, if cue is ancestor of token; chain of dependency labels and chain of PoS from cue to token, if token is ancestor of cue; chain of dependency labels and PoS from cue to ROOT and from token to ROOT.

  Features indicating whether token is a candidate to be the first token of scope (FEAT-FIRST), and whether token is a candidate to be the last token of the scope (FEAT-LAST). These features are calculated by a heuristics that takes into account detailed information of the dependency tree. The value of FEAT-FIRST depends on whether the clause is in active or in passive voice, on the PoS of the cue, and on the lemma in some cases (for example, verbs *appear, seem*). The value of FEAT-LAST depends on the PoS of the cue.

5.2 Postprocessing

In the corpora provided for this task, scopes are annotated as continuous sequences of tokens that include the cue. However, the classifiers only predict the first and last element of the scope. In order to guarantee that all scopes are continuous sequences of tokens we apply a first postprocessing step (P-SCOPE) that builds the sequence of scope based on the following rules:

1. If one token has been predicted as FIRST and one as LAST, the sequence is formed by the tokens between FIRST and LAST.

2. If one token has been predicted as FIRST and none has been predicted as LAST, the sequence is formed by the tokens between FIRST and the first token that has value 1 for FEAT-LAST.

3. If one token has been predicted as FIRST and more than one as LAST, the sequence is formed by the tokens between FIRST and the first token predicted as LAST that is located after cue.

4. If one token has been predicted as LAST and none as FIRST, the sequence will start at the hedge cue and it will finish at the token predicted as LAST.

5. If no token has been predicted as FIRST and more than one as LAST, the sequence will start at the hedge cue and will end at the first token predicted as LAST after the hedge signal.

6. If one token has been predicted as LAST and more than one as FIRST, the sequence will start at the cue.

7. If no tokens have been predicted as FIRST and no tokens have been predicted as LAST, the sequence will start at the hedge cue and will end at the first token that has value 1 for FEAT-LAST.

The system predicts 987 scopes in total. Of these, 1 FIRST and 1 LAST are predicted in 762 cases; a different number of predictions is made for FIRST and for LAST in 217 cases; no FIRST and no LAST are predicted in 5 cases, and 2 FIRST and 2 LAST are predicted in 3 cases. In 52 cases no FIRST is predicted, in 93 cases no LAST is predicted.

Additionally, as exemplified in Example 1 in Section 1, bibliographic references and references to tables and figures do not always fall under the scope of cues, when the references appear at the end of the scope sequence. If references that appear at the end of the sentence have been predicted by the classifier within the scope of the cue, these references are set out of the scope in a second postprocessing step (P-REF).

5.3 Results

The official results of Task 2 are presented in Table 5. The system scores 57.32 F1, which is the highest score of the systems that participated in this task.

	In-domain		
	P	R	F1
BIO	59.62	55.18	57.32

Table 5: Scope resolution official results (Task 2 - closed track).

In order to know what is the effect of the postprocessing steps, we evaluate the output of the system before performing step P-REF and before performing step P-SCOPE. Table 6 shows the results of the evaluation. Without P-REF, the performance decreases in 7.30 F1. This is caused by the fact that a considerable proportion of scopes end in a reference to bibliography, tables, or figures. Without P-SCOPE it decreases 4.50 F1 more. This is caused, mostly, by the cases in which the classifier does not predict the LAST class.

	In-domain		
	P	R	F1
BIO before P-REF	51.98	48.20	50.02
BIO before P-SCOPE	48.82	44.43	46.52

Table 6: Scope resolution results before postprocessing steps.

It is not really possible to compare the scores obtained in this task to existing research previous to the CoNLL-2010 Shared Task, namely the results obtained by Özgür and Radev (2009) on the BioScope corpus with a rule-based system and by Morante and Daelemans (2009) on the same corpus with a combination of classifiers. Özgür and Radev (2009) report accuracy scores (61.13 on full text), but no F measures are reported. Morante and Daelemans (2009) report percentage of correct scopes for the full text data set (42.37), obtained by training on the abstracts data set, whereas the results presented in Table 5 are reported in F measures and obtained in by training and testing on other corpora. Additionally, the system has been trained on a corpus that contains abstracts and full text articles, instead of only abstracts. However, it is possible to confirm that, even with information on dependency syntax, resolving the scopes of hedge cues in biological texts is not a trivial task. The scores obtained in this task are much lower than the scores obtained in other tasks that involve semantic processing, like semantic role labeling.

The errors of the system in Task 2 are caused by different factors. First, there is error propagation from the system that finds cues. Second, the system heavily relies on information from the syntactic dependency tree. The parser used to preprocess the data (GDep) has been trained on abstracts, instead of full articles, which means that the performance on full articles will be lower, since sentence are longer and more complex. Third, encoding the information of the dependency tree in features for the learner is not a straightforward process. In particular, some errors in resolving the scope are caused by keeping subordinate clauses within the scope, as in sentence (2), where, apart from not identifying *speculated* as a cue, the system wrongly includes *resulting in fewer high-confidence sequence assignments* within the scope of *may*. This error is caused in the instance construction phase, because token *assignments* gets value 1 for feature FEAT-LAST and token *algorithm* gets value 0, whereas it should have been otherwise.

(2) We speculated that the presence of multiple isotope peaks per fragment ion in the high resolution Orbitrap MS/MS scans <xcope id=1><cue ref=1>may </cue> degrade the sensitivity of the search algorithm, resulting in fewer high-confidence sequence assignments</xcope>.

Additionally, the test corpus contains an article about the annotation of a corpus of hedge cues, thus, an article that contains metalanguage. Our system can not deal with sentences like the one in (3), in which all cues with their scopes are false positives.

(3) For example, the word <xcope id=1><cue ref=1> may</cue> in sentence 1</xcope>) <xcope id=2> <cue ref=2>indicates that</cue> there is some uncertainty about the truth of the event, whilst the phrase Our results show that in 2) <xcope id=3> <cue ref=3>indicates that</cue> there is experimental evidence to back up the event described by encodes</xcope></xcope>.

6 Conclusions and future research

In this paper we presented the machine learning systems that we submitted to the CoNLL-2010 Shared Task on Learning to Detect Hedges and Their Scope in Natural Language Text. The BIO data were processed by memory-based systems in Task 1 and Task 2. The system that performs Task 2 relies on information from syntactic dependencies. This system scored the highest F1 (57.32) of Task 2.

As for Task 1, in-domain results confirm that uncertain sentences in Wikipedia text are more difficult to detect than uncertain sentences in biological text. One of the reasons is that the number of weasels is much higher and diverse than the number of hedge cues. BIO cross-domain results show that adding WIKI data to the training set causes a slight decrease in precision and a slight increase in recall. The errors of the BIO system show that some cues, like *or* are difficult to identify, because they are ambiguous. As for Task 2, results indicate that resolving the scopes of hedge cues in biological texts is not a trivial task. The scores obtained in this task are much lower than the scores obtained in other tasks that involve semantic processing, like semantic role labeling. The results are influenced by propagation of errors from identifying cues, errors in the dependency tree, the extraction process of syntactic information from the dependency tree to encode it in the features, and the presence of metalanguage on hedge cues in the test corpus. Future research will focus on improving the identification of hedge cues and on using different machine learning techniques to resolve the scope of cues.

Acknowledgements

The research reported in this paper was made possible through financial support from the University of Antwerp (GOA project BIOGRAPH).

References

Sabine Buchholz and Erwin Marsi. 2006. CoNLL-X shared task on multilingual dependency parsing. In *Proceedings of the CoNLL-X Shared Task*, New York. SIGNLL.

Thomas M. Cover and Peter E. Hart. 1967. Nearest neighbor pattern classification. *Institute of Electrical and Electronics Engineers Transactions on Information Theory*, 13:21–27.

Walter Daelemans and Antal van den Bosch. 2005. *Memory-based language processing*. Cambridge University Press, Cambridge, UK.

Walter Daelemans, Jakub Zavrel, Ko Van der Sloot, and Antal Van den Bosch. 2009. *TiMBL: Tilburg Memory Based Learner, version 6.2, Reference Guide*. Number 09-01 in Technical Report Series. Tilburg, The Netherlands.

Chrysanne Di Marco and Robert E. Mercer, 2005. *Computing attitude and affect in text: Theory and applications*, chapter Hedging in scientific articles as a means of classifying citations. Springer-Verlag, Dordrecht.

Richárd Farkas, Veronika Vincze, György Móra, János Csirik, and György Szarvas. 2010. The CoNLL-2010 Shared Task: Learning to Detect Hedges and their Scope in Natural Language Text. In *Proceedings of the Fourteenth Conference on Computational Natural Language Learning (CoNLL-2010): Shared Task*, pages 1–12, Uppsala, Sweden, July. Association for Computational Linguistics.

Carol Friedman, Philip Alderson, John Austin, James J. Cimino, and Stephen B. Johnson. 1994. A general natural–language text processor for clinical radiology. *Journal of the American Medical Informatics Association*, 1(2):161–174.

Ken Hyland. 1998. *Hedging in scientific research articles*. John Benjamins B.V, Amsterdam.

Thorsten Joachims. 2002. *Learning to Classify Text Using Support Vector Machines*, volume 668 of *The Springer International Series in Engineering and Computer Science*. Springer.

Halil Kilicoglu and Sabine Bergler. 2008. Recognizing speculative language in biomedical research articles: a linguistically motivated perspective. *BMC Bioinformatics*, 9(Suppl 11):S10.

George Lakoff. 1972. Hedges: a study in meaning criteria and the logic of fuzzy concepts. *Chicago Linguistics Society Papers*, 8:183–228.

Marc Light, Xin Y.Qiu, and Padmini Srinivasan. 2004. The language of bioscience: facts, speculations, and statements in between. In *Proceedings of the BioLINK 2004*, pages 17–24.

Ben Medlock and Ted Briscoe. 2007. Weakly supervised learning for hedge classification in scientific literature. In *Proceedings of ACL 2007*, pages 992–999.

Ben Medlock. 2008. Exploring hedge identification in biomedical literature. *Journal of Biomedical Informatics*, 41:636–654.

Roser Morante and Walter Daelemans. 2009. Learning the scope of hedge cues in biomedical texts. In *Proceedings of BioNLP 2009*, pages 28–36, Boulder, Colorado.

Joakim Nivre. 2006. *Inductive Dependency Parsing*, volume 34 of *Text, Speech and Language Technology*. Springer.

Arzucan Özgür and Dragomir R. Radev. 2009. Detecting speculations and their scopes in scientific text. In *Proceedings of EMNLP 2009*, pages 1398–1407, Singapore.

Frank R. Palmer. 1986. *Mood and modality*. CUP, Cambridge, UK.

Kenji Sagae and Jun'ichi Tsujii. 2007. Dependency parsing and domain adaptation with LR models and parser ensembles. In *Proceedings of CoNLL 2007: Shared Task*, pages 82–94, Prague, Czech Republic.

György Szarvas. 2008. Hedge classification in biomedical texts with a weakly supervised selection of keywords. In *Proceedings of ACL 2008*, pages 281–289, Columbus, Ohio, USA. ACL.

Paul Thompson, Giulia Venturi, John McNaught, Simonetta Montemagni, and Sophia Ananiadou. 2008. Categorising modality in biomedical texts. In *Proceedings of the LREC 2008 Workshop on Building and Evaluating Resources for Biomedical Text Mining 2008*, pages 27–34, Marrakech. LREC.

Veronika Vincze, György Szarvas, Richárd Farkas, György Móra, and János Csirik. 2008. The BioScope corpus: biomedical texts annotated for uncertainty, negation and their scopes. *BMC Bioinformatics*, 9(Suppl 11):S9.

Resolving Speculation: MaxEnt Cue Classification and Dependency-Based Scope Rules*

Erik Velldal♣ and **Lilja Øvrelid**♠♣ and **Stephan Oepen**♣
♣ University of Oslo, Department of Informatics (Norway)
♠Universität Potsdam, Institut für Linguistik (Germany)
erikve@ifi.uio.no and ovrelid@uni-potsdam.de and oe@ifi.uio.no

Abstract

This paper describes a hybrid, two-level approach for resolving hedge cues, the problem of the CoNLL-2010 shared task. First, a maximum entropy classifier is applied to identify cue words, using both syntactic- and surface-oriented features. Second, a set of manually crafted rules, operating on dependency representations and the output of the classifier, is applied to resolve the scope of the hedge cues within the sentence.

1 Introduction

The CoNLL-2010 shared task[1] comprises two sub-tasks. Task 1 is described as *learning to detect sentences containing uncertainty*, while the object of Task 2 is *learning to resolve the in-sentence scope of hedge cues* (Farkas et al., 2010). Paralleling this two-fold task definition, the architecture of our system naturally decomposes into two main steps. First, a maximum entropy (MaxEnt) classifier is applied to automatically detect cue words. For Task 1, a given sentence is labeled as *uncertain* if it contains a word classified as a cue. For Task 2, we then go on to determine the scope of the identified cues using a set of manually crafted rules operating on dependency representations.

For both Task 1 and Task 2, our system participates in the stricter category of 'closed' or 'in-domain' systems. This means that we do not use any additional uncertainty-annotated material beyond the supplied training data, consisting of 14541 sentences from biomedical abstracts and articles (see Table 2). In the official ranking of results, and considering systems in all categories together (closed/open/cross-domain), our system is ranked 4 out of 24 for Task 1 and 3 out of 15 for Task 2, resulting in highest average rank (and F_1) overall. We detail the implementation of the cue classifier and the syntactic rules in Sections 3 and 4, respectively. Results for the held-out testing are provided in Section 5. First, however, the next section describes the various resources that we used for pre-processing the CoNLL data sets, to prepare the input to our hedge analysis systems.

2 Architecture and Set-Up

2.1 Preprocessing

To ease integration of annotations across system components, we converted the XML training data to plain-text files, with stand-off annotation linked to the raw data by virtue of character start and end positions (dubbed *characterization* in the following). Thus, hedge cues, scope boundaries, tokenization, Part-of-Speech (PoS) assignments, etc. are all represented in a uniform fashion: as potentially overlapping annotations on sub-strings of the raw input.

The GENIA tagger (Tsuruoka et al., 2005) takes an important role in our pre-processing set-up. However, maybe somewhat surprisingly, we found that its tokenization rules are not always optimally adapted for the BioScope corpus. GENIA unconditionally introduces token boundaries for some punctuation marks that can also occur token-internally. For example, it wrongly splits tokens like '3,926.50', 'methlycobamide:CoM', or 'Ca(2+)'. Conversely, GENIA fails to isolate some kinds of opening single quotes, because the quoting conventions assumed in BioScope differ from those used in the GENIA Corpus; furthermore, it mis-tokenizes LaTeX-style n- and m-dashes.

On average, one in five sentences in the CoNLL training data exhibited GENIA tokenization prob-

*We are grateful to our colleagues at the University of Oslo and the University of Potsdam, for many useful discussions, constructive critique, and encouragment. We specifically thank Woodley Packard for careful proof-reading.

[1]The CoNLL-2010 shared task website: http://www.inf.u-szeged.hu/rgai/conll2010st/.

Proceedings of the Fourteenth Conference on Computational Natural Language Learning: Shared Task, pages 48–55, Uppsala, Sweden, 15-16 July 2010. ©2010 Association for Computational Linguistics

<table>
<tr><th>ID</th><th>FORM</th><th>LEMMA</th><th>POS</th><th>FEATS</th><th>HEAD</th><th>DEPREL</th><th>XHEAD</th><th>XDEP</th></tr>
<tr><td>1</td><td>The</td><td>the</td><td>DT</td><td>_</td><td>4</td><td>NMOD</td><td>4</td><td>SPECDET</td></tr>
<tr><td>2</td><td>unknown</td><td>unknown</td><td>JJ</td><td>degree:attributive</td><td>4</td><td>NMOD</td><td>4</td><td>ADJUNCT</td></tr>
<tr><td>3</td><td>amino</td><td>amino</td><td>JJ</td><td>degree:attributive</td><td>4</td><td>NMOD</td><td>4</td><td>ADJUNCT</td></tr>
<tr><td>4</td><td>acid</td><td>acid</td><td>NN</td><td>pers:3|case:nom|num:sg|ntype:common</td><td>5</td><td>SBJ</td><td>3</td><td>SUBJ</td></tr>
<tr><td>5</td><td>may</td><td>may</td><td>MD</td><td>mood:ind|subcat:MODAL|tense:pres|clauseType:decl|passive:-</td><td>0</td><td>ROOT</td><td>0</td><td>ROOT</td></tr>
<tr><td>6</td><td>be</td><td>be</td><td>VB</td><td>_</td><td>5</td><td>VC</td><td>7</td><td>PHI</td></tr>
<tr><td>7</td><td>used</td><td>use</td><td>VBN</td><td>subcat:V-SUBJ-OBJ|vtype:main|passive:+</td><td>6</td><td>VC</td><td>5</td><td>XCOMP</td></tr>
<tr><td>8</td><td>by</td><td>by</td><td>IN</td><td>_</td><td>7</td><td>LGS</td><td>9</td><td>PHI</td></tr>
<tr><td>9</td><td>these</td><td>these</td><td>DT</td><td>deixis:proximal</td><td>10</td><td>NMOD</td><td>10</td><td>SPECDET</td></tr>
<tr><td>10</td><td>species</td><td>specie</td><td>NNS</td><td>num:pl|pers:3|case:obl|common:count|ntype:common</td><td>8</td><td>PMOD</td><td>7</td><td>OBL-AG</td></tr>
<tr><td>11</td><td>.</td><td>.</td><td>.</td><td>_</td><td>5</td><td>P</td><td>0</td><td>PUNC</td></tr>
</table>

Table 1: Enhanced dependency representation of the example sentence *The unknown amino acid may be used by these species* with GENIAPoS-tags (POS), Malt parses (HEAD, DEPREL) and XLE parses (XHEAD, XDEP).

lems. Our pre-processing approach therefore deploys a home-grown, cascaded finite-state tokenizer (borrowed and adapted from the open-source English Resource Grammar; Flickinger (2000)), which aims to implement the tokenization decisions made in the Penn Treebank (Marcus et al., 1993) – much like GENIA, in principle – but properly treating corner cases like the ones above. Synchronized via characterization, this tokenization is then enriched with the output of no less than two PoS taggers, as detailed in the next section.

2.2 PoS Tagging and Lemmatization

For PoS tagging and lemmatization, we combine GENIA (with its built-in, occasionally deviant tokenizer) and TnT (Brants, 2000), which operates on pre-tokenized inputs but in its default model is trained on financial news from the Penn Treebank. Our general goal here is to take advantage of the higher PoS accuracy provided by GENIA in the biomedical domain, while using our improved tokenization and producing inputs to the parsing stage (see Section 2.3 below) that as much as possible resemble the conventions used in the original training data for the parser – the Penn Treebank, once again.

To this effect, for the vast majority of tokens we can align the GENIA tokenization with our own, and in these cases we typically use GENIA PoS tags and lemmas (i.e. base forms). For better normalization, we downcase base forms for all parts of speech except proper nouns. However, GENIA does not make a PoS distinction between proper and common nouns, as in the Penn Treebank, and hence we give precedence to TnT outputs for tokens tagged as nominal by both taggers. Finally, for the small number of cases where we cannot establish a one-to-one alignment from an element in our own tokenization to a GENIA token, we rely on TnT annotation only. In the merging of annotations across components, and also in downstream processing we have found it most convenient to operate predominantly in terms of characterization, i.e. sub-strings of the raw input that need not align perfectly with token boundaries.

2.3 Dependency Parsing with LFG Features

For syntactic parsing we employ a data-driven dependency parser which incorporates the predictions from a large-scale LFG grammar. A technique of *parser stacking* is employed, which enables a data-driven parser to learn from the output of another parser, in addition to gold standard treebank annotations (Nivre and McDonald, 2008). This technique has been shown to provide significant improvements in accuracy for both English and German (Øvrelid et al., 2009), and a similar approach employing an HPSG grammar has been shown to increase domain independence in data-driven dependency parsing (Zhang and Wang, 2009). For our purposes, we decide to use a parser which incorporates analyses from two quite different parsing approaches – data-driven dependency parsing and "deep" parsing with a hand-crafted grammar – providing us with a range of different types of linguistic features which may be used in hedge detection.

We employ the freely available MaltParser (Nivre et al., 2006), which is a language-independent system for data-driven dependency parsing.[2] It is based on a deterministic parsing strategy in combination with treebank-induced classifiers for predicting parse transitions. It supports a rich feature representation of the parse history in order to guide parsing and may easily be extended to take into account new features of the

[2]See http://maltparser.org.

	Sentences	Hedged Sentences	Cues	Multi-Word Cues	Tokens	Cue Tokens
Abstracts	11871	2101	2659	364	309634	3056
Articles	2670	519	668	84	68579	782
Total	14541	2620	3327	448	378213	3838

Table 2: Some descriptive figures for the shared task training data. Token-level counts are based on the tokenization described in Section 2.1.

parse history.

Parser stacking The procedure to enable the data-driven parser to learn from the grammar-driven parser is quite simple. We parse a treebank with the XLE platform (Crouch et al., 2008) and the English grammar developed within the ParGram project (Butt et al., 2002). We then convert the LFG output to dependency structures, so that we have two parallel versions of the treebank – one gold standard and one with LFG-annotation. We extend the gold standard treebank with additional information from the corresponding LFG analysis and train the data-driven dependency parser on the enhanced data set. See Øvrelid et al. (2010) for details of the conversion and training of the parser.

Table 1 shows the enhanced dependency representation of the English sentence *The unknown amino acid may be used by these species*, taken from the training data. For each token, the parsed data contains information on the surface form, lemma, and PoS tag, as well as on the head and dependency relation in columns 6 and 7. The dependency analysis suggested by XLE is contained in columns 8 and 9, whereas additional XLE information, such as morphosyntactic properties like number and voice, as well as more semantic properties detailing, e.g., subcategorization frames, semantic conceptual categories such as human, time and location, etc., resides in the FEATS column. The parser outputs, which in turn form the basis for our scope resolution rules discussed in Section 4, also take this same form.

The parser employed in this work is trained on the Wall Street Journal sections 2 – 24 of the Penn Treebank, converted to dependency format (Johansson and Nugues, 2007) and extended with XLE features, as described above. Parsing is performed using the arc-eager mode of MaltParser (Nivre, 2003) and an SVM with a polynomial kernel. When tested using 10-fold cross-validation on this data set, the parser achieves a labeled accuracy score of 89.8 (Øvrelid et al., 2010).

3 Identifying Hedge Cues

For the task of identifying hedge cues, we developed a binary maximum entropy (MaxEnt) classifier. The identification of cue words is used for (*i*) classifying sentences as certain/uncertain (Task 1), and (*ii*) providing input to the syntactic rules that we later apply for resolving the in-sentence scope of the cues (Task 2). We also report evaluation scores for the sub-task of cue detection in isolation.

As annotated in the training data, it is possible for a hedge cue to span multiple tokens, e.g. as in *whether or not*. The majority of the multi-word cues in the training data are very infrequent, however, most occurring only once, and the classifier itself is not sensitive to the notion of multi-word cues. A given word token in the training data is simply considered to be either a cue or a non-cue, depending on whether it falls within the span of a cue annotation. The task of determining whether a cue word forms part of a larger multi-word cue, is performed by a separate post-processing step, further described in Section 3.2.

3.1 Maximum Entropy Classification

In the MaxEnt framework, each training example – in our case a paired word and label $\langle w_i, y_i \rangle$ – is represented as a feature vector $f(w_i, y_i) = f_i \in \Re^d$. Each dimension or feature function f_{ij} can encode arbitrary properties of the data. The particular feature functions we are using for the cue identification are described under Section 3.4 below. For model estimation we use the TADM[3] software (Malouf, 2002). For feature extraction and model tuning, we build on the experimentation environment developed by Velldal (2008) (in turn extending earlier work by Oepen et al.

[3]Toolkit for Advanced Discriminative Modeling; available from `http://tadm.sourceforge.net/`.

(2004)). Among other things, its highly optimized feature handling – where the potentially expensive feature extraction step is performed only once and then combined with several levels of feature caching – make it computationally feasible to perform large-scale 'grid searches' over different configurations of features and model parameters when using many millions of features.

3.2 Multi-Word Cues

After applying the classifier, a separate post-processing step aims to determine whether tokens identified as cue words belong to a larger multi-word cue. For example, when the classifier has already identified one or more of the tokens in a phrase such as *raises the possibility* to be part of a hedge cue, a heuristic rule (viz. basically lemma-level pattern-matching, targeted at only the most frequently occurring multi-word cues in the training data) makes sure that the tokens are treated as part of one and the same cue.

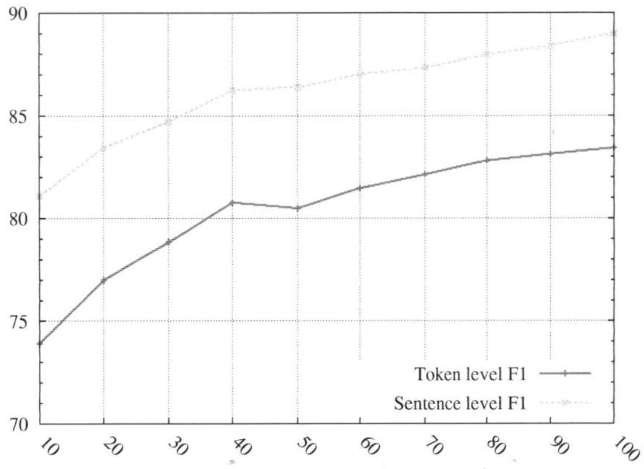

Figure 1: Learning curves showing, for both token- and sentence-level F-scores, the effect of incrementally including a larger percentage of training data into the 10-fold cycles. (As described also for the other development results, while we are training on both the articles and the abstracts, we are testing only on the articles.)

3.3 Model Development, Data Sets and Evaluation Measures

While the training data made available for the shared task consisted of both abstracts and full articles from the BioScope corpus (Vincze et al., 2008), the test data were pre-announced to consist of biomedical articles only. In order to make the testing situation during development as similar as possible to what could be expected for the held-out testing, we only tested on sentences taken from the articles part of the training data. When developing the classifiers we performed 10-fold training and testing over the articles, while always including all sentences from the abstracts in the training set as well. Table 2 provides some basic descriptive figures summarizing the training data.

As can be seen in Table 3, we will be reporting precision, recall and F-scores for three different levels of evaluation for the cue classifiers: the sentence-level, token-level and cue-level. The sentence-level scores correspond to Task 1 of the shared task, i.e. correctly identifying sentences as being *certain* or *uncertain*. A sentence is labeled *uncertain* if it contains at least one token classified as a hedge cue. The token-level scores indicate how well the classifiers succeed in identifying individual cue words (this score does not take into account the heuristic post-processing rules for finding multi-word cues). Finally, the cue-level scores are based on the exact-match counts for full hedge cues (possibly spanning multiple tokens). These latter scores are computed using the official shared task scorer script.

3.4 Feature Types

We trained cue classifiers using a wide variety of feature types, both syntactic and surface-oriented. However, to better assess the contribution of the different features, we first trained two baseline models using only features defined for non-normalized surface forms as they occur in the training data. The most basic baseline model (Baseline 1) included only unigram features. The behavior of this classifier is similar to what we would expect from simply compiling a list of cue words from the training data, based on the majority usage of each word as cue or non-cue. Baseline 2 additionally included 2 words to the left and 3 to the right of the focus word (after first performing a search for the optimal spans of n-grams up to 5). As shown in Table 3, this model achieved a sentence-level F1 of 87.14 and a token-level F1 of 81.97. The corresponding scores for Baseline 1 are 79.20 and 69.59.

A general goal in our approach to hedge analysis is to evaluate the contribution of syntactic information, both in cue detection and scope resolution. After applying the parser described in Section 2.3, we extracted a range of classifier features on the basis of the dependency structures (both as proposed by the stacked MaltParser and converted from XLE) as well as the deep grammar (XLE). Additionally we defined various features on the basis of base forms and PoS information provided by the GENIA pre-processing (see Section 2.2).

For a quick overview, the feature types we experimented with include the following:

GENIA features n-gram features over the base forms and PoS tags from the GENIA information described in Section 2.2.

Dependency features A range of features extracted from dependency structures produced by MaltParser and XLE (see Section 2.3), designed to capture the syntactic properties and environment of a token: **deprel** – dependency relation (Malt and XLE), **deppath** – dependency path to root, **deppattern** – ordered set of co-dependents/siblings, including focus token (Malt), **lextriple/postriple** – lexicalized and unlexicalized dependency triplet for token (Malt), **coord** – binary feature expressing coordination (XLE), **coordLevel** – phrase-structural level of coordination (XLE).

Lexical parser features Other features constructed on the basis of the parser output: **subcat** – subcategorization frame for verbs (XLE), **advType** – type of adverbial, e.g. sentence, VP (XLE), **adjType** – adjectival function, e.g. attributive vs. predicative (XLE)

When added to Baseline 2 in isolation, most of these features resulted in a boost in classifier performance. For the dependency-based features, the contribution was more pronounced for *lexicalized* versions of the features. This also points to the fact that lexical information seems to be the key for the task of cue identification, where the model using only n-grams over surface forms proved a strong baseline. As more feature types were added to the classifier together, we also saw a clear trend of diminishing returns, in that many of the features seemed to contribute overlapping information. After several rounds of grid-search over different feature configurations, the best-performing classifier (as used for the shared task) used only the following feature types: n-grams over surface forms (including up to 2 tokens to the right), n-grams over base forms (up to 3 tokens left and right), PoS of the target word, 'subcat', 'coord', and 'coordLevel'. The 'subcat' feature contains information taken from XLE regarding the subcategorization requirements of a verb in a specific context, e.g., whether a verb is modal, takes an expletive subject etc., whereas the coordination features signal coordination ('coord') and detail the phrase-structural level of coordination ('coordLevel'), e.g., NP, VP, etc. This defines the feature set used for the model referred to as *final* in Table 3.

Recall that for Baseline 2, the F-score is 87.14 for the sentence-level evaluation and 81.97 for the token-level. For our best and final feature configuration, the corresponding F-scores are 89.00 and 83.42, respectively. At both the sentence-level and the token-level, the differences in classifier performance were found to be statistically significant at $p < 0.005$, using a two-tailed sign-test. After also applying the heuristic rules for detecting multi-word cues, the cue-level F-score for our final model is 84.60, compared to 82.83 for Baseline 2.

3.5 The Effect of Data Size

In order to asses the effect of the size of the training set, we computed learning curves showing how classifier performance changes as more training data is added. Starting with only 10% of the training data included in the 10-fold cycle, Figure 1 shows the effect on both token level and sentence-level F-scores as we incrementally include larger portions of the available training data.

Unsurprisingly, we see that the performance of the classifier is steadily improving up to the point where 100% of the data is included, and by extrapolating from the curves shown in Figure 1 it seems reasonable to assume that this improvement would continue if more data were available. We therefore tried to further increase the size of the training set by also using the hedge-annotated *clinical reports* that form part of the BioScope corpus. This provided us with an additional 855 hedged sentences. However, the classifiers did not seem able to benefit from the additional training examples, and across several feature configurations performance was found to be consistently lower (though not significantly so). The reason is probably that the type of text is quite different – the clinical reports have a high ratio of fragments and also shows other patterns of cue usage, being somewhat more jargon-based. This seems to underpin the findings of previous studies that hedge cue learners appear quite sensitive to text type (Morante and Daele-

Model	Sentence Level			Token Level			Cue Level		
	Prec	Rec	F1	Prec	Rec	F1	Prec	Rec	F1
Baseline 1	79.25	79.45	79.20	77.71	63.41	69.59	77.37	71.70	74.43
Baseline 2	86.83	87.54	87.14	86.86	77.69	81.97	85.34	80.21	82.69
Final	91.39	86.78	89.00	91.20	76.95	83.42	90.18	79.47	84.49

Table 3: Averaged 10-fold cross-validation results on the articles in the official shared task training data, always including the abstracts in the training portion. The model listed as *final* includes features such as n-grams over surface forms and base forms (both left and right), PoS, subcategorization frames, and phrase-structural coordination level. The feature types are further described in Section 3.4.

PoS	Description	Source
CC	Coordinations scope over their conjuncts	M
IN	Prepositions scope over their arguments with its descendants	M
$\texttt{JJ}_{attr}$	Attributive adjectives scope over their nominal head and its descendants	M
$\texttt{JJ}_{pred}$	Predicative adjectives scope over referential subjects and clausal arguments, if any	M, X
MD	Modals inherit subj-scope from their lexical verb and scope over their descendants	M, X
RB	Adverbs scope over their heads with its descendants	M
$\texttt{VB}_{pass}$	Passive verbs scope over referential subjects and the verbal descendants	M, X
$\texttt{VB}_{rais}$	Raising verbs scope over referential subjects and the verbal descendants	M, X
*	For multi-word cues, the head determines scope for all elements	
*	Back off from final punctuation and parentheses	

Table 4: Overview of dependency-based scope rules with information source (MaltParser or XLE), organized by PoS of the cue.

mans, 2009).

4 Resolving Cue Scope

In our approach to scope resolution we rely heavily on syntactic information, taken from the dependency structures proposed by both MaltParser and XLE, as well as various additional features from the XLE parses relating to specific syntactic constructions.

4.1 Scope Rules

We construct a small set of heuristic rules which define the scope for each cue detected in Stage 1. In the construction of these rules, we made use of the information provided by the guidelines for scope annotation in the BioScope corpus (Vincze et al., 2008) as well as manual inspection of the training data in order to arrive at reasonable scope hypotheses for various types of cues.

The rules take as input a parsed sentence which has been tagged with hedge cues and operate over the dependency structures and additional features provided by the parser. Default scope is set to start at the cue word and span to the end of the sentence (not including final puctuation), and this scope also provides the baseline for the evaluation of our rules. Table 4 provides an overview of the rules employed for scope resolution.

In the case of multi-word cues, such as *indicate that*, and *either ... or*, which share scope, we need to determine the head of the multi-word unit. We then set the scope of the whole unit to the scope of the head token.

As an example, the application of the rules in Table 4 to the sentence with the parsed output in Table 1 correctly determine the scope of the cue *may* as shown in example (1), using a variety of syntactic cues regarding part-of-speech, argumenthood, voice, etc. First, the scope of the sentence is set to default scope. Then the MD rule is applied, which checks the properties of the lexical verb *used*, located through a chain of verbal dependents from the modal verb. Since it is passive (`passive:+`), initial scope is set to include the cue's subject (SBJ) argument with all its descendants (*The unknown amino acid*).

Task 1			Task 2			Cue Detection		
Prec	**Rec**	**F1**	**Prec**	**Rec**	**F1**	**Prec**	**Rec**	**F1**
85.48	84.94	85.21	56.71	54.02	55.33	81.20	76.31	78.68

Table 6: Evaluation results for the official held-out testing.

Scope	Prec	Rec	F1
Default w/gold cues	45.21	45.21	45.21
Rules w/gold cues	72.31	72.31	72.31
Rules w/classified cues	68.56	61.38	64.77

Table 5: Evaluation of the scope resolution rules on the training articles, using both gold standard cues and predicted cues. For the row labeled *Default*, the scope for each cue is always taken to span rightward to the end of the sentence. In the rows labeled *Rules*, the scopes have been resolved using the dependency-based rules.

(1) (The unknown amino acid <may> be **used** by these species).

4.2 Rule Evaluation

Table 5 shows the evaluation of the set of scope rules on the articles section of the data set, using gold standard cues.[4] This gives us an indication of the performance of the rules, isolated from errors in cue detection.

First of all, we may note that the baseline is a strong one: choosing to extend the scope of a cue to the end of the sentence provides an F-score of 45.21. Given gold standard cue information, the set of scope rules improves on the baseline by 27 percentage points on the articles section of the data set, giving us an F-score of 72.31. Comparing to the evaluation using classified cues (the bottom row of Table 5), we find that the use of automatically assigned cues causes a drop in performance of 7.5 percentage points, to a result of 64.77.

5 Held-Out Testing

Table 6 presents the final results as obtained on the held-out test data, which constitute the official results for our system in the CoNLL-2010 shared task. The held-out test set comprises biomedical articles with a total of 5003 sentences (790 of them hedged).

For Task 1 we obtain an F-score of 85.21. The corresponding result for the training data, which is reported as 'Sentence Level' in Table 3, is 89.00. Although we experience a slight drop in performance (3.8 percentage points), the system seems to generalize quite well to unseen data when it comes to the detection of sentence-level uncertainty.

For Task 2, the result on the held-out data set is an F-score of 55.33, with quite balanced values for precision and recall, 56.7 and 54.0, respectively. If we compare this to the end-to-end evaluation on the training data, provided in the bottom row of Table 5, we find a somewhat larger drop in performance (9.5 percentage points), from an F-score of 64.77 to the held-out 55.3. There are several possible reasons for this drop. First of all, there might be a certain degree of overfitting of our system to the training data. The held-out data may contain hedging constructions that are not covered by our set of scope rules. Moreover, the performance of the scope rules is also influenced by the cue detection, which is reported in the final columns of Table 6. The cue-level performance of our system on the held-out data set is 78.68, whereas the same evaluation on the training data is 84.49. We find that it is the precision, in particular, which suffers in the application to the held-out data set. A possible strategy for future work is to optimize both components of the Task 2 system, the cue detection and the scope rules, on the entire training set, instead of just on the articles.

6 Conclusions – Outlook

We have described a hybrid, two-level approach for resolving hedging in biomedical text, as submitted for the stricter track of 'closed' or 'in-domain' systems in the CoNLL-2010 shared task. For the task of identifying hedge cues, we train a MaxEnt classifier, which, for the held-out test

[4]This evaluation was carried out using the official scorer script of the CoNLL shared task. When cue information is kept constant, as in our case, the values for false positives and false negatives will be identical, hence the precision and recall values will always be identical as well.

data, achieves an F-score of 78.68 on the cue-level and 85.21 on the sentence-level (Task 1). For the task of resolving the in-sentence scope of the identified cues (Task 2), we apply a set of manually crafted rules operating on dependency representations, resulting in an end-to-end F-score of 55.33 (based on exact match of both cues and scopes). In the official shared task ranking of results, and considering systems in all tracks together, our system is ranked 4 out of 24 for Task 1 and 3 out of 15 for Task 2, resulting in the highest average rank overall. For future work we aim to further improve the cue detection, in particular with respect to multi-word cues, and also continue to refine the scope rules. Instead of defining the scopal rules only at the level of dependency structure, one could also have rules operating on constituent structure – perhaps even combining alternative resolution candidates using a statistical ranker.

References

Thorsten Brants. 2000. TnT. A statistical Part-of-Speech tagger. In *Proceedings of the Sixth Conference on Applied Natural Language Processing*, pages 224–231.

Miriam Butt, Helge Dyvik, Tracy Holloway King, Hiroshi Masuichi, and Christian Rohrer. 2002. The Parallel Grammar Project. In *Proceedings of COLING Workshop on Grammar Engineering and Evaluation*, pages 1–7.

Dick Crouch, Mary Dalrymple, Ron Kaplan, Tracy King, John Maxwell, and Paula Newman. 2008. *XLE documentation*. Palo Alto Research Center.

Richárd Farkas, Veronika Vincze, György Móra, János Csirik, and György Szarvas. 2010. The CoNLL-2010 Shared Task: Learning to Detect Hedges and their Scope in Natural Language Text. In *Proceedings of the Fourteenth Conference on Computational Natural Language Learning (CoNLL-2010): Shared Task*, pages 1–12.

Dan Flickinger. 2000. On building a more efficient grammar by exploiting types. *Natural Language Engineering*, 6 (1):15–28.

Richard Johansson and Pierre Nugues. 2007. Extended constituent-to-dependency conversion for English. In Joakim Nivre, Heiki-Jaan Kaalep, and Mare Koit, editors, *Proceedings of NODALIDA 2007*, pages 105–112.

Robert Malouf. 2002. A comparison of algorithms for maximum entropy parameter estimation. In *Proceedings of the 6th Conference on Natural Language Learning*, pages 49–55.

Mitchell P. Marcus, Beatrice Santorini, and Mary Ann Marcinkiewicz. 1993. Building a large annotated corpus of English. The Penn Treebank. *Computational Linguistics*, 19:313–330.

Roser Morante and Walter Daelemans. 2009. Learning the scope of hedge cues in biomedical texts. In *Proceedings of the BioNLP 2009 Workshop*, pages 28–36.

Joakim Nivre and Ryan McDonald. 2008. Integrating graph-based and transition-based dependency parsers. In *Proceedings of the 46th Meeting of the Association for Computational Linguistics*, pages 950–958.

Joakim Nivre, Johan Hall, and Jens Nilsson. 2006. MaltParser: A data-driven parser-generator for dependency parsing. In *Proceedings of the Fifth International Conference on Language Resources and Evaluation*, pages 2216–2219.

Joakim Nivre. 2003. An efficient algorithm for projective dependency parsing. In *Proceedings of the Eighth International Workshop on Parsing Technologies*, pages 149–160.

Stephan Oepen, Daniel Flickinger, Kristina Toutanova, and Christopher D. Manning. 2004. LinGO Redwoods. A rich and dynamic treebank for HPSG. *Journal of Research on Language and Computation*, 2(4):575–596.

Lilja Øvrelid, Jonas Kuhn, and Kathrin Spreyer. 2009. Improving data-driven dependency parsing using large-scale LFG grammars. In *Proceedings of the 47th Meeting of the Association for Computational Linguistics*, pages 37–40.

Lilja Øvrelid, Jonas Kuhn, and Kathrin Spreyer. 2010. Cross-framework parser stacking for data-driven dependency parsing. *TAL 2010 special issue on Machine Learning for NLP*, 50(3).

Yoshimasa Tsuruoka, Yuka Tateishi, Jin-Dong Kim, Tomoko Ohta, John McNaught, Sophia Ananiadou, and Jun'ichi Tsujii. 2005. Developing a robust Part-of-Speech tagger for biomedical text. In *Advances in Informatics*, pages 382–392. Springer, Berlin, Germany.

Erik Velldal. 2008. *Empirical Realization Ranking*. Ph.D. thesis, University of Oslo, Institute of Informatics, Oslo.

Veronika Vincze, György Szarvas, Richárd Farkas, György Móra, and János Csirik. 2008. The BioScope corpus: Annotation for negation, uncertainty and their scope in biomedical texts. In *Proceedings of the BioNLP 2008 Workshop*.

Yi Zhang and Rui Wang. 2009. Cross-domain dependency parsing using a deep linguistic grammar. In *Proceedings of the 47th Meeting of the Association for Computational Linguistics*, Singapore.

Combining Manual Rules and Supervised Learning for Hedge Cue and Scope Detection

Marek Rei
Computer Laboratory
University of Cambridge
United Kingdom
Marek.Rei@cl.cam.ac.uk

Ted Briscoe
Computer Laboratory
University of Cambridge
United Kingdom
Ted.Briscoe@cl.cam.ac.uk

Abstract

Hedge cues were detected using a supervised Conditional Random Field (CRF) classifier exploiting features from the RASP parser. The CRF's predictions were filtered using known cues and unseen instances were removed, increasing precision while retaining recall. Rules for scope detection, based on the grammatical relations of the sentence and the part-of-speech tag of the cue, were manually-developed. However, another supervised CRF classifier was used to refine these predictions. As a final step, scopes were constructed from the classifier output using a small set of post-processing rules. Development of the system revealed a number of issues with the annotation scheme adopted by the organisers.

1 Introduction

Speculative or, more generally, "hedged" language is a way of weakening the strength of a statement. It is usually signalled by a word or phrase, called a hedge cue, which weakens some clauses or propositions. These weakened portions of a sentence form the scope of the hedge cues.

Hedging is an important tool in scientific language allowing scientists to guide research beyond the evidence without overstating what follows from their work. Vincze et al. (2008) show that 19.44% of all sentences in the full papers of the BioScope corpus contain hedge cues. Detecting these cues is potentially valuable for tasks such as scientific information extraction or literature curation, as typically only definite information should be extracted and curated. Most work so far has been done on classifying entire text sentences as hedged or not, but this risks losing valuable information in (semi-)automated systems. More recent approaches attempt to find the specific parts of a text sentence that are hedged.

Here we describe a system that is designed to find hedge cues and their scopes in biomedical research papers. It works in three stages:

1. Detecting the cues using a token-level supervised classifier.

2. Finding the scopes with a combination of manual rules and a second supervised token-level classifier.

3. Applying postprocessing rules to convert the token-level annotation into predictions about scope.

Parts of the system are similar to that of Morante and Daelemans (2009) — both make use of machine learning to tag tokens as being in a cue or a scope. The most important differences are the use of manually defined rules and the inclusion of grammatical relations from a parser as critical features.

2 Data

A revised version of the BioScope corpus (Vincze et al., 2008), containing annotation of cues and scopes, was provided as training data for the CoNLL-2010 shared task (Farkas et al., 2010). This includes 9 full papers and 1273 abstracts from biomedical research fields. A separate new set of full papers was released for evaluation as part of the task. Table 1 contains an overview of the training corpus statistics.

(1) provides an example sentence from the corpus illustrating the annotation provided for training.

(2) shows the same sentence, representing cues with angle brackets and scopes with round brackets.

Proceedings of the Fourteenth Conference on Computational Natural Language Learning: Shared Task, pages 56–63, Uppsala, Sweden, 15-16 July 2010.

	Papers	Abstracts
Documents	9	1273
Sentences	2670	11871
Cues	682	2694
Scopes	668	2659
Unique cues	100	112
Cues with multiple words	10.70%	12.25%
Scopes start with cue	72.00%	80.59%
Scopes with multiple cues	2.10%	1.28%

Table 1: Training data statistics.

(1) <sentence id="S1.166">We <xcope id="X1.166.2"><cue ref="X1.166.2" type="speculation">expect</cue> that this cluster <xcope id="X1.166.1"><cue ref="X1.166.1" type="speculation">may</cue> represent a novel selenoprotein family</xcope></xcope>.</sentence>

(2) We (<expect> that this cluster (<may> represent a novel selenoprotein family)).

There are a number of conditions on the annotation that are imposed:

- Every cue has one scope.
- Every scope has one or more cues.
- The cue must be contained within its scope.
- Cues and scopes have to be continuous.

For development of the system, before the evaluation data were released, we used 60% of the available corpus for training and 40% for testing. The results we give below measure the system performance on the evaluation data while using all of the training data to build the supervised classifiers. The manually-developed rules are based on the 60% of the development data we originally reserved for training.

All of the training and test data sentences were tokenised and parsed using the RASP system (Briscoe et al., 2006). Multiple part-of-speech (POS) tag outputs were passed to the parser (to compensate for the high number of unseen words in biomedical text), retaining just the highest ranked directed graph of grammatical relations (GRs). Each node in the graph represents a word token annotated with POS, lemma, and positional order information. In the case of parse failure the set of unconnected graphs returned by the highest-ranked spanning subanalyses for each sentence were retained.

3 Speculation cues

The hedge cues are found using a Conditional Random Field (CRF) (Lafferty et al., 2001) classifier, implemented using CRF++ [1]. We chose the CRF model because we framed the task as one of token-level sequential tagging and CRFs are known to achieve state-of-the-art performance on related text classification tasks. Each word token is assigned one of the following tags: **F** (first word of a cue), **I** (inside a cue), **L** (last word of a cue), **O** (outside, not a cue), hereafter referred to as the FILO scheme.

The feature types used for classification are defined in terms of the grammatical relations output provided by the RASP system. We use binary features that indicate whether a word token is a head or a dependent in specific types of grammatical relation (GR). This distinguishes between different functions of the same word (when used as a subject, object, modifier, etc.). These features are combined with POS and lemma of the word to distinguish between uses of different cues and cue types. We also utilise features for the lemma and POS of the 3 words before and after the current word.

The list of feature types for training the classifier is:

- string
- lemma
- part-of-speech
- broad part-of-speech
- incoming GRs + POS
- outgoing GRs + POS
- incoming GRs + POS + lemma
- outgoing GRs + POS + lemma
- lemma + POS + POS of next word
- lemma + POS + POS of previous word
- 3 previous lemma + POS combinations
- 3 following lemma + POS combinations.

Outgoing GRs are grammatical relations where the current word is the head, incoming GRs where it is the dependent.

The predictions from the classifier are compared to the list of known cues extracted from the training data; the longest possible match is marked as a cue. For example, the classifier could output the following tag sequence:

(3) This[O] indicates[F] that[O] these[O] two[O] lethal[O] mutations[O] ...

[1] http://crfpp.sourceforge.net

indicates is classified as a cue but *that* is not. The list of known cues contains "indicates that" which matches this sentence, therefore the system prediction is:

(4) This <indicates that> these two lethal mutations ...

Experiments in section 5.1 show that our system is not good at finding previously unseen cues. Lemma is the most important feature type for cue detection and when it is not available, there is not enough evidence to make good predictions. Therefore, we compare all system predictions to the list of known cues and if there is no match, they are removed. The detection of unseen hedge cues is a potential topic for future research.

4 Speculation scopes

We find a scope for each cue predicted in the previous step. Each word token in the sentence is tagged with either **F** (first word of a scope), **I** (inside a scope), **L** (last word of a scope) or **O** (outside, not in a scope). Using our example sentence (2) the correct tagging is:

	expect	**may**
We	O	O
expect	F	O
that	I	O
this	I	O
cluster	I	O
may	I	F
represent	I	I
a	I	I
novel	I	I
selenoprotein	I	I
family	L	L
.	O	O

Table 2: Example of scope tagging.

If a cue contains multiple words, they are each processed separately and the predictions are later combined by postprocessing rules.

As the first step, manually written rules are applied that find the scope based on GRs and POS tags. We refine these predictions using a second CRF classifier and further feature types extracted from the RASP system output. Finally, postprocessing rules are applied to convert the tagging sequence into scopes. By default, the minimal scope returned is the cue itself.

4.1 Manual rules

Manual rules were constructed based on the development data and annotation guidelines. In the following rules and examples:

- "below" refers to nodes that are in the subgraph of GRs rooted in the current node.
- "parent" refers to the node that is the head of the current node in the directed, connected GR graph.
- "before" and "after" refer to word positions in the text centered on the current node.
- "mark everything below" means mark all nodes in the subgraph as being in the scope (i.e. tag as F/I/L as appropriate). However, the traversal of the graph is terminated when a text adjunct (TA) GR boundary or a word POS-tagged as a clause separator is found, since they often indicate the end of the scope.

The rules for finding the scope of a cue are triggered based on the generalised POS tag of the cue:

- **Auxiliary — VM**
  Mark everything that is below the parent and after the cue.
  If the parent verb is passive, mark everything below its subject (i.e. the dependent of the subj GR) before the cue.
- **Verb — VV**
  Mark everything that is below the cue and after the cue.
  If cue is *appear* or *seem*, mark everything below subject before the cue.
  If cue is passive, mark everything below subject before the cue.
- **Adjective — JJ**
  Find parent of cue. If there is no parent, the cue is used instead.
  Mark everything that is below the parent and after the cue.
  If parent is passive, mark everything below subject before the cue.
  If cue is *(un)likely* and the next word is *to*, mark everything below subject before the cue.
- **Adverb — RR**
  Mark everything that is below the parent and after the cue.

- **Noun — NN**
  Find parent of cue. If there is no parent, the cue is used instead.
  Mark everything that is below the parent and after the cue.
  If parent is passive, mark everything below subject before the cue.
- **Conjunction — CC**
  Mark everything below the conjunction.
  If the cue is *or* and there is another cue *either* before, combine them together.
- **"Whether" as a conjunction — CSW**
  Mark everything that is below the cue and after the cue.
- **Default — anything else**
  Mark everything that is below the parent and after the cue.
  If parent verb is passive, mark everything below subject before the cue.

Either... *or*... is a frequent exception containing two separate cues that form a single scope. An additional rule combines these cues when they are found in the same sentence.

The partial GR graph for (5) is given in Figure 1 (with positional numbering suppressed for readability).

(5) Lobanov et al. thus developed a sensitive search method to deal with this problem, but they also admitted that it (<would> fail to identify highly unusual tRNAs).

Following the rules, *would* is identified as a cue word with the part-of-speech VM; this triggers the first rule in the list. The parent of *would* is *fail* since they are connected with a GR where *fail* is the head. Everything that is below *fail* in the GR graph and positioned after *would* is marked as being in the scope. Since *fail* is not passive, the subject *it* is left out. The final scope returned by the rule is then *would fail to identify highly unusual tRNAs*.

4.2 Machine learning

The tagging sequence from the manual rules is used as input to a second CRF classifier, along with other feature types from RASP. The output of the classifier is a modified sequence of FILO tags.

The list of features for each token, used both alone and as sequences of 5-grams before and after the token, is:

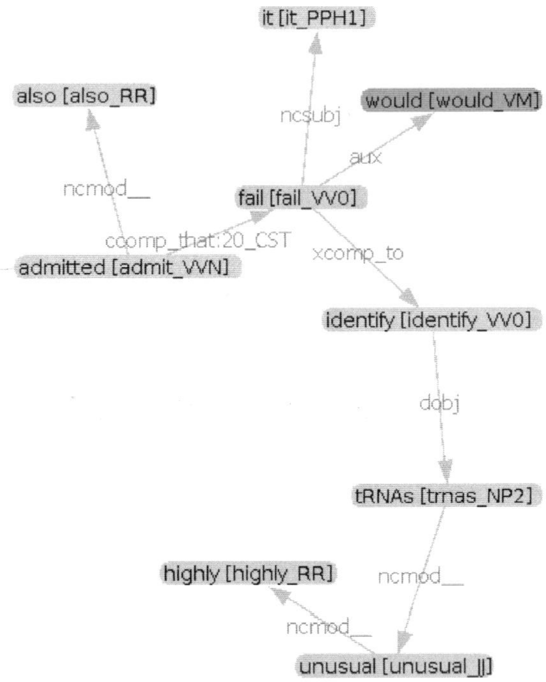

Figure 1: Partial GR graph for sample sentence (5)

- tag from manual rules
- lemma
- POS
- is the token also the cue
- distance from the cue
- absolute distance from the cue
- relative position to the cue
- are there brackets between the word and the cue
- is there any other punctuation between the word and the cue
- are there any special (clause ending) words between the word and cue
- is the word in the GR subtree of the cue
- is the word in the GR subtree of the main verb
- is the word in the GR subject subtree of the main verb

Features of the current word, used in combination with the POS sequence of the cue:

- POS
- distance from the cue
- absolute distance from the cue
- relative position to the cue
- is the word in the GR subtree of the cue
- is the word in the GR subtree of the main verb
- is the word in the GR subject subtree of the main verb

Additional features:

- GR paths between the word and the cue: full path plus subpaths with up to 5 nodes
- GR paths in combination with the lemma sequence of the cue

The scope of the hedge cue can often be found by tracking the sequence of grammatical relations in the GR graph of a sentence, as described by the manual rules. To allow the classifier to learn such regularities, we introduce the concept of a GR path.

Given that the sentence has a full parse and connected graph, we can find the shortest connected path between any two words. We take the connected path between the word and the cue and convert it into a string representation to use it as a feature value in the classifier. Path sections of different lengths allow the system to find both general and more specific patterns. POS tags are used as node values to abstract away from word tokens.

An example for the word *unusual*, using the graph from Figure 1, is given below. Five features representing paths with increasing lengths plus one feature containing the full path are extracted.

(6) 1: VM
2: VM<–aux–VV0
3: VM<–aux–VV0–xcomp–>VV0
4: VM<–aux–VV0–xcomp–>VV0–dobj–>NP2
5: VM<–aux–VV0–xcomp–>VV0–dobj–>NP2–ncmod–>JJ
6: VM<–aux–VV0–xcomp–>VV0–dobj–>NP2–ncmod–>JJ

Line 1 shows the POS of the cue *would* (VM). On line 2, this node is connected to *fail* (VV0) by an auxiliary GR type. More links are added until we reach *unusual* (JJ).

The presence of potential clause ending words, used by Morante and Daelemans (2009), is included as a feature type with values: *whereas, but, although, nevertheless, notwithstanding, however, consequently, hence, therefore, thus, instead, otherwise, alternatively, furthermore, moreover, since*.

4.3 Post-processing

If the cue contains multiple words, the tag sequences have to be combined. This is done by overlapping the sequences and choosing the preferred tag for each word, according to the hierarchy F > L > I > O.

Next, scopes are constructed from tag sequences using the following rules:

- Scope start point is the first token tagged as F before the cue. If none are found, the first word of the cue is used as the start point.
- Scope end point is the last token tagged as L after the cue. If none are found, look for tags I and F. If none are found, the last word of the cue is used as end point.

The scopes are further modified until none of the rules below return any updates:

- If the last token of the scope is punctuation, move the endpoint before the token.
- If the last token is a closing bracket, move the scope endpoint before the opening bracket.
- If the last token is a number and it is not preceded by a capitalised word (e.g. *Table 16*), move the scope endpoint before the token. This is a heuristic rule to handle trailing citations which are frequent in the training data and often misattached by the parser.

Finally, scopes are checked for partial overlap and any instances are corrected. For example, the system might return a faulty version (7) of the sentence (2) in which one scope is only partially contained within the other.

(7) We [<expect> that this cluster (<may> represent a novel] selenoprotein family).

This prediction cannot be represented within the format specified for the shared task and we were unable to find cases where such annotation would be needed. These scopes are modified by moving the end of the first scope to the end of the second scope. The example above would become:

(8) We [<expect> that this cluster (<may> represent a novel selenoprotein family)].

5 Results

5.1 Hedge cues

In evaluation a predicted cue is correct if it contains the correct substring of the sentence. Token-level evaluation would not give accurate results because of varying tokenisation rules. A sentence is classified as hedged if it contains one or more cues.

The results below are obtained using the scorers implemented by the organisers of the shared task.

As our baseline system, we use simple string matching. The list of known cues is collected from the training data and compared to the evaluation sentences. The longest possible match is always marked as a cue. ML1 to ML3 are variations of the system described in section 3. All available data, from papers and abstracts, were used to train the CRF classifier. ML1 uses the results of the classifier directly. The longest sequence of tokens tagged as being part of a cue is used to form the final prediction. ML2 incorporates the list of known cues, constructing a cue over the longest sequence of matching tokens where at least one token has been tagged as belonging to a cue. ML3 uses the list of known cues and also removes any predicted cues not seen in the training data.

	Baseline	ML1	ML2	ML3
Total cues	1047	1047	1047	1047
Predicted cues	3062	995	1006	995
Correctly predicted cues	1018	785	810	810
Cue precision	0.332	0.789	0.805	0.814
Cue recall	0.972	0.750	0.774	0.774
Cue F-measure	0.495	0.769	0.789	0.793
Sentence precision	0.413	0.831	0.831	0.838
Sentence recall	0.995	0.843	0.843	0.842
Sentence F-measure	0.584	0.837	0.837	0.840

Table 3: Cue detection results.

The baseline system returns nearly all cues but since it matches every string, it also returns many false positives, resulting in low precision. ML1 delivers more realistic predictions and increases precision to 0.79. This illustrates how the use of a word as a hedge cue depends on its context and not only on the word itself. ML2 incorporates known cues and increases both precision and recall. ML3 removes any unseen cue predictions further improving precision. This shows the system is unable to accurately predict cues that have not been included in the training data.

Table 4 lists the ten most common cues in the test data and the number of cues found by the ML3 system.

In the cases of *may* and *suggest*, which are also the most common cues in the development data, the system finds all the correct instances. *Can* and *or* are not detected as accurately because they are both common words that in most cases are not functioning as hedges. For example, there are 1215 occurrences of *or* in the training data and only 146 of them are hedge cues; *can* is a cue in 64 out of 506 instances. We have not found any extractable features that reliably distinguish between the different uses of these words.

	TP	FP	Gold
may	161	5	161
suggest	124	0	124
can	2	1	61
or	9	12	52
indicate that	49	2	50
whether	42	6	42
might	42	1	42
could	30	17	41
would	37	14	37
appear	31	14	31

Table 4: True and false positives of the ten most common cues in the evaluation data, using ML3 system.

5.2 Hedge scopes

A scope is counted as correct if it has the correct beginning and end points in the sentence and is associated with the correct cues. Scope prediction systems take cues as input, therefore we present two separate evaluations – one with gold standard cues and the other with cues predicted by the ML3 system from section 4.

The baseline system looks at each cue and marks a scope from the beginning of the cue to the end of the sentence, excluding the full stop. The system using manual rules applies a rule for each cue to find its scope, as described in section 4.1. The POS tag of the cue is used to decide which rule should be used and the GRs determine the scope.

The final system uses the result from the manual rules to derive features, adds various further features from the parser and trains a CRF classifier to refine the predictions.

We hypothesized that the speculative sentences in abstracts may differ from the ones in full papers and a 10-fold cross-validation of the development data supported this intuition. Therefore, the original system (CRF1) only used data from the full papers to train the scope detection classifier. We present here also the system trained on all of the available data (CRF2).

Post-processing rules are applied equally to all of these systems.

The baseline system performs remarkably well.

	Baseline	Manual rules	Manual rules + CRF1	Manual rules + CRF2
Total scopes	1033	1033	1033	1033
Predicted	1047	1035	1035	1035
Correctly predicted	596	661	686	683
Precision	0.569	0.639	0.663	0.660
Recall	0.577	0.640	0.664	0.661
F-measure	0.573	0.639	0.663	0.661

Table 5: Scope detection results using gold standard cues.

	Baseline	Manual rules	Manual rules + CRF1	Manual rules + CRF2
Total scopes	1033	1033	1033	1033
Predicted	995	994	994	994
Correctly predicted	507	532	564	567
Precision	0.510	0.535	0.567	0.570
Recall	0.491	0.515	0.546	0.549
F-measure	0.500	0.525	0.556	0.559

Table 6: Scope detection results using predicted cues.

It does not use any grammatical or lexical knowledge apart from the cue and yet it delivers an F-score of 0.50 with predicted and 0.57 with gold standard cues.

Manual rules are essentially a more fine-grained version of the baseline. Instead of a single rule, one of 8 possible rules is selected based on the POS tag of the cue. This improves the results, increasing the F-score to 0.53 with predicted and 0.64 with gold standard cues. The improvement suggests that the POS tag of a cue is a good indicator of how it behaves in the sentence.

Error analysis showed that 35% of faulty scopes were due to incorrect or unconnected GR graphs output by the parser, and 65% due to exceptions that the rules do not cover. An example of an exception, the braces { } showing the scopes predicted by the rules, is given in (9).

(9) Contamination is {(<probably> below 1%)}, which is {(<likely> lower than the contamination rate of the positive dataset) as discussed in 47}.

as discussed in 47 is a modifier of the clause which is usually included in the scope but in this case should be left out.

Finally, the last system combines features from the rule-based system with features from RASP to train a second classifier and improves our results further, reaching 0.56 with predicted cues.

Inclusion of the abstracts as training data gave a small improvement with predicted cues but not with gold standard cues. It is part of future work to determine if and how the use of hedges differs across text sources.

6 Annotation scheme

During analysis of the data, several examples were found that could not be correctly annotated due to the restrictions of the markup. This leads us to believe that the current rules for annotation might not be best suited to handle complex constructions containing hedged text.

Most importantly, the requirement for the hedge scope to be continuous over the surface form of text sentence does not work for some examples drawn from the development data. In (10) below it is uncertain whether fat body disintegration is independent of the AdoR. In contrast, it is stated with certainty that fat body disintegration is promoted by action of the hemocytes, yet the latter assertion is included in the scope to keep it continuous.

(10) (The block of pupariation <appears> to involve signaling through the adenosine receptor (AdoR)) , but (fat body disintegration , which is promoted by action of the hemocytes , <seems> to be independent of the AdoR) .

Similarly, according to the guidelines, the subject of *be likely* should be included in its scope, as shown in example (11). In sentence (12), however, the subject *this phenomenon* is separated by two non-speculative clauses and is therefore left out of the scope.

(11) Some predictors make use of the observation that (neighboring genes whose relative location is conserved across several prokaryotic organisms are <likely> to interact).

(12) This phenomenon, which is independent of tumour necrosis factor, is associated with HIV replication, and (is thus <likely> to explain at least in part the perpetuation of HIV infection in monocytes).

In (13), arguably, there is no hedging as the sentence precisely describes a statistical technique for predicting interaction given an assumption.

(13) More recently, other groups have come up with sophisticated statistical methods to estimate (<putatively> interacting domain pairs), based on the (<assumption> of domain reusability).

Ultimately, dealing effectively with these and related examples would involve representing hedge scope in terms of sets of semantic propositions recovered from a logical semantic representation of the text, in which anaphora, word sense, and entailments had been resolved.

7 Related work

Most of the previous work has been done on classifying sentences as hedged or not, rather than finding the scope of the hedge.

The first linguistically and computationally motivated study of hedging in biomedical texts is Light et al. (2004). They present an analysis of the problem based on Medline abstracts and construct an initial experiment for automated classification.

Medlock and Briscoe (2007) propose a weakly supervised machine learning approach to the hedge classification problem. They construct a classifier with single words as features and use a small amount of seed data to bootstrap the system, achieving the precision/recall break-even point (BEP) of 0.76. Szarvas (2008) extends this work by introducing bigrams and trigrams as feature types, improving feature selection and using external data sources to construct lists of cue words, achieving a BEP of 0.85.

Kilicoglu and Bergler (2008) apply a combination of lexical and syntactic methods, improving on previous results and showing that quantifying the strength of a hedge can be beneficial for classification of speculative sentences.

Vincze et al. (2008) created a publicly available annotated corpus of biomedical papers, abstracts and clinical data called BioScope, parts of which were also used as training data for the CoNLL10 shared task, building on the dataset and annotation scheme used for evaluation by Medlock and Briscoe (2007).

Morante and Daelemans (2009) use the BioScope corpus to approach the problem of identifying cues and scopes via supervised machine learning. They train a selection of classifiers to tag each word and combine the results with a final classifier, finding 65.6% of the scopes in abstracts and 35.9% of the scopes in papers.

8 Conclusions

We have shown that the GRs output by the RASP system can be effectively used as features for detecting cues in a supervised classifier and also as the basis for manual rules and features for scope detection. We demonstrated that a small number of manual rules can provide competitive results, but that these can be further improved using machine learning techniques and post-processing rules. The generally low ceiling for the scope detection results demonstrates the difficulty of both annotating and detecting the hedge scopes in terms of surface sentential forms.

Future work could usefully be directed at improving performance on unseen cue detection and on learning rules of the same form as those developed manually from annotated training data. However, perhaps the most pressing issue is that of establishing the best possible annotation and consequent definition of the scope detection task.

References

Ted Briscoe, John Carroll, and Rebecca Watson. 2006. The second release of the RASP system. In *Proceedings of the COLING/ACL 2006 on Interactive Presentation Sessions*.

Richárd Farkas, Veronika Vincze, György Móra, János Csirik, and György Szarvas. 2010. The CoNLL-2010 Shared Task: Learning to Detect Hedges and their Scope in Natural Language Text. In *Proceedings of the Fourteenth Conference on Computational Natural Language Learning (CoNLL-2010): Shared Task*, pages 1–12.

Halil Kilicoglu and Sabine Bergler. 2008. Recognizing speculative language in biomedical research articles: a linguistically motivated perspective. *BMC Bioinformatics*, 9 Suppl 11.

John Lafferty, Andrew McCallum, and Fernando Pereira. 2001. Conditional random fields: Probabilistic models for segmenting and labeling sequence data. In *Proceedings of ICML 2001*.

Marc Light, Xin Y. Qiu, and Padmini Srinivasan. 2004. The language of bioscience: Facts, speculations, and statements in between. In *Proceedings of BioLink 2004*.

Ben Medlock and Ted Briscoe. 2007. Weakly supervised learning for hedge classification in scientific literature. In *Proceedings of ACL 2007*.

Roser Morante and Walter Daelemans. 2009. Learning the scope of hedge cues in biomedical texts. In *Proceedings of the Workshop on BioNLP*.

György Szarvas. 2008. Hedge classification in biomedical texts with a weakly supervised selection of keywords. In *Proceedings of ACL 2008*.

Veronika Vincze, György Szarvas, Richárd Farkas, György Móra, and János Csirik. 2008. The BioScope corpus: biomedical texts annotated for uncertainty, negation and their scopes. *BMC Bioinformatics*, 9 Suppl 11.

Hedge Detection Using the *RelHunter* Approach*

Eraldo R. Fernandes† and **Carlos E. M. Crestana**‡ and **Ruy L. Milidiú**§
Departamento de Informática, PUC-Rio
Rio de Janeiro, Brazil
{efernandes, ccrestana, milidiu}@inf.puc-rio.br

Abstract

RelHunter is a Machine Learning based method for the extraction of structured information from text. Here, we apply *RelHunter* to the Hedge Detection task, proposed as the CoNLL-2010 Shared Task[1]. *RelHunter*'s key design idea is to model the target structures as a relation over entities. The method decomposes the original task into three subtasks: (i) Entity Identification; (ii) Candidate Relation Generation; and (iii) Relation Recognition. In the Hedge Detection task, we define three types of entities: *cue chunk*, *start scope token* and *end scope token*. Hence, the Entity Identification subtask is further decomposed into three token classification subtasks, one for each entity type. In the Candidate Relation Generation subtask, we apply a simple procedure to generate a *ternary* candidate relation. Each instance in this relation represents a hedge candidate composed by a cue chunk, a start scope token and an end scope token. For the Relation Recognition subtask, we use a binary classifier to discriminate between true and false candidates. The four classifiers are trained with the *Entropy Guided Transformation Learning* algorithm. When compared to the other hedge detection systems of the CoNLL shared task, our scheme shows a competitive performance. The F-score of our system is 54.05 on the evaluation corpus.

* This work is partially funded by CNPq and FAPERJ grants 557.128/2009-9 and E-26/170028/2008.

† Holds a CNPq doctoral fellowship and has financial support from IFG, Brazil.

‡ Holds a CAPES doctoral fellowship.

§ Holds a CNPq research fellowship.

[1] *Closed Task 2*: detection of hedge cues and their scopes.

1 Introduction

Hedges are linguistic devices that indicate uncertain or unreliable information within a text. The detection of hedge structures is important for many applications that extract facts from textual data. The CoNLL-2010 Shared Task (Farkas et al., 2010) is dedicated to hedge detection.

A hedge structure consists of a *cue* and a *scope*. In Figure 1, we present a sentence with two hedge instances. The hedge cues are highlighted and their scopes are delimited by brackets. The hedge cue comprises one or more keywords that indicate uncertainty. The hedge scope is the uncertain statement which is hedged by the cue. The scope always includes the corresponding cue.

> [They **indicate that** [the demonstration is **possible** in this context] and there is a correlation]

Figure 1: Sentence with two hedge instances.

Over the last two decades, several Computational Linguistic problems have been successfully modeled as local token classification tasks (Brill, 1995; Milidiú et al., 2009). Nevertheless, the harder problems consist in identifying complex structures within a text. These structures comprise many tokens and show non local token dependencies.

Phrase chunking (Sang and Buchholz, 2000) is a task that involves structure recognition. Punyakanok and Roth decompose this task into four subtasks, that are sequentially solved (Punyakanok and Roth, 2001). They use Hidden Markov Models for the first three subtasks. They find out that task decomposition improves the overall token classification modeling.

Clause identification (Sang and Déjean, 2001) is another task that requires structure recognition. As clauses may embed other clauses, these struc-

Proceedings of the Fourteenth Conference on Computational Natural Language Learning: Shared Task, pages 64–69,
Uppsala, Sweden, 15-16 July 2010.

tures involve stronger dependencies than phrase chunks. Carreras et al. propose an approach that extends Punyakanok and Roth's previous work (Carreras et al., 2002). Their system comprises complex methods for training and extraction, in order to exploit the specific dependency aspects of clause structures.

Phrase Recognition is a general type of task that includes both phrase chunking and clause identification. Carreras et al. propose the Filtering-Ranking Perceptron (FRP) system for this general task (Carreras et al., 2005). The FRP task modeling is strongly related to previous proposals (Punyakanok and Roth, 2001; Carreras et al., 2002). However, it simultaneously learns to solve three subtasks. FRP is very effective, although computationally expensive at both training and prediction time. Currently, FRP provides the best performing clause identification system.

In Morante and Daelemans (2009), the hedge detection task is solved as two consecutive classification tasks. The first one consists of classifying the tokens of a sentence as hedge cues using the IOB tagging style. The second task consists of classifying tokens of a sentence as being the start of a hedge scope, the end of one, or neither. The result of those two tasks is combined using a set of six rules to solve the hedge detection task.

Here, we describe *RelHunter*, a new method for the extraction of structured information from text. Additionally, we apply it to the Hedge Detection task. *RelHunter* extends the modeling strategy used both in Carreras et al. (2005) and Punyakanok et al. (2001). Other applications of this method are presented in Fernandes at al. (2009b; 2010).

The remainder of this text is organized as follows. In Section 2, we present an overview of the *RelHunter* method. The modeling approach for the Hedge Detection task is presented in Sections 3 and 4. The experimental findings are depicted and discussed in Section 5. Finally, in Section 6, we present our final remarks.

2 RelHunter Overview

The central idea of *RelHunter* is to model the target structures as a relation over entities. To learn how to extract this relation from text, *RelHunter* uses two additional schemes: task decomposition and interdependent classification.

We decompose the original task into three subtasks: (i) *Entity Identification*; (ii) *Candidate Relation Generation*; and (iii) *Relation Recognition*. In Figure 2, we illustrate the application of *RelHunter* to hedge detection. We use the sentence introduced by Figure 1.

Entity Identification is a local subtask, in which simple entities are detected without any concern about the structures they belong to. The outcome of this subtask is the *entity set*. For instance, for hedge detection, we identify three types of entities: hedge cues, tokens that start a scope and tokens that end a scope.

The second subtask is performed by a simple procedure that generates the *candidate relation* over the entity set. This relation includes true and false *candidates*. This procedure considers domain specific knowledge to avoid the generation of all possible candidates. In the hedge detection task, we define the candidate relation as the set of entity triples that comprise a hedge cue, a start scope token and an end scope token, such that the start token does not occur after the end token and the hedge cue occurs between the start and the end tokens.

The Relation Recognition subtask is a binary classification problem. In this subtask, we discriminate between true and false candidates. The *output relation* produced in this subtask contains the identified hedge instances.

3 Hedge Detection using RelHunter

In this section, we detail the *RelHunter* method and describe its application to hedge detection.

3.1 Entity Identification

We consider three specific entity types: cue chunk, start scope token, and end scope token. We divide entity identification into three token classification tasks, one for each entity type. Thus, we use the original corpus to train three classifiers.

The *cue chunk* subtask is approached as a token classification problem by using the IOB tagging style. The token tag is defined as follows: I, when it is inside a hedge cue; O, when it is outside a hedge cue; and B, when it begins a hedge cue immediately after a distinct cue. As the baseline classifier, we use the Cue Dictionary proposed in Morante and Daelemans (2009), classifying each occurrence of those words as a cue.

The *start scope* and *end scope* subtasks are modeled as binary token classification problems.

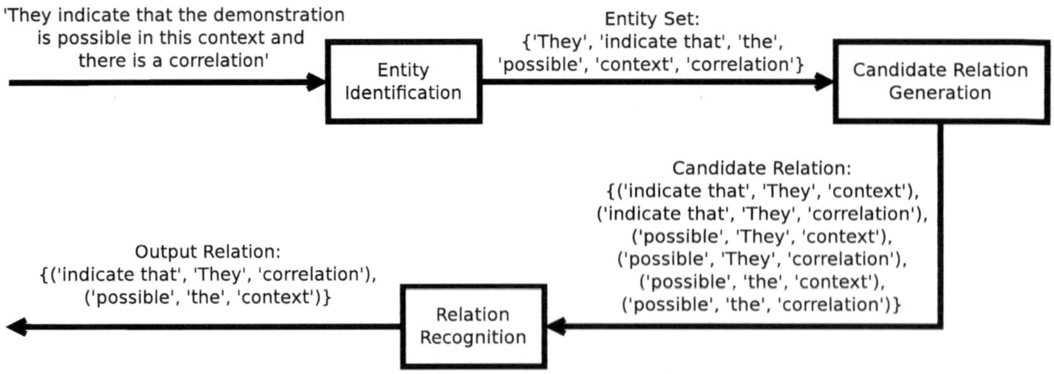

Figure 2: Diagram of the *RelHunter* method.

As the baseline classifier for the start scope subtask, we assign the first token of each hedge cue as the start of a scope.

We have two baseline classifiers for the end scope subtask: *END* and *END-X*. The *END* system classifies as an end token the second to the last token of each sentence that contains a cue. Due to the frequent occurrence of parenthesized clauses at the end of sentences in full articles, the *END-X* system extends the *END* system with an additional operation. It reassigns an end scope tag, from a close parentheses token, to the token before its corresponding open parentheses.

3.2 Candidate Relation Generation

We define as the candidate hedge relation the set of entity triples that comprise a hedge cue, a start scope token and an end scope token, such that the start token does not occur after the end token and the hedge cue occurs between the start and the end tokens.

3.3 Relation Recognition

We train a binary classifier to discriminate between positive and negative candidates within the candidate relation. This classifier is trained on the *relation dataset*, which is built by a general procedure. This dataset contains an entry for each candidate. For each candidate, we generate two feature sets: *local features* and *global features*.

The local features include local information about each candidate entity, namely: cue chunk, start scope token and end scope token. These features are retrieved from the original corpus. For the start and end tokens, we use all their features in the original corpus. For the cue chunk, we use the features of the rightmost token within the chunk.

The global features follow Carreras et al. (2002). These features are generated by considering the whole sentence where the candidate lies in. They inform about the occurrence of *relevant elements* within sentence *fragments*. We consider as relevant elements the three entity types and verbal chunks.

For each candidate entity, we consider three fragments. The first one contains all the tokens before the entity. The second, all the entity tokens, and the third all the tokens after the entity. Similarly, for the whole candidate, we have three more fragments: one containing all the tokens before the candidate, another containing all the candidate tokens, and the third one containing all the tokens after the candidate. Thus, there are 12 fragments for each candidate, three for each entity plus three for the whole candidate.

For each relevant element and fragment, we generate two global features in the relation dataset: a flag indicating the occurrence of the element within the fragment and a counter showing its frequency.

The relation dataset has km local features and $6r(k+1)$ global features, where k is the relation cardinality (number of entities), m is the number of features in the original corpus, and r is the number of relevant elements.

Our current *RelHunter* implementation uses the Entropy Guided Transformation Learning (ETL) as its learning engine (Milidiú et al., 2008; dos Santos and Milidiú, 2009). For instance, we train four ETL based classifiers: one for each Entity Identification subtask and one for the Relation Recognition subtask. In the next section, we describe an important issue explored by the ETL algorithm.

4 Interdependent Classification

The input to the Relation Recognition subtask is the candidate relation, i.e., a set of hedge candidates. The corresponding classifier must discriminate positive from negative candidates. However, identifying one candidate as positive implies that some other candidates must be negatives. This involves a special modeling issue: *interdependent classification*. The learning engine may explore these dependencies, when building the classifier for this subtask.

Interdependent classification is usually assumed for neighboring examples. When the learning model adopts a Markovian Property, then the neighborhood is given by a context window. This is the case for Markovian Fields such as Hidden Markov Models. Another model that also explores interdependent examples is ETL.

ETL is a very attractive modeling tool and has been applied to several classification tasks (Milidiú et al., 2008; dos Santos and Milidiú, 2009; Fernandes et al., 2009a; Fernandes et al., 2010). ETL uses an annotated corpus, where the corresponding class is attached to each example. The corpus is partitioned into segments. Each segment is a sequence of examples. Examples within the same segment are considered dependent. Conversely, examples within different segments are considered independent. Moreover, an example classification depends only on the features of the examples from its corresponding *context window*. Hence, to apply ETL we need to provide three modeling ingredients: segment definition, example ordering within a segment and the context window size. Given that, classification dependencies are explored by the ETL classifier. Hence, *RelHunter* uses ETL as its learning engine.

We include in the same segment the hedge candidates that have the same cue and start scope tokens. Within a segment, we order the candidates by the order of the end token in the original corpus. We use a context window of 7 candidates, i.e., three candidates before the current, the current candidate and three candidates after the current.

5 Experimental Results

We use the corpus provided in the CoNLL-2010 Shared Task to train and evaluate our hedge detection system. We add the following annotation to the corpus: word stems, part-of-speech tags, phrase chunks, and clause annotations. Word stems have been generated by the Porter stemmer (Porter, 1980). The additional annotation has been generated by ETL based systems (dos Santos and Milidiú, 2009; Fernandes et al., 2009b; Milidiú et al., 2008).

The CoNLL corpus is based on the *BioScope* corpus (Vincze et al., 2008). Since it contains documents of two different kinds – paper abstracts and full papers – we split it into two subcorpora. The first subcorpus is called *ABST* and contains all the paper abstracts. The second is called *FULL* and contains all the full papers.

We have two experimental setups: *Development* and *Evaluation*. In the Development Setup, we use *ABST* as the training corpus and *FULL* as the development corpus. This is a conservative decision since the CoNLL Evaluation Corpus is comprised only of full articles. In the Evaluation Setup, we use the union of *ABST* and *FULL* as the training corpus and report the performance over the CoNLL Evaluation Corpus.

5.1 Development

Here, we report the development setup experimental findings. In Table 1, we show the performance of the three baseline classifiers. The start and end classifiers are evaluated with golden standard cue chunks. All results are obtained with the *END-X* baseline system, except when explicitly stated.

Task	*Precision*	*Recall*	*F-score*
Cue	51.96	51.65	51.80
Start scope	72.01	72.22	72.11
End scope	65.90	58.97	62.24

Table 1: Development performance of the three Baseline Classifiers.

In Table 2, we report the performance of the three entity identification ETL classifiers. Again, the start and end classifiers are evaluated with golden standard cue chunks. These results indicate that the end scope subtask is the hardest one. Indeed, our ETL classifier is not able to improve the baseline classifier performance. The last table line shows the performance of the *RelHunter* method on the target task – hedge detection.

5.2 Evaluation

Here, we report the evaluation setup findings. In Table 3, we show the performance of the three

Task	*Precision*	*Recall*	*F-score*
Cue	81.23	73.20	77.01
Start scope	91.81	72.37	80.94
End scope	65.90	58.97	62.24
Hedge	53.49	34.43	41.89

Table 2: Development performance of the three entity identification ETL classifiers and the *RelHunter* method to hedge detection.

baseline classifiers. The start and end classifiers are evaluated with golden standard cue chunks.

Task	*Precision*	*Recall*	*F-score*
Cue	45.12	60.02	51.52
Start scope	75.51	75.73	75.62
End scope	81.01	72.56	76.55

Table 3: Evaluation performance of the three Baseline Classifiers.

In Table 4, we report the performance of the three entity identification ETL classifiers. Again, the start and end classifiers are evaluated with golden standard cue chunks. The last table line shows the performance of the *RelHunter* method on the target task – hedge detection.

Task	*Precision*	*Recall*	*F-score*
Cue	78.73	77.05	77.88
Start scope	89.21	77.86	83.15
End scope	81.01	72.56	76.55
Hedge	57.84	50.73	54.05

Table 4: Evaluation performance of the three entity identification ETL classifiers and the *RelHunter* method to hedge detection.

In Table 5, we report the Hedge Detection performances when using *END* and *END-X*, as the baseline classifier for the end scope subtask. The use of *END-X* improves the overall system *F-score* by more than ten twelve.

In Table 6, we report the Final Results of the CoNLL-2010 Shared Task – Closed Task 2. For the sake of comparison, we also include the performance of the *RelHunter* system with *END-X*, that has been developed and tested after the competition end. The version with the END baseline holds rank 7 at the competition.

End scope	*Precision*	*Recall*	*F-score*
END	45.96	38.04	41.63
END-X	57.84	50.73	54.05

Table 5: Evaluation performance of the *RelHunter* system when using *END* and *END-X*.

Official Rank	*System*	*P*	*R*	*F*
1	Morante	59.62	55.18	57.32
2	Rei	56.74	54.60	55.65
3	Velldal	56.71	54.02	55.33
-	***RelHunter***	**57.84**	**50.73**	**54.05**
4	Li	57.42	47.92	52.24
5	Zhou	45.32	43.56	44.42
6	Zhang	45.94	42.69	44.25
7	**Fernandes**	**45.96**	**38.04**	**41.63**
8	Vlachos	41.18	35.91	38.37
9	Zhao	34.78	41.05	37.66
10	Tang	34.49	31.85	33.12
11	Ji	21.87	17.23	19.27
12	Täckström	02.27	02.03	02.15

Table 6: Evaluation performance of the CoNLL-2010 systems and the *RelHunter* method with the *END-X* end scope classifier.

6 Conclusion

We propose *RelHunter*, a new machine learning based method for the extraction of structured information from text. *RelHunter* consists in modeling the target structures as a relation over entities. To learn how to extract this relation from text, *RelHunter* uses two main schemes: task decomposition and interdependent classification.

RelHunter decomposes the identification of entities into several but simple token classification subtasks. Additionally, the method generates a candidate relation over the identified entities and discriminates between true and false candidates within this relation.

RelHunter uses the Entropy Guided Transformation Learning algorithm as its learning engine. As Hidden Markov Models, ETL is able to consider interdependent examples. *RelHunter* exploits this powerful feature in order to tackle dependencies among the hedge candidates.

RelHunter is easily applied to many complex Computational Linguistic problems. We show its effectiveness by applying it to hedge detection. Other successful applications of this method are presented in Fernandes et al. (2009b; 2010).

RelHunter explores the dependency among linguistic structures by using a powerful feature of the ETL algorithm. Nevertheless, this feature is restricted to sequentially organized examples, since ETL has been initially proposed for token classification problems. Linguistic structures involve topologies that are frequently more complex than that. The ETL algorithm may be extended to consider more complex topologies. We conjecture that it is possible to consider quite general topologies. This would contribute to the construction of better solutions to many Computational Linguistic tasks.

Acknowledgments

The authors thank Evelin Amorim and Eduardo Motta for coding dataset normalization procedures that are very handy for Hedge Detection.

References

Eric Brill. 1995. Transformation-based error-driven learning and natural language processing: a case study in part-of-speech tagging. *Computational Linguistics*, 21(4):543–565.

Xavier Carreras, Lluís Màrquez, Vasin Punyakanok, and Dan Roth. 2002. Learning and inference for clause identification. In *Proceedings of the Thirteenth European Conference on Machine Learning*, pages 35–47.

Xavier Carreras, Lluís Màrquez, and Jorge Castro. 2005. Filtering-ranking perceptron learning for partial parsing. *Machine Learning*, 60(1–3):41–71.

Cícero N. dos Santos and Ruy L. Milidiú, 2009. *Foundations of Computational Intelligence, Volume 1: Learning and Approximation*, volume 201 of *Studies in Computational Intelligence*, chapter Entropy Guided Transformation Learning, pages 159–184. Springer.

Richárd Farkas, Veronika Vincze, György Móra, János Csirik, and György Szarvas. 2010. The CoNLL-2010 Shared Task: Learning to Detect Hedges and their Scope in Natural Language Text. In *Proceedings of the Fourteenth Conference on Computational Natural Language Learning (CoNLL-2010): Shared Task*, pages 1–12, Uppsala, Sweden, July. Association for Computational Linguistics.

Eraldo R. Fernandes, Cícero N. dos Santos, and Ruy L. Milidiú. 2009a. Portuguese language processing service. In *Proceedings of the Web in Ibero-America Alternate Track of the 18th World Wide Web Conference (WWW'2009)*, Madrid.

Eraldo R. Fernandes, Bernardo A. Pires, Cícero N. dos Santos, and Ruy L. Milidiú. 2009b. Clause identification using entropy guided transformation learning. In *Proceedings of the 7th Brazilian Symposium in Information and Human Language Technology (STIL)*, São Carlos, Brazil.

Eraldo R. Fernandes, Bernardo A. Pires, Cícero N. dos Santos, and Ruy L. Milidiú. 2010. A machine learning approach to Portuguese clause identification. In *Proceedings of the Nineth International Conference on Computational Processing of the Portuguese Language (PROPOR)*, volume 6001 of *Lecture Notes in Artificial Intelligence*, pages 55–64, Porto Alegre, Brazil. Springer.

Ruy L. Milidiú, Cícero N. dos Santos, and Julio C. Duarte. 2008. Phrase chunking using entropy guided transformation learning. In *Proceedings of ACL-08: HLT*, pages 647–655, Columbus, USA. Association for Computational Linguistics.

Ruy L. Milidiú, Cícero N. dos Santos, and Carlos E. M. Crestana. 2009. A token classification approach to dependency parsing. In *Proceedings of the 7th Brazilian Symposium in Information and Human Language Technology (STIL'2009)*, São Carlos, Brazil.

Roser Morante and Walter Daelemans. 2009. Learning the scope of hedge cues in biomedical texts. In *Proceedings of the BioNLP 2009 Workshop*, pages 28–36, Boulder, USA, June. Association for Computational Linguistics.

Martin F. Porter. 1980. An algorithm for suffix stripping. *Program*, 14(3):130–137.

Vasin Punyakanok and Dan Roth. 2001. The use of classifiers in sequential inference. In *Proceedings of the Conference on Advances in Neural Information Processing Systems (NIPS)*, pages 995–1001. MIT Press.

Erik F. Tjong Kim Sang and Sabine Buchholz. 2000. Introduction to the CoNLL-2000 shared task: Chunking. In *Proceedings of CoNLL-2000 and LLL-2000*, Lisbon, Portugal.

Erik F. T. K. Sang and Hervé Déjean. 2001. Introduction to the CoNLL-2001 shared task: Clause identification. In *Proceedings of Fifth Conference on Computational Natural Language Learning*, Toulouse, France.

Veronika Vincze, György Szarvas, Richárd Farkas, György Móra, and János Csirik. 2008. The BioScope corpus: biomedical texts annotated for uncertainty, negation and their scopes. *BMC Bioinformatics*, 9 (Suppl 11):S9.

A High-Precision Approach to Detecting Hedges and Their Scopes

Halil Kilicoglu and Sabine Bergler
Department of Computer Science and Software Engineering
Concordia University
1455 de Maisonneuve Blvd. West
Montréal, Canada
{h_kilico,bergler}@cse.concordia.ca

Abstract

We extend our prior work on speculative sentence recognition and speculation scope detection in biomedical text to the CoNLL-2010 Shared Task on Hedge Detection. In our participation, we sought to assess the extensibility and portability of our prior work, which relies on linguistic categorization and weighting of hedging cues and on syntactic patterns in which these cues play a role. For Task 1B, we tuned our categorization and weighting scheme to recognize hedging in biological text. By accommodating a small number of vagueness quantifiers, we were able to extend our methodology to detecting vague sentences in Wikipedia articles. We exploited constituent parse trees in addition to syntactic dependency relations in resolving hedging scope. Our results are competitive with those of closed-domain trained systems and demonstrate that our high-precision oriented methodology is extensible and portable.

1 Introduction

Natural language is imbued with uncertainty, vagueness, and subjectivity. However, information extraction systems generally focus on extracting factual information, ignoring the wealth of information expressed through such phenomena. In recent years, the need for information extraction and text mining systems to identify and model such extra-factual information has increasingly become clear. For example, online product and movie reviews have provided a rich context for analyzing sentiments and opinions in text (see Pang and Lee (2008) for a recent survey), while tentative, speculative nature of scientific writing, particularly in biomedical literature, has provided impetus for recent research in speculation detection (Light et al., 2004). The term *hedging* is often used as an umbrella term to refer to an array of extra-factual phenomena in natural language and is the focus of the CoNLL-2010 Shared Task on Hedge Detection.

The CoNLL-2010 Shared Task on Hedge Detection (Farkas et al., 2010) follows in the steps of the recent BioNLP'09 Shared Task on Event Extraction (Kim et al., 2009), in which one task (speculation and negation detection) was concerned with notions related to hedging in biomedical abstracts. However, the CoNLL-2010 Shared Task differs in several aspects. It sheds light on the pervasiveness of hedging across genres and domains: in addition to biomedical abstracts, it is concerned with biomedical full text articles as well as with Wikipedia articles. Both shared tasks have been concerned with scope resolution; however, their definitions of scope are fundamentally different: the BioNLP'09 Shared Task takes the scope of a speculation instance to be an abstract semantic object (an *event*), thus a normalized logical form. The CoNLL-2010 Shared Task, on the other hand, defines it as a textual unit based on syntactic considerations. It is also important to note that hedging in scientific writing is a core aspect of the genre (Hyland, 1998), while it is judged to be a flaw which has to be eradicated in Wikipedia articles. Therefore, hedge detection in these genres serves different purposes: explicitly encoding the factuality of a scientific claim (*doubtful*, *probable*, etc.) versus flagging unreliable text.

We participated in both tasks of the CoNLL-2010 Shared Task: namely, detection of sentences with uncertainty (Task 1) and resolution of uncertainty scope (Task 2). Since we pursued both of these directions in prior work, one of our goals in participating in the shared task was to assess how our approach generalized to previously unseen texts, even genres. Towards this goal, we adopted

Proceedings of the Fourteenth Conference on Computational Natural Language Learning: Shared Task, pages 70–77,
Uppsala, Sweden, 15-16 July 2010.

an open-domain approach, where we aimed to use previously developed techniques to the extent possible. Among all participating groups, we distinguished ourselves as the one that fully worked in an open-domain setting. This approach worked reasonably well for uncertainty detection (Task 1); however, for the scope resolution task, we needed to extend our work more substantially, since the notion of scope was fundamentally different than what we adopted previously. The performance of our system was competitive; in terms of F-measure, we were ranked near the middle in Task 1, while a more significant focus on scope resolution resulted in fourth place ranking among fifteen systems. We obtained the highest precision in tasks focusing on biological text. Considering that we chose not to exploit the training data provided to the full extent, we believe that our system is viable in terms of extensibility and portability.

2 Related Work

Several notions related to hedging have been previously explored in natural language processing. In the news article genre, these have included *certainty*, *modality*, and *subjectivity*. For example, Rubin et al. (2005) proposed a four dimensional model to categorize *certainty* in news text: *certainty level*, *focus*, *perspective* and *time*. In the context of TimeML (Pustejovsky et al., 2005), which focuses on temporal expressions in news articles, *event modality* is encoded using subordination links (SLINKs), some of which (MODAL,EVIDENTIAL) indicate hedging (Saurí et al., 2006). Saurí (2008) exploits modality and polarity to assess the *factuality degree* of events (whether they correspond to facts, counter-facts or possibilities), and reports on FactBank, a corpus annotated for event factuality (Saurí and Pustejovsky, 2009). Wiebe et al. (2005) consider subjectivity in news articles, and focus on the notion of *private states*, encompassing speculations, opinions, and evaluations in their subjectivity frames.

The importance of speculative language in biomedical articles was first acknowledged by Light et al. (2004). Following work in this area focused on detecting speculative sentences (Medlock and Briscoe, 2007; Szarvas, 2008; Kilicoglu and Bergler, 2008). Similar to Rubin et al.'s (2005) work, Thompson et al. (2008) proposed a categorization scheme for *epistemic modality* in biomedical text according to the type of information expressed (e.g., *certainty level*, *point of view*, *knowledge type*). With the availability of the BioScope corpus (Vincze et al., 2008), in which negation, hedging and their scopes are annotated, studies in detecting speculation scope have also been reported (Morante and Daelemans, 2009; Özgür and Radev, 2009). Negation and uncertainty of bio-events are also annotated to some extent in the GENIA event corpus (Kim et al., 2008). The BioNLP'09 Shared Task on Event Extraction (Kim et al., 2009) dedicated a task to detecting negation and speculation in biomedical abstracts, based on the GENIA event corpus annotations.

Ganter and Strube (2009) elaborated on the link between *vagueness* in Wikipedia articles indicated by *weasel words* and hedging. They exploited word frequency measures and shallow syntactic patterns to detect weasel words in Wikipedia articles.

3 Methods

Our methodology for hedge detection is essentially rule-based and relies on a combination of lexical and syntactic information. Lexical information is encoded in a simple dictionary, and relevant syntactic information is identified using the Stanford Lexicalized Parser (Klein and Manning, 2003). We exploit constituent parse trees as well as corresponding collapsed dependency representations (deMarneffe et al., 2006), provided by the parser.

3.1 Detecting Uncertainty in Biological Text

For detecting uncertain sentences in biological text (Task 1B), we built on the linguistically-inspired system previously described in detail in Kilicoglu and Bergler (2008). In summary, this system relies on a dictionary of lexical speculation cues, derived from a set of core surface realizations of hedging identified by Hyland (1998) and expanded through WordNet (Fellbaum, 1998) synsets and UMLS SPECIALIST Lexicon (McCray et al., 1994) nominalizations. A set of lexical certainty markers (*unhedgers*) are also included, as they indicate hedging when they are negated (e.g., *know*). These hedging cues are categorized by their type (*modal auxiliaries*, *epistemic verbs*, *approximative adjectives*, etc.) and are weighted to reflect their central/peripheral contribution to hedging, inspired by the fuzzy model of Hyland (1998). We use a scale of 1-5, where 5 is assigned to cues most central to hedging and 1 to those that are most peripheral. For example, the modal auxiliary *may* has a weight of 5, while a relatively weak hedging cue, the epistemic adverb *apparently*, has a weight of 2. The weight sum of cues in a sentence in combination with a predetermined threshold determines whether the sentence in question is uncertain. Syntax, generally ignored in other studies on hedging, plays a prominent role in our approach. Certain syntactic constructions act as cues (e.g., *whether*- and *if*-complements), while others strengthen or weaken the effect of the cue associated with them. For example, a *that*-complement taken by an epistemic verb increases the hedging score contributed by the verb by 2, while lack of any complement decreases the score by 1.

For the shared task, we tuned this categorization and weighting scheme, based on an analysis of the biomedical full text articles in training data. We also adjusted the threshold. We eliminated some hedging cue categories completely and adjusted the weights of a small number of the remaining cues. The eliminated cue categories included *approximative adverbs* (e.g., *generally*, *largely*, *partially*) and *approximative adjectives* (e.g., *partial*), often used to "manipulate precision in quantification" (Hyland, 1998). The other eliminated category included verbs of *effort* (e.g., *try*, *attempt*, *seek*), also referred to as *rationalising narrators* (Hyland, 1998). The motivation behind eliminating these categories was that cues belonging to these categories were never annotated as hedging cues in the training data. The elimination process resulted in a total of 147 remaining hedging cues. Additionally, we adjusted the weights of several other cues that were not consistently annotated as cues in the training data, despite our view that they were strong hedging cues. One example is the epistemic verb *predict*, previously assigned a weight of 4 based on Hyland's analysis. We found its annotation in the training data somewhat inconsistent, and lowered its weight to 3, thus requiring a syntactic strengthening effect (an infinitival complement, for example) for it to qualify as a hedging cue in the current setting (threshold of 4).

3.2 Detecting Uncertainty in Wikipedia Articles

Task 1W was concerned with detecting uncertainty in Wikipedia articles. Uncertainty in this context refers more or less to *vagueness* indicated by *weasel words*, an undesirable feature according to Wikipedia policy. Analysis of Wikipedia training data provided by the organizers revealed that there is overlap between *weasel words* and hedging cues described in previous section. We, therefore, sought to adapt our dictionary of hedging cues to the task of detecting vagueness in Wikipedia articles. Similar to Task 1B, changes involved eliminating cue categories and adjusting cue weights. In addition, however, we also added a previously unconsidered category of cues, due to their prominence in Wikipedia data as *weasel words*. This category (*vagueness quantifiers* (Lappin, 2000)) includes words, such as *some*, *several*, *many* and *various*, which introduce imprecision when in modifier position. For instance, in the example below, both *some* and *certain* contribute to vagueness of the sentence.

(1) Even today, *some cultures* have *certain instances* of their music intending to imitate natural sounds.

For Wikipedia uncertainty detection, eliminated categories included verbs and nouns concerning *tendencies* (e.g., *tend*, *inclination*) in addition to verbs of *effort*. The only modal auxiliary consistently considered a *weasel word* was *might*; therefore, we only kept *might* in this category and eliminated the rest (e.g., *may*, *would*). *Approximative adverbs*, eliminated in detecting uncertainty in biological text, not only were revived for this task, but also their weights were increased as they were more central to vagueness expressions. Besides these changes in weighting and categorization, the methodology for uncertainty detection in Wikipedia articles was essentially the same as that for biological text. The threshold we used in our submission was, similarly, 4.

3.3 Scope Resolution for Uncertainty in Biological Text

Task 2 of the shared task involved hedging scope resolution in biological text. We previously tackled this problem within the context of biological text in the BioNLP'09 Shared Task (Kilicoglu and Bergler, 2009). That task defined the scope of speculation instances as abstract, previously extracted *bio-events*. Our approach relied on finding an appropriate syntactic dependency relation between the bio-event trigger word identified in earlier steps and the speculation cue. The category of the hedging cue constrained the dependency relations that are deemed appropriate. For example, consider the sentence in (2a), where *involves* is a bio-event trigger for a `Regulation` event and *suggest* is a speculation cue of epistemic verb type. The first dependency relation in (2b) indicates that the epistemic verb takes a clausal complement headed by the bio-event trigger. The second indicates that *that* is the complementizer. This cue category/dependency combination licenses the generation of a speculation instance where the event indicated by the event trigger represents the scope.

(2) (a) The results *suggest* that M-CSF induction of M-CSF *involves* G proteins, PKC and NF kappa B.

(b) *ccomp(suggest,involves)*
complm(involves,that)

Several other cue category/dependency combinations sought for speculation scope resolution are given in Table 1. *X* represents a token that is neither a cue nor a trigger (*aux*: auxiliary, *dobj*: direct object, *neg*: negation modifier).

Cue Category	**Dependency**
Modal auxiliary (*may*)	*aux(Trigger,Cue)*
Conditional (*if*)	*complm(Trigger,Cue)*
Unhedging noun (*evidence*)	*dobj(X,Cue)* *ccomp(X,Trigger)* *neg(Cue,no)*

Table 1: Cue categories with examples and the dependency relations to search

In contrast to this notion of scope being an abstract semantic object, Task 2 (BioScope corpus, in general) conceptualizes hedge scope as a continuous textual unit, including the hedging cue itself and the biggest syntactic unit the cue is involved in (Vincze et al., 2008). This fundamental difference in conceptualization limits the direct applicability of our prior approach to this task. Nevertheless, we were able to use our work as a building block in extending scope resolution heuristics. We further augmented it by exploiting constituent parse trees provided by Stanford Lexicalized Parser. These extensions are summarized below.

3.3.1 Exploiting parse trees

The constituent parse trees contribute to scope resolution uniformly across all hedging cue categories. We simply determine the phrasal node that dominates the hedging cue and consider the tokens within that phrase as being in the scope of the cue, unless they meet one of the following exclusion criteria:

1. Exclude tokens within post-cue sentential complements (indicated by S and SBAR nodes) introduced by a small number of discourse markers (*thus*, *whereas*, *because*, *since*, *if*, and *despite*).

2. Exclude punctuation marks at the right boundary of the phrase

3. Exclude pre-cue determiners and adverbs at the left boundary of the phrase

For example, in the sentence below, the verb phrase that included the modal auxiliary *may* also included the complement introduced by *thereby*. Using the exclusion criteria 1 and 2, we excluded the tokens following *SPACER* from the scope:

(3) (a) ... motifs *may* be easily compared with the results from BEAM, PRISM and SPACER, thereby extending the SCOPE ensemble to include a fourth class of motifs.

(b) CUE: *may*
SCOPE: motifs may be easily compared with the results from BEAM, PRISM and SPACER

3.3.2 Extending dependency-based heuristics

The new scope definition was also accommodated by extending the basic dependency-based heuristics summarized earlier in this section. In addition to finding the trigger word that satisfies the appropriate dependency constraint with the hedging cue (we refer to this trigger word as *scope head*, henceforth), we also considered the other dependency relations that the *scope head* was involved in. These relations, then, were used in *right expansion* and *left expansion* of the scope. *Right expansion* involves finding the rightmost token that is in a dependency relation with the *scope head*. Consider the sentence below:

(4) The surprisingly low correlations between Sig and accuracy may *indicate* that the objective functions employed by motif finding

programs are only a first *approximation* to biological *significance*.

The epistemic verb *indicate* has as its *scope head* the token *approximation*, due to the existence of a clausal complement dependency (*ccomp*) between them. On the other hand, the rightmost token of the sentence, *significance*, has a prepositional modifier dependency (*prep_to*) with *approximation*. It is, therefore, included in the scope of *indicate*. Two dependency types, adverbial clause modifier (*advcl*) and conjunct (*conj*), were excluded from consideration when the rightmost token is sought, since they are likely to signal new discourse units outside the scope.

In contrast to *right expansion*, which applies to all hedging cue categories, *left expansion* applies only to a subset. Left expansion involves searching for a subject dependency governed by the *scope head*. The dependency types descending from the subject (*subj*) type in the Stanford dependency hierarchy are considered: *nsubj* (nominal subject), *nsubjpass* (passive nominal subject), *csubj* (clausal subject) and *csubjpass* (passive clausal subject). In the following example, the first token, *This*, is added to the scope of *likely* through left expansion (*cop*: copula).

(5) (a) This is most *likely* a conservative estimate since a certain proportion of interactions remain unknown ...

(b) *nsubj(likely,This)*
cop(likely,is)

Left expansion was limited to the following cue categories, with the additional constraints given:

1. *Modal auxiliaries*, only when their *scope head* takes a passive subject (e.g., *they* is added to the scope of *may* in *they may be annotated as pseudogenes*).

2. Cues in adjectival categories, when they are in copular constructions (e.g., Example (5)).

3. Cues in several adjectival ad verbal categories, when they take infinitival complements (e.g., *this* is added to the scope of *appears* in *However, this appears to add more noise to the prediction without increasing the accuracy*).

After scope tokens are identified using the parse tree as well as via left and right expansion, the algorithm simply sets as scope the continuous textual unit that includes all the scope tokens and the hedging cue. Since, *likely* is the hedging cue and *This* and *estimate* are identified as scope tokens in Example (5), the scope associated with *likely* becomes *This is most likely a conservative estimate*.

We found that citations, numbers and punctuation marks occurring at the end of sentences caused problems in scope resolution, specifically in biomedical full text articles. Since they are rarely within any scope, we implemented a simple stripping algorithm to eliminate them from scopes in such documents.

4 Results and Discussion

The official evaluation results regarding our submission are given in Table 2. These results were achieved with the threshold 4, which was the optimal threshold on the training data.

	Prec.	Recall	F-score	Rank
Task 1B	92.07	74.94	82.62	12/24
Task 1W	67.90	46.02	54.86	10/17
Task 2	62.47	49.47	55.21	4/15

Table 2: Evaluation results

In Task 1B, we achieved the highest precision. However, our relatively low recall led to the placement of our system in the middle. Our system allows adjusting precision versus recall by setting the threshold. In fact, setting the threshold to 3 after the shared task, we were able to obtain overall better results (Precision=83.43, Recall=84.81, F-score=84.12, Rank=8/24). However, we explicitly targeted precision, and in that respect, our submission results were not surprising. In fact, we identified a new type of hedging signalled by coordination (*either* ... *or* ... as well as just *or*) in the training data. An example is given below:

(6) (a) It will be *either* a sequencing error *or* a pseudogene.

(b) CUE: *either-or*
SCOPE: *either a seqeuncing error or a pseudogene*

By handling this class to some extent, we could have increased our recall, and therefore, F-score (65 out of 1,044 cues in the evaluation data for biological text involved this class). However, we decided against treating this class, as we believe it requires a slightly different treatment due to its special semantics.

In participating in Task 1W, our goal was to test the ease of extensibility of our system. In that regard, our results show that we were able to exploit the overlap between our hedging cues and the weasel words. The major difference we noted between hedging in two genres was the class of vagueness quantifiers, and, with little effort, we extended our system to consider them. We also note that setting the threshold to 3 after the shared task, our recall and F-score improved significantly (Precision=63.21, Recall=53.67, F-score=58.05, Rank=3/17).

Our more substantial effort for Task 2 resulted in a better overall ranking, as well as the highest precision in this task. In contrast to Task 1, changing the threshold in this task did not have a positive effect on the outcome. We also measured the relative contribution of the enhancements to scope resolution. The results are presented in Table 3. Baseline is taken as the scope resolution algorithm we developed in prior work. These results show that: a) scope definition we adopted earlier is essentially incompatible with the BioScope definition b) simply taking the phrase that the hedging cue belongs to as the scope provides relatively good results c) left and right expansion heuristics are needed for increased precision and recall.

	Prec.	**Recall**	**F-score**
Baseline	3.29	2.61	2.91
Baseline+ Left/ right expansion	25.18	20.03	22.31
Parse tree	49.20	39.10	43.58
Baseline+ Parse tree	50.66	40.27	44.87
All	62.47	49.47	55.21

Table 3: Effect of scope resolution enhancements

4.1 Error Analysis

In this section, we provide a short analysis of the errors our system generated, focusing on biological text.

Since our dictionary of hedging cues is incomplete and we did not attempt to expand it for Task 1B, we had a fair number of recall errors. As we mentioned above, *either-or* constructions occur frequently in the training and evaluation data, and we did not attempt to handle them. Additionally, some lexical cues, such as *feasible* and *implicate*, do not appear in our dictionary, causing further recall errors. The weighting scheme also affects recall. For example, the adjective *apparent* has a weight of 2, which is not itself sufficient to qualify a sentence as uncertain (with a threshold of 4) (7a). On the other hand, when it takes a clausal complement, the sentence is considered uncertain (7b). The first sentence (7a) causes a recall error.

(7) (a) An *apparent* contradiction between the previously reported number of cycling genes ...
(b) ... it is *apparent* that the axonal termini contain a significantly reduced number of varicosities ...

In some cases, syntactic constructions that play a role in determining the certainty status of a sentence cannot be correctly identified by the parser, often leading to recall errors. For example, in the sentence below, the clausal complement construction is missed by the parser. Since the verb *indicate* has weight 3, this leads to a recall error in the current setting.

(8) ... *indicating* that dMyc overexpression can substitute for PI3K activation ...

Adjusting the weights of cues worked well generally, but also caused unexpected problems, due to what seem like inconsistencies in annotation. The examples below highlight the effect of lowering the weight of *predict* from 4 to 3. Examples (9a) and (9b) are almost identical on surface and our system predicted both to be uncertain, due to the fact that *predicted* took infinitival complements in both cases. However, only (9a) was annotated as uncertain, leading to a precision error in (9b).

(9) (a) ... include all protein pairs *predicted* to have posterior odds ratio ...
(b) Protein pairs *predicted* to have a posterior odds ratio ...

The error cases in scope resolution are more varied. Syntax has a larger role in this task, and therefore, parsing errors tend to affect the results more directly. In the following example, during left-expanding the scope of the modal auxiliary *could*, *RNAi screens*, rather than the full noun phrase *fruit fly RNAi screens*, is identified as the passive subject of the scope head (*associated*), because an appropriate modifier dependency cannot be found between the noun phrase head *screens* and either of the modifiers, *fruit* and *fly*.

(10) ...was to investigate whether fruit fly RNAi screens of conserved genes *could* be associated with similar tick phenotypes and tick gene function.

In general, the simple mechanism to exploit constituent parse trees was useful in resolving scope. However, it appears that a nuanced approach based on cue categories could enhance the results further. In particular, the current mechanism does not contribute much to resolving scopes of adverbial cues. In the following example, parse tree mechanism does not have any effect, leading to both a precision and a recall error in scope resolution.

(11) (a) ...we will consider tightening the definitions and *possibly* splitting them into different roles.
(b) FP: possibly
FN: possibly splitting them into different roles

Left/right expansion strategies were based on the analysis of training data. However, we encountered errors caused by these strategies where we found the annotations contradictory. In Example (12a), the entire fragment is in the scope of *thought*, while in (12b), the scope of *suggested* does not include *it was*, even though on surface both fragments are very similar.

(12) (a) ...the kinesin-5 motor is *thought* to play a key role.
(b) ...it was *suggested* to enhance the nuclear translocation of NF-κB.

Post-processing in the form of citation stripping was simplistic, and, therefore, was unable to handle complex cases, as the one shown in the example below. The algorithm is only able to remove one reference at the end.

(13) (a) ...it is possible that some other signalling system may operate with Semas to confine dorsally projecting neurons to dorsal neuropile [3],[40],[41].
(b) FP: may operate with Semas to confine dorsally projecting neurons to dorsal neuropile [3],[40],
FN: may operate with Semas to confine dorsally projecting neurons to dorsal neuropile

5 Conclusions

Rather than developing a dedicated methodology that exclusively relies on the data provided by organizers, we chose to extend and refine our prior work in hedge detection and used the training data only in a limited manner: to tune our system in a principled way. With little tuning, we achieved the highest precision in Task 1B. We were able to capitalize on the overlap between hedging cues and weasel words for Task 1W and achieved competitive results. Adapting our previous work in scope resolution to Task 2, however, was less straightforward, due to the incompatible definitions of scope. Nevertheless, by refining the prior dependency-based heuristics with left and right expansion strategies and utilizing a simple mechanism for parse tree information, we were able to accommodate the new definition of scope to a large extent. With these results, we conclude that our methodology is portable and easily extensible.

While the results show that using the parse tree information for scope resolution benefited our performance greatly, error analysis presented in the previous sections also suggests that a finer-grained approach based on cue categories could further improve results, and we aim to explore this extension further.

References

Marie-Catherine deMarneffe, Bill MacCartney, and Christopher D. Manning. 2006. Generating typed dependency parses from phrase structure parses. In *Proceedings of the 5th International Conference on Language Resources and Evaluation*, pages 449–454.

Richárd Farkas, Veronika Vincze, György Móra, János Csirik, and György Szarvas. 2010. The CoNLL-2010 Shared Task: Learning to Detect Hedges and their Scope in Natural Language Text. In *Proceedings of the Fourteenth Conference on Computational Natural Language Learning (CoNLL-2010): Shared Task*, pages 1–12, Uppsala, Sweden, July. Association for Computational Linguistics.

Christiane Fellbaum. 1998. *WordNet: an electronic lexical database*. MIT Press, Cambridge, MA.

Viola Ganter and Michael Strube. 2009. Finding Hedges by Chasing Weasels: Hedge Detection Using Wikipedia Tags and Shallow Linguistic Features. In *Proceedings of the ACL-IJCNLP 2009 Conference Short Papers*, pages 173–176.

Ken Hyland. 1998. *Hedging in scientific research articles*. John Benjamins B.V., Amsterdam, Netherlands.

Halil Kilicoglu and Sabine Bergler. 2008. Recognizing speculative language in biomedical research articles: a linguistically motivated perspective. *BMC Bioinformatics*, 9 Suppl 11:s10.

Halil Kilicoglu and Sabine Bergler. 2009. Syntactic dependency based heuristics for biological event extraction. In *Proceedings of Natural Language Processing in Biomedicine (BioNLP) NAACL 2009 Workshop*, pages 119–127.

Jin-Dong Kim, Tomoko Ohta, and Jun'ichi Tsujii. 2008. Corpus annotation for mining biomedical events from literature. *BMC Bioinformatics*, 9:10.

Jin-Dong Kim, Tomoko Ohta, Sampo Pyysalo, Yoshinobu Kano, and Jun'ichi Tsujii. 2009. Overview of BioNLP'09 Shared Task on Event Extraction. In *Proceedings of Natural Language Processing in Biomedicine (BioNLP) NAACL 2009 Workshop*, pages 1–9.

Dan Klein and Christopher D Manning. 2003. Accurate unlexicalized parsing. In *Proceedings of the 41th Meeting of the Association for Computational Linguistics*, pages 423–430.

Shalom Lappin. 2000. An intensional parametric semantics for vague quantifiers. *Linguistics and Philosophy*, 23(6):599–620.

Marc Light, Xin Y. Qiu, and Padmini Srinivasan. 2004. The language of bioscience: facts, speculations, and statements in between. In *BioLINK 2004: Linking Biological Literature, Ontologies and Databases*, pages 17–24.

Alexa T. McCray, Suresh Srinivasan, and Allen C. Browne. 1994. Lexical methods for managing variation in biomedical terminologies. In *Proceedings of the 18th Annual Symposium on Computer Applications in Medical Care*, pages 235–239.

Ben Medlock and Ted Briscoe. 2007. Weakly supervised learning for hedge classification in scientific literature. In *Proceedings of the 45th Meeting of the Association for Computational Linguistics*, pages 992–999.

Roser Morante and Walter Daelemans. 2009. Learning the scope of hedge cues in biomedical texts. In *Proceedings of the BioNLP 2009 Workshop*, pages 28–36.

Arzucan Özgür and Dragomir R. Radev. 2009. Detecting speculations and their scopes in scientific text. In *Proceedings of the 2009 Conference on Empirical Methods in Natural Language Processing*, pages 1398–1407.

Bo Pang and Lillian Lee. 2008. *Sentiment Analysis and Opinion Mining*. Now Publishers Inc, Boston, MA.

James Pustejovsky, Robert Knippen, Jessica Littman, and Roser Saurí. 2005. Temporal and event information in natural language text. *Language Resources and Evaluation*, 39(2):123–164.

Victoria L. Rubin, Elizabeth D. Liddy, and Noriko Kando. 2005. Certainty identification in texts: Categorization model and manual tagging results. In James G. Shanahan, Yan Qu, and Janyce Wiebe, editors, *Computing Attitude and Affect in Text: Theories and Applications*, volume 20, pages 61–76. Springer Netherlands, Dordrecht.

Roser Saurí and James Pustejovsky. 2009. FactBank: a corpus annotated with event factuality. *Language Resources and Evaluation*, 43(3):227–268.

Roser Saurí, Marc Verhagen, and James Pustejovsky. 2006. Annotating and recognizing event modality in text. In *Proceedings of 19th International FLAIRS Conference*.

Roser Saurí. 2008. *A Factuality Profiler for Eventualities in Text*. Ph.D. thesis, Brandeis University.

György Szarvas. 2008. Hedge classification in biomedical texts with a weakly supervised selection of keywords. In *Proceedings of the 46th Meeting of the Association for Computational Linguistics*, pages 281–289.

Paul Thompson, Giulia Venturi, John McNaught, Simonetta Montemagni, and Sophia Ananiadou. 2008. Categorising modality in biomedical texts. In *Proceedings of LREC 2008 Workshop on Building and Evaluating Resources for Biomedical Text Mining*.

Veronika Vincze, György Szarvas, Richárd Farkas, György Móra, and János Csirik. 2008. The BioScope corpus: biomedical texts annotated for uncertainty, negation and their scopes. *BMC Bioinformatics*, 9 Suppl 11:S9.

Janyce Wiebe, Theresa Wilson, and Claire Cardie. 2005. Annotating expressions of opinions and emotions in language. *Language Resources and Evaluation*, 39(2):165–210.

Exploiting Rich Features for Detecting Hedges and Their Scope

Xinxin Li, Jianping Shen, Xiang Gao, Xuan Wang
Harbin Institute of Technology Shenzhen Graduate School
Shenzhen, Guangdong, China
{lixxin2, jpshen2008}@gmail.com,
sky0306201@163.com, wangxuan@insun.hit.edu.cn

Abstract

This paper describes our system about detecting hedges and their scope in natural language texts for our participation in CoNLL-2010 shared tasks. We formalize these two tasks as sequence labeling problems, and implement them using conditional random fields (CRFs) model. In the first task, we use a greedy forward procedure to select features for the classifier. These features include part-of-speech tag, word form, lemma, chunk tag of tokens in the sentence. In the second task, our system exploits rich syntactic features about dependency structures and phrase structures, which achieves a better performance than only using the flat sequence features. Our system achieves the third score in biological data set for the first task, and achieves 0.5265 F1 score for the second task.

1 Introduction

In recent years, a fair amount of approaches have been developed on detecting speculative and negative information from biomedical and natural language texts, for its benefit to the applications like information extraction. These approaches evolve from hand-crafted rule-based approaches, which use regular expressions to match the sentences or its grammatical parsing, such as NegEx (Chapman et al., 2001), Negfinder (Mutalik et al., 2001), and NegExpander (Aronow et al., 1999), to machine learning approaches, including semi-supervised methods (Medlock and Briscoe, 2007; Szarvas, 2008), and supervised methods (Morante and Daelemans, 2009).

In this paper, we describe the machine learning system submitted to CoNLL-2010 Shared task (Farkas et al., 2010). Our system formalizes these two tasks as consecutive sequence labeling problems, and learns the classifiers using conditional random fields approach. In the first task, a model is trained to identify the hedge cues in sentences, and in the second task, another model is used to find the corresponding scope for each hedge cue generated in the first task. Our system follows the study of Morante and Daelemans (2009), but applies more refined feature selection. In the first task, we use a greedy forward procedure to select features for the classifier. In the second task, we exploit rich syntactic information to improve the performance of the model, from dependency structures and phrase structures. A rule-based post processing procedure is used to eliminate the errors brought by the classifier for each task.

The remainder of the paper is organized as follows. In section 2, we briefly describe the task and the details of our system, including how to select features for the hedge cue detection system, and how to find the corresponding scope for each hedge cue. The experimental results are discussed in section 3. In section 4 we put forward some conclusion.

2 System Description

We model these two tasks for identifying the hedge cues and finding their scope as two consecutive sequence labeling problems, such as chunking, segmentation and named entity recognition, and train the classifiers using conditional random fields approach (Lafferty et al., 2001). For each task, a post-processing procedure is used to refine the results from the classifier.

In the first task, we detect the hedge cue by classifying the tokens of a sentence as being at the beginning of, inside or outside of the hedge signal. In the second task, we find the scope of a hedge cue by classifying the tokens of a sentence as being the first one of, the last one or neither of the scope.

A sentence from biological full articles data set omitting the id number is shown below in Figure 1. In this sentence, there is only one hedge cue, the phrase "raises an interesting question", and its corresponding scope is the sequence from token "raises" to token "acid".

Proceedings of the Fourteenth Conference on Computational Natural Language Learning: Shared Task, pages 78–83,
Uppsala, Sweden, 15-16 July 2010.

<sentence>This <xcope><cue>raises an interesting question</cue>: "Is there a 23rd amino acid</xcope>?".</sentence>

Figure 1: A sentence with hedge cue and scope annotation in biological full articles data set

2.1 Hedge detection

Since hedge cues usually consist of one or more tokens, we predict the tokens in BIO representation, whether the token is the first token of a hedge cue (B-cue), inside a hedge cue (I-cue), or outside of the hedge cue (O-cue). For the sentence in Figure 1, token "raises" is denoted as B-cue, tokens "an interesting question" all as I-cue, and the other tokens in the sentence as O-cue.

The classifier is trained using conditional random fields (Lafferty et al., 2001), which combines the benefits of conditional models with the global normalization of random field models, and avoid the label bias problem that exists in maximum entropy Markov models (MEMMs). The CRF model we use is implemented as CRF++ 0.51 [1]. The parameters of the CRF classifier are set as defaults.

We use a greedy forward procedure to select a better feature sets for the classifier according to the evaluation results in the development set. We first start from a basic feature set, and then add each feature outside the basic set and remove each feature inside the basic set one by one to check the effectiveness of each feature by the performance change in the development set. This procedure is repeated until no feature is added or removed or the performance is not improved.

The selected features are listed below:

- C_n (n=-2,-1, 0, 1, 2)
- C_nC_{n+1} (n=-1,0)
- $C_{n-1}C_nC_{n+1}$ (n=-1,0,1)
- $C_{n-2}C_{n-1}C_nC_{n+1}$ (n=0,1)

Where C denote features of each token, including FORM, LEMMA, and POS (in Table 1), C_0 represents the feature of current token and $C_n(C_{-n})$ represents the feature of the token n positions to the right (left) of current token. C_nC_{n+1} denote the combination of C_n and C_{n+1}. So are $C_{n-1}C_nC_{n+1}$ and $C_{n-2}C_{n-1}C_nC_{n+1}$.

[1] http://crfpp.sourceforge.net/

Feature Name	Description
FORM	Word form or punctuation symbol.
LEMMA	Lemma or stem of word form.
POS	Part-of-speech tag of the token.
CHUNK	Chunk tag of the token, e.g. B_NP, B_ SBAR, and I_NP.
TCHUNK	Chunk type of the token, e.g. NP.

Table 1: Description of features of each token

Although our system is based on token, chunk features are also important. Analyzing the training data set, it is shown that if one token in a chunk is in the hedge cue, the other tokens in the chunk are usually in the same hedge cue. The chunk feature can provide more information for the multiword hedge cues. The LEMMA, POS, and CHUNK of each token used in our system are determined using GENIA tagger (Tsuruoka et al., 2005).

The selected CHUNK features in our system are listed as follows:

- C_n (n=-3, -2,-1, 0, 1, 2, 3)
- C_nC_{n+1} (n=-3, -2,-1, 0, 1, 2, 3)
- $C_{n-1}C_nC_{n+1}$ (n=-2,-1,0,1,-2)
- $C_{n-2}C_{n-1}C_nC_{n+1}$ (n=-1,0,1,2)

We can obtain the preliminary results using the CRF model-based classifier, but there are some missed or incorrectly classified hedge cues which can be recognized by rule-based patterns. Through statistical analysis on the training and development data sets, we obtain some effective rules for post processing, including:

- If the first token of a NP chunk tag is annotated as I-cue, the whole NP chunk is in the hedge cues.
- If the B-VP chunk tag of a token is followed by a B-SBAR chunk tag, the token is annotated as B-cue.
- If token "that" follows token "indicate" and the POS of token "that" is IN, the chunk tag of token "that" is B-SBAR, then the "indicate" will be annotated with B-cue and "that" will be annotated with I-cue.
- If token "indicate" is followed by token "an" or token "a", then the token "indicate" is annotated as B-cue.

2.2 Scope finding

In this task, we train a classifier to predict whether each token in the sentence is in the scope by classifying them as the first one (F-scope), the last one (L-scope), or neither (NONE) of the scope, which is the same as Morante and Daelemans (2009). For the sentence in Figure 1, token "raises" is denoted as F-scope, token "acid" as L-scope, and the other tokens in the sentence as NONE.

After the classification, a post processing procedure is used to match the scope to each hedge, guaranteeing that each hedge has only one corresponding scope sequence, and must be inside its scope sequence. There is no cross between different scope sequences, but inclusion is allowed. The hedges are selected from the first task.

The classifier is also implemented using conditional random fields model, and the parameters of the CRF classifier are set as defaults. We first build a set of baseline sequence features for the classifier, some borrowed from Morante and Daelemans (2009). The selected baseline sequence features are:

- Of the token in focus: FORM, POS, LEMMA, CHUNK, TCHUNK, combination of FORM and POS; POS, LEMMA, CHUNK, TCHUNK of two tokens to the left and three tokens to the right; first word, last word, chain of FORM, POS of two chunks to the left and two chunks to the right; All combination of POS in the window of length less than 3; All combination of CHUNK in the window of length 2.
- Of the left closest hedge: chain of the FORM, POS, LEMMA, CHUNK, and TCHUNK; All combination of POS and FORM in the window of length 2.
- Of the right closest hedge: chain of the FORM, POS, LEMMA, CHUNK, and TCHUNK; All combination of POS and FORM in the window of length 2.
- Of the tokens between the left closest hedge and the token in focus: chain of FORM, POS, LEMMA, CHUNK and TCHUNK; the number.
- Of the tokens between the right closest hedge and the token in focus: chain of FORM, POS, LEMMA, CHUNK and TCHUNK; the number.
- Others: the number of hedge cues in the sentence; the sequence relation between the token in focus and hedge cues (LEFT, RIGHT, MIDDLE, IN, NULL)

Besides the sequence features listed above, syntactic features between the token in focus and hedge cues are explored in our classifier. Huang and Low (2007) notes that structure information stored in parse trees helps identifying the scope of negative hedge cues, and Szarvas (2008) points out that the scope of a keyword can be determined on the basic of syntax. Thus we believe that a highly accurate extraction of syntactic structure would be beneficial for this task.

For sentences in the dataset, their dependency structures are extracted using GENIA Dependency parser (Sagae and Tsujii, 2007), and phrase structure using Brown self-trained biomedical parser (McClosky, 2009). Figure 2 shows the corresponding dependency tree and Figure 3 shows the corresponding phrase structure tree for the sentence in Figure 1. In the following part in the section, we will illustrate these syntactic features and give examples for their value. We take the token "acid" as the token in focus, to determine whether it is classified as F-scope, L-scope or NONE.

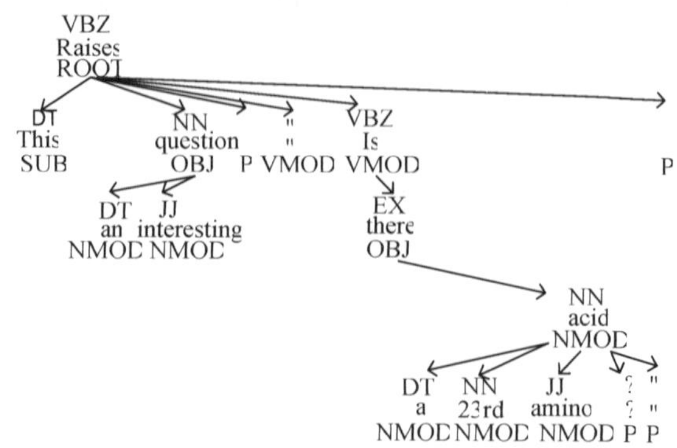

Figure 2: Dependency tree of the sentence in Figure 1

For the token "acid" in the dependency trees in Figure 2, its father node is the token "there", and the dependency relation between these two token is "NMOD".

Dependency features between the token in focus and the left closest hedge cue are:

- Dependency relation of the token in focus to its father, left closest hedge to its father and the dependency relation pair: NOMD, ROOT, ROOT+NMOD.

- Chain of POS: ->VBZ<-VBZ<-EX<-NN
- Chain of POS without consecutive redundant POS: ->VBZ <-EX<-NN
- POS of their nearest co-father: VBZ
- Whether it is a linear relation (self, up , down, no): up
- Kinship (grandfather, grandson, father, son, brother, self, no): no.
- The number of tokens in the chain: 4

Similar features are extracted for dependency relation between the token in focus and its right closest hedge cue. There is no right hedge cue for token "acid". Thus these features are set as "NULL".

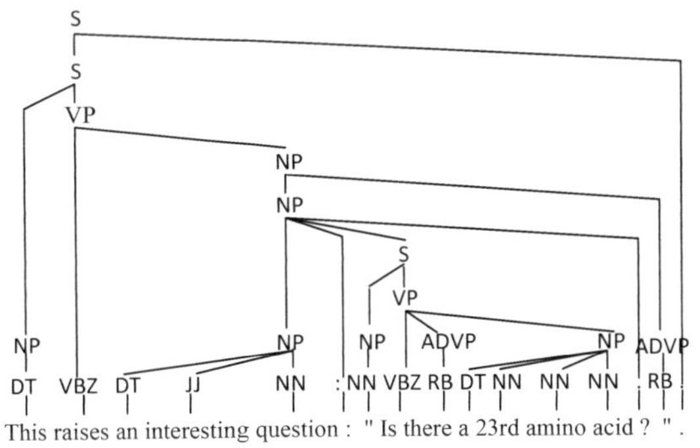

Figure 3: Phrase structure tree of the sentence in Figure 1

Phrase structure features between the token in focus and its left closest hedge cue are:

- Chain of syntactic categories: VBZ->VP<- NP <-NP <-S<-VP <-NP<-NN
- syntactic categories without consecutive redundant ones: VBZ->VP<-NP<-S<-VP<- NP<-NN
- Syntactic category of their nearest co-father: VP
- The number of syntactic categories in the chain: 8

The phrase structure features between the token in focus and the nearest right hedge cue are similar, setting as "NULL".

Scope finding requires each hedge cue has only one corresponding scope. A hedge-scope pair is true positive only if the hedge cue and its corresponding scope are correctly identified. We perform the post processing procedure in sequence:

- For each hedge cue from the beginning to the end of the sentence, find its left closest F-scope which has not been identified by other hedge cues, and identify it as its F-scope.
- For each hedge cue from the end to the beginning of the sentence, find its right closest L-scope which has not been identified by other hedge cues, and identify it as its L-scope.
- For each hedge:
    - If both its F-scope and L-scope is identified, then done;
    - If only its F-scope is identified, then its L-scope is set as L-scope of the last hedge cue in the sentence if it exists or according to the dictionary which we build with training data set;
    - If only its L-scope is identified, then its F-scope is set as its first token;
    - If none of its F-scope and L-scope is identified, then discard the hedge cue.

3 Overall Results

In this section we will present our experimental results for these two tasks. In the first task, the chief evaluation is carried on sentence level: whether a sentence contains hedge/weasel cue or not. Our system compares the performance of different machine learning algorithm, CRF and SVM-HMM on hedge cue detection. A post processing procedure is used to increase the recall measure for our system.

In the second task, three experiments are performed. The first experiment is used to validate the benefit of dependency features and phrase structure features for scope finding. The second experiment is designed to evaluate the effect of abstract dataset on full article dataset. These two experiments are all performed using gold hedge cues. The performance of our scope finding system with predicted hedge cues is presented in the third experiment.

3.1 Hedge detection

The first experiment is used to compare two machine learning algorithms, SVM-HMM and CRF. We train the classifiers on abstract and full articles data sets. The results of the classifier on evaluation data set are shown in Table 2.

Model	Precision	Recall	F1
SVM-HMM	88.71	81.52	84.96
CRF	90.4	81.01	85.45

Table 2: Results of hedge cues detection using CRF and SVM-HMM

From Table 1, it is shown that CRF model outperforms SVM-HMM model in both precision and recall measure. The results are obtained without post processing. The experimental result with post processing is shown in Table 3.

Feature	Precision	Recall	F1
Without Post processing	90.4	81.01	85.45
Post processing	90.1	82.05	85.89

Table 3: Result of biological evaluation data set without/with post processing

By post processing, some mislabeled or incorrectly classified hedge cues can be recognized, especially the recall of the I-cue improved largely, from 55.26% to 68.51%. Though the precision is a little lower, the F1 measure increases 0.44%.

3.2 Scope finding

To measure the benefit of syntactic features on scope finding task, we perform the experiment with different features on abstract data set, of which we split two-thirds as training data, and the other one third as testing data. The results are presented in Table 4.

We take the classifier with sequence features as baseline classifier. From Table 4, it is shown that adding dependency features achieves a slightly better performance than the baseline classifier, and adding phrase structure features improve much better, about 1.2% F1-score. The classifier with all syntactic features achieves the best F1-score, 2.19% higher than baseline classifier. However, in later experiment on evaluation dataset after the shared task, we observed that dependency features actually harmed the performance for full articles dataset.

Feature set	Precision	Recall	F1
Sequence (Baseline)	82.20	81.61	81.90
Sequence + Dependency	82.28	82.09	82.19
Sequence + Phrase structure	83.14	83.04	83.09
All	84.19	83.99	84.09

Table 4: Results of scope finding system with different feature sets on abstract data set

Three experiments are designed to evaluate the benefit of abstract dataset for full articles dataset. The first one is performed on full articles data set, of which we split two-thirds for training, and the other one third for testing. The second experiment is trained on abstract data set, and evaluated on full articles data set. In the third experiment, we take abstract data set and one third of full articles as training data, and evaluate on the remaining full articles data set. The results are shown below in Table 5.

Training data	Testing data	Prec.	Recall	F1
Part Art.	Part Art.	53.14	51.80	52.46
Abs.	Full Art.	54.32	54.64	54.48
Mix	Part Art.	59.59	59.74	59.66

Table 5: Results of scope finding system with gold-standard hedge cues

Results in Table 5 reveal that more abstract and full article dataset are added to the classifier as training data, better performance the system achieve. Thus we use the combination of abstract and full articles as training data for the final evaluation.

Table 6 presents the results of our scope finding system with or without dependency features, using both gold-standard hedge cues and predicated hedge cues generated by our hedge cue finding system.

Comparing the results in Table 4, 5, and 6, we observe that the performance of scope finding classifier on full article dataset is much lower than on abstract dataset, and dependency features are beneficial for the abstract dataset, but useless for full article dataset. We ascribe this phenomenon to the lack of enough full articles training data and the different properties of abstract and full articles data sets. Deep research is expected to continue.

Hedge cues	Dep. features	Prec.	Recall	F1
Predicted	with	57.42	47.92	52.24
	without	58.13	48.11	52.65
Gold standard	with	59.43	58.28	58.85
	without	60.20	58.86	59.52

Table 6: Results of scope finding system with/without dependency features using both gold-standard and predicated hedge cues

4 Conclusion

In this paper, we describe a machine learning system for detecting hedges and their scope in natural language texts. These two tasks are formalized as sequence labeling problems, and implemented using conditional random fields approach. We use a greedy forward procedure to select features for the classifier, and exploit rich syntactic features to achieve a better performance. In the in-domain evaluation, our system achieves the third score in biological data set for the first task, and achieves 0.5265 F1 score for the second task.

Acknowledgments

The authors would like to thank Buzhou Tang for useful discussions of the paper. This work is supported by the National High-tech R&D Program of China (863 Program, No. 2007AA01Z194).

References

David B. Aronow, Fangfang Feng, and W. Bruce Croft. 1999. Ad Hoc Classification of Radiology Reports. *Journal of the American Medical Informatics Association*, 6(5):393–411.

Wendy W. Chapman, Will Bridewell, Paul Hanbury, Gregory F. Cooper, and Bruce G. Buchanan. 2001. A Simple Algorithm for Identifying Negated Findings and Diseases in Discharge Summaries. *Journal of Biomedical Informatics*, 34:301–310.

Richárd Farkas, Veronika Vincze, György Móra, János Csirik, and György Szarvas. 2010. The CoNLL-2010 Shared Task: Learning to Detect Hedges and their Scope in Natural Language Text. In *Proceedings of the Fourteenth Conference on Computational Natural Language Learning (CoNLL-2010): Shared Task*, pages 1–12.

Yang Huang, and Henry J. Lowe. 2007. A novel hybrid approach to automated negation detection in clinical radiology reports. *Journal of the American Medical Informatics Association*, 14(3):304–311.

John Lafferty, Andrew McCallum, and Fernando Pereira. 2001. Conditional random fields: Probabilistic models for segmenting and labeling sequence data. In *Proceedings of the Eighteenth International Conference on Machine Learning*, pages 282–289.

David McClosky. 2009. *Any Domain Parsing: Automatic Domain Adaptation for Natural Language Parsing*. Ph.D. thesis, Department of Computer Science, Brown University.

Ben Medlock, and Ted Briscoe. 2007. Weakly supervised learning for hedge classification in scientific literature. In *Proc. of ACL 2007*, pages 992–999.

Roser Morante, and Walter Daelemans. 2009. Learning the scope of hedge cues in biomedical texts. In *Proceedings of the Workshop on BioNLP*, pages 28–36.

Pradeep G. Mutalik, Aniruddha Deshpande, and Prakash M. Nadkarni. 2001. Use of general-purpose negation detection to augment concept indexing of medical documents: a quantitative study using the UMLS. *Journal of the American Medical Informatics Association*, 8(6):598–609.

Kenji Sagae, and Jun'ichi Tsujii. 2007. Dependency parsing and domain adaptation with LR models and parser ensembles. In *Proceedings of the CoNLL-2007 Shared Task*, pages 82–94

György Szarvas. 2008. Hedge classification in biomedical texts with a weakly supervised selection of keywords. In *Proc. of ACL 2008*, pages 281–289, Columbus, Ohio, USA. ACL.

György Szarvas, Veronika Vincze, Richárd Farkas, and János Csirik. 2008. The BioScope corpus: annotation for negation, uncertainty and their scope in biomedical texts. In *Proc. of BioNLP 2008*, pages 38–45, Columbus, Ohio. ACL.

Yoshimasa Tsuruoka, Yuka Tateishi, Jin-Dong Kim, Tomoko Ohta, John McNaught, Sophia Ananiadou, and Jun'ichi Tsujii. 2005. Developing a Robust Part-of-Speech Tagger for Biomedical Text. *Advances in Informatics - 10th Panhellenic Conference on Informatics,* LNCS 3746, pages 382–392.

Uncertainty Detection as Approximate Max-Margin Sequence Labelling

Oscar Täckström
SICS / Uppsala University
Kista / Uppsala, Sweden
oscar@sics.se

Sumithra Velupillai
DSV, Stockholm University
Kista, Sweden
sumithra@dsv.su.se

Martin Hassel
DSV, Stockholm University
Kista, Sweden
xmartin@dsv.su.se

Gunnar Eriksson
SICS
Kista, Sweden
guer@sics.se

Hercules Dalianis
DSV, Stockholm University
Kista, Sweden
hercules@dsv.su.se

Jussi Karlgren
SICS
Kista, Sweden
jussi@sics.se

Abstract

This paper reports experiments for the CoNLL-2010 shared task on learning to detect hedges and their scope in natural language text. We have addressed the experimental tasks as supervised linear maximum margin prediction problems. For sentence level hedge detection in the biological domain we use an L_1-regularised binary support vector machine, while for sentence level weasel detection in the Wikipedia domain, we use an L_2-regularised approach. We model the in-sentence uncertainty cue and scope detection task as an L_2-regularised approximate maximum margin sequence labelling problem, using the BIO-encoding. In addition to surface level features, we use a variety of linguistic features based on a functional dependency analysis. A greedy forward selection strategy is used in exploring the large set of potential features. Our official results for Task 1 for the biological domain are 85.2 F_1-score, for the Wikipedia set 55.4 F_1-score. For Task 2, our official results are 2.1 for the entire task with a score of 62.5 for cue detection. After resolving errors and final bugs, our final results are for Task 1, biological: 86.0, Wikipedia: 58.2; Task 2, scopes: 39.6 and cues: 78.5.

1 Introduction

This paper reports experiments to detect uncertainty in text. The experiments are part of the two shared tasks given by CoNLL-2010 (Farkas et al., 2010). The first task is to identify uncertain sentences; the second task is to detect the cue phrase which makes the sentence uncertain and to mark its scope or span in the sentence.

Uncertainty as a target category needs to be addressed with some care. Sentences, utterances, statements are not uncertain – their producer, the speaker or author, is. Statements may explicitly indicate this uncertainty, employing several different linguistic and textual mechanisms to encode the speaker's attitude with respect to the veracity of an utterance. The absence of such markers does not necessarily indicate certainty – the opposition between certain and uncertain is not clearly demarkable, but more of a dimensional measure. Uncertainty on the part of the speaker may be difficult to differentiate from a certain assessment of an uncertain situation, *It is unclear whether this specimen is an X or a Y* vs. *The difference between X and Y is unclear*.

In this task, the basis for identifying uncertainty in utterances is almost entirely lexical. *Hedges*, the main target of this experiment, are an established category in lexical grammar analyses - see e.g. Quirk et al. (1985), for examples of English language constructions. Most languages use various verbal markers or modifiers for indicating the speaker's beliefs in what is being said, most prototypically using conditional or optative verb forms, *Six Parisiens seraient morts*, or auxiliaries, *This mushroom may be edible*, but aspectual markers may also be recruited for this purpose, more indirectly, *I'm hoping you will help* vs. *I hope you will help*; *Do you want to see me now* vs. *Did you want to see me now*. Besides verbs, there are classes of terms that through their presence, typically in an adverbial role, in an utterance make explicit its tentativeness: *possibly, perhaps...* and more complex constructions *with some reservation*, especially such that explicitly mention the speaker and the speaker's beliefs or doubts, *I suspect that X*.

Weasels, the other target of this experiment, on the other hand, do not indicate uncertainty.

Proceedings of the Fourteenth Conference on Computational Natural Language Learning: Shared Task, pages 84–91,
Uppsala, Sweden, 15-16 July 2010. ©2010 Association for Computational Linguistics

Weasels are employed when speakers attempt to convince the listener of something they most likely are certain of themselves, by anchoring the truthfulness of the utterance to some outside fact or authority (*Most linguists believe in the existence of an autonomous linguistic processing component*), but where the authority in question is so unspecific as not to be verifiable when scrutinised.

We address both CoNLL-2010 shared tasks (Farkas et al., 2010). The first, detecting uncertain information on a sentence level, we solve by using an L_1-regularised support vector machine with hinge loss for the biological domain, and an L_2-regularised maximum margin model for the Wikipedia domain. The second task, resolution of in-sentence scopes of hedge cues, we approach as an approximate L_2-regularized maximum margin structured prediction problem. Our official results for Task 1 for the biological domain are 85.2 F_1-score, for the Wikipedia set 55.4 F_1-score. For Task 2, our official results were 2.1 for the entire task with a score of 62.5 for cue detection. After resolving errors and unfortunate bugs, our final results are for Task 1, biological: 86.0, Wikipedia: 58.2; Task 2: 39.6 and 78.5 for cues.

2 Detecting Sentence Level Uncertainty

On the sentence level, word- and lemma-based features have been shown to be useful for uncertainty detection (see e.g. Light et al. (2004), Medlock and Briscoe (2007), Medlock (2008), and Szarvas (2008)). Medlock (2008) and Szarvas (2008) employ probabilistic, weakly supervised methods, where in the former, a stemmed single term and bigram representation achieved best results (0.82 BEP), and in the latter, a more complex n-gram feature selection procedure was applied using a Maximum Entropy classifier, achieving best results when adding reliable keywords from an external hedge keyword dictionary (0.85 BEP, 85.08 F_1-score on biomedical articles). More linguistically motivated features are used by Kilicoglu and Bergler (2008), such as negated "unhedging" verbs and nouns and *that* preceded by epistemic verbs and nouns. On the fruit-fly dataset (Medlock and Briscoe, 2007) they achieve 0.85 BEP, and on the BMC dataset (Szarvas, 2008) they achieve 0.82 BEP. Light et al. (2004) also found that most of the uncertain sentences appeared towards the end of the abstract, indicating that the position of an uncertain sentence might be a useful feature.

Ganter and Strube (2009) consider weasel tags in Wikipedia articles as hedge cues, and achieve results of 0.70 BEP using word- and distance based features on a test set automatically derived from Wikipedia, and 0.69 BEP on a manually annotated test set using syntactic patterns as features. These results suggest that syntactic features are useful for identifying weasels that ought to be tagged. However, evaluation is performed on balanced test sets, which gives a higher baseline.

2.1 Learning and Optimization Framework

A guiding principle in our approach to this shared task has been to focus on highly computationally efficient models, both in terms of training and prediction times. Although kernel based non-linear separators may sometimes obtain better prediction performance, compared to linear models, the speed penalty at prediction time is often substantial, since the number of support patterns often grows linearly with the size of the training set. We therefore restrict ourselves to linear models, but allow for a restricted family of explicit non-linear mappings by feature combinations.

For sentence level hedge detection in the biological domain, we employ an L_1-regularised support vector machine with hinge loss, as provided by the library implemented by Fan et al. (2008), while for weasel detection in the Wikipedia domain, we instead use the L_2-regularised maximum margin model described in more detail in section 3.1. In both cases, we approximately optimise the F_1-measure by weighting each class by the inverse of its proportion in the training data.

The reason for using L_1-regularisation in the biological domain is that the annotation is heavily biased towards a rather small number of lexical cues, making most of the potential surface features irrelevant. The Wikipedia weasel annotation, on the other hand, is much more noisy and less determined by specific lexical markers. Regularising with respect to the L_1-norm is known to give preference to sparse models and for the special case of logistic regression, Ng (2004) proved that the sample complexity grows only logarithmically in the number of irrelevant features, instead of linearly as when regularising with respect to the L_2-norm. Our preliminary experiments indicated that L_1-regularisation is superior to L_2-regularisation in the biological domain, while slightly inferior in the Wikipedia domain.

2.2 Feature Definitions

The asymmetric relationship between certain and uncertain sentences becomes evident when one tries to learn this distinction based on surface level cues. While the UNCERTAIN category is to a large extent explicitly anchored in lexical markers, the CERTAIN category is more or less defined implicitly as the complement of the UNCERTAIN category. To handle this situation, we use a bias feature to model the weight of the CERTAIN category, while explicit features are used to model the UNCERTAIN category.

The following list describes the feature templates explored for sentence level uncertainty detection. Some features are based on a linguistic analysis by the Connexor Functional Dependency (FDG) parser (Tapanainen and Järvinen, 1997).

SENLEN Preliminary experiments indicated that taking sentence length into account is beneficial. We incorporate this by using three different bias terms, according to the length (in tokens) of the sentences. This feature takes the following values: $\text{S} < 18 \leq \text{M} \leq 32 < \text{L}$.

DOCPT Document part, e.g., TITLE, ABSTRACT and BODY TEXT, allowing for different models for different document parts.

TOKEN, LEMMA Tokens in most cases equals words, but may in some special cases also be multiword units, e.g. *of course*, as defined by the FDG tokenisation. Lemmas are base forms of words, with some special features introduced for numeric tokens, e.g., year, short number, and long number.

QUANT Syntactic function of a noun phrase with a quantifier head (*at least* ***some of the isoforms*** *are conserved between mouse and humans*), or a modifying quantifier (*Recently,* ***many investigators*** *have been interested in the study on eosinophil biology*).

HEAD, DEPREL Functional dependency head of the token, and the type of dependency relation between the head and the token, respectively.

SYN Phrase-level and clause-level syntactic functions of a word.

MORPH Part-of-speech and morphological traits of a word.

Each feature template defines a set of features when applied to data. The TOKEN, LEMMA, QUANT, HEAD, DEPREL templates yield singleton sets of features for each token, while the SYN and MORPH templates extends to sets consisting of several features for each token. A sentence is represented as the union of all active token level features and the SENLEN and DOCPT, if active. In addition to the linear combination of concrete features, we allow combined features by the Cartesian product of the feature set extensions of two or more feature templates.

2.3 Feature Template Selection

Although regularised maximum margin models often cope well even in the presence of irrelevant features, it is a good idea to search the large set of potential features for an optimal subset.

In order to make this search feasible we make two simplifications. First, we do not explore the full set of individual features, but instead the set of feature templates, as defined above. Second, we perform a greedy search in which we iteratively add the feature template that gives the largest performance improvement, when added to the current optimal set of templates. The performance of a feature set for sentence level detection is measured as the mean F_1-score, with respect to the UNCERTAIN class, minus one standard deviation – the mean and standard deviation are computed by three fold cross-validation on the training set. We subtract one standard deviation from the mean in order to promote stable solutions over unstable ones.

Of course, these simplifications do not come for free. The solution of the optimisation problem might be quite unstable with respect to the optimal hyper-parameters of the learning algorithm, which in turn may depend on the feature set used. This risk could be reduced by conducting a more thorough parameter search for each candidate feature set, however, this was simply too time consuming for the present work. A further risk of using forward selection is that feature interactions are ignored. This issue is handled better with backward elimination, but that is also more time consuming.

The full set of explored feature templates is too large to be listed here; instead we list the features selected in each iteration of the search, together with their corresponding scores, in Table 1.

3 Detecting In-sentence Uncertainty

When it comes to the automatic identification of hedge cues and their linguistic scopes, Morante and Daelemans (2009) and Özgür and Radev (2009) report experiments on the BioScope corpus (Vincze et al., 2008), achieving best results (10-fold cross evaluation) on the identification of hedge cues of 71.59 F-score (using IGTree with current, preceding and subsequent word and cur-

Task	Template set	Dev F_1	Test F_1
Bio	SENLEN	-	-
	∪ LEMMA	88.9 (.25)	78.79
	∪ LEMMABI	90.3 (.19)	85.86
	∪ LEMMA⊗QUANT	90.3 (.07)	85.97
Wiki	SENLEN	-	-
	∪ TOKEN⊗DOCPT	59.0 (.76)	60.12
	∪ TOKENBI⊗SENLEN	59.9 (.09)	58.26

Table 1: Top feature templates for sentence level hedge and weasel detection.

rent lemma as features) and 82.82 F-score (using a Support Vector Machine classifier and a complex feature set including keyword and dependency relation information), respectively. On the task of automatic scope resolution, best results are reported as 59.66 (F-score) and 61.13 (accuracy), respectively, on the full paper subset. Özgür and Radev (2009) use a rule-based method for this subtask, while Morante and Daelemans (2009) use three different classifiers as input to a CRF-based meta-learner, with a complex set of features, including hedge cue information, current and surrounding token information, distance information and location information.

3.1 Learning and Optimisation Framework

In recent years, a wide range of different approaches to general structured prediction problems, of which sequence labelling is a special case, have been suggested. Among others, Conditional Random Fields (Lafferty et al., 2001), Max-Margin Markov Networks (Taskar et al., 2003), and Structured Support Vector Machines (Tsochantaridis et al., 2005). A drawback of these approaches is that they are all quite computationally demanding. As an alternative, we propose a much more computationally lenient approach based on the regularised margin-rescaling formulation of Taskar et al. (2003), which we instead optimise by stochastic subgradient descent as suggested by Ratliff et al. (2007). In addition we only perform approximate decoding, using beam search, which allows arbitrary complex joint feature maps to be employed, without sacrificing speed.

3.1.1 Technical Details

Let $\mathcal{X}$ denote the pattern set and let $\mathcal{Y}$ denote the set of structured labels. Let $\mathcal{A}$ denote the set of atomic labels and let each label $y \in \mathcal{Y}$ consist of an indexed sequence of atomic labels $y_i \in \mathcal{A}$. Denote by $\mathcal{Y}_x \subseteq \mathcal{Y}$ the set of possible label assignments to pattern $x \in \mathcal{X}$ and by $y_x \in \mathcal{Y}_x$ its correct label. In the specific case of BIO-sequence labelling, $\mathcal{A} = \{\text{BEGIN}, \text{INSIDE}, \text{OUTSIDE}\}$ and $\mathcal{Y}_x = \mathcal{A}^{|x|}$, where $|x|$ is the length of the sequence $x \in \mathcal{X}$.

A structured classification problem amounts to learning a mapping from patterns to labels, $f : \mathcal{X} \mapsto \mathcal{Y}$, such that the expected loss $\mathrm{E}_{\mathcal{X}\times\mathcal{Y}}[\Delta(y_x, f(x))]$ is minimised. The prediction loss, $\Delta : \mathcal{Y} \times \mathcal{Y} \mapsto \Re^+$, measures the loss of predicting label $y = f(x)$ when the correct label is y_x, with $\Delta(y_x, y_x) = 0$. Here we assume the Hamming loss, $\Delta_H(y, y') = \sum_{i=1}^{|y|} \delta(y_i, y'_i)$, where $\delta(y_i, y'_i) = 1$ if $y_i \neq y'_i$ and 0 otherwise.

The idea of the margin-rescaling approach is to let the *structured margin* between the correct label y_x and a hypothesis $y \in \mathcal{Y}_x$ scale linearly with the prediction loss $\Delta(y_x, y)$ (Taskar et al., 2003). The structured margin is defined in terms of a score function $S : \mathcal{X} \times \mathcal{Y} \mapsto \Re$, in our case the linear score function $S(x, y) = \boldsymbol{w}^T \Phi(x, y)$, where $\boldsymbol{w} \in \Re^m$ is a vector of parameters and $\Phi : \mathcal{X}\times\mathcal{Y} \mapsto \Re^m$ is a joint feature function. The learning problem then amounts to finding parameters $\boldsymbol{w}$ such that $S(x, y_x) \geq S(x, y) + \Delta(y_x, y)$ for all $y \in \mathcal{Y}_x \setminus \{y_x\}$ over the training data $\mathcal{D}$. In other words, we want the score of the correct label to be higher than the score *plus the loss*, of all other labels, for each instance. In order to balance margin maximisation and margin violation, we add the L_2-regularisation term $\|\boldsymbol{w}\|^2$.

By making use of the *loss augmented* decoding function

$$f_\Delta(x, y_x) = \operatorname*{argmax}_{y \in \mathcal{Y}_x} [S(x, y) + \Delta(y_x, y)], \quad (1)$$

we get the following regularised risk functional:

$$Q_{\lambda,\mathcal{D}}(\boldsymbol{w}) = \sum_{i=1}^{|\mathcal{D}|} S_\Delta(x^{(i)}, y_{x^{(i)}}) + \frac{\lambda}{2}\|\boldsymbol{w}\|^2, \quad (2)$$

where

$$S_\Delta(x, y_x) = \max_{y \in \mathcal{Y}_x} [S(x, y) + \Delta(y_x, y)] - S(x, y_x) \quad (3)$$

We optimise (2) by stochastic approximate subgradient descent with step size sequence $[\eta_0/\sqrt{t}]_{t=1}^{\infty}$ (Ratliff et al., 2007). The initial step size η_0 and the regularisation factor λ are data dependent hyper-parameters, which we tune by cross-validation.

This framework is highly efficient both at learning and prediction time. Training cues and scopes on the biological data, takes about a minute, while prediction times are in the order of seconds, using a Java based implementation on a standard laptop; the absolute majority of that time is spent on reading and extracting features from an inefficient internal JSON-based format.

3.1.2 Hashed Feature Functions

Joint feature functions enable encoding of dependencies between labels and relations between pattern and label. Most feature templates are defined based on input only, while some are defined with respect to output features as well. Let $\Psi(x, y_{1:i-1}, i) \in \Re^m$ denote the joint feature function corresponding to the application of all active feature templates to pattern $x \in \mathcal{X}$ and partially decoded label $y_{1:i-1} \in \mathcal{A}^{i-1}$ when decoding at position i. The feature mapping used in scoring candidate label $y_i \in \mathcal{A}$ is then computed as the Cartesian product $\Phi(x, y, i) = \Psi(x, y_{1:i-1}, i) \otimes \Lambda(y_i)$, where $\Lambda(y_i) \in \Re^m$ is a unique unitary feature vector representation of label y_i. The feature representation for a complete sequence x and its associated label y is then computed as

$$\Phi(x, y) = \sum_{i=1}^{|x|} \Phi(x, y, i)$$

When employing joint feature functions and combined features, the number of unique features may grow very large. This is a problem when the amount of internal memory is limited. Feature hashing, as described by Weinberger et al. (2009), is a simple trick to circumvent this problem. Assume that we have an original feature function $\phi : \mathcal{X} \times \mathcal{Y} \mapsto \Re^m$, where m might be arbitrarily large. Let $h : \mathbb{N}^+ \mapsto [1, n]$ be a hash function and let $h^{-1}(i) \subseteq [1, m]$ be the set of integers such that $j \in h^{-1}(i)$ iff $h(j) = i$. We now use this hash function to map the index of each feature in $\phi(x, y)$ to its corresponding index in $\Phi(x, y)$, as $\Phi_i(x, y) = \sum_{j \in h^{-1}(i)} \phi_j(x, y)$. The features in Φ are thus unions of multisets of features in ϕ. Given a hash function with good collision properties, we can expect that the subset of features mapped to any index in $\Phi(x, y)$ is small and composed of elements drawn at random from $\phi(x, y)$. Weinberger et al. (2009) contains proofs of bounds on these distributions. Furthermore, by using a k-valued hash function $h : \mathbb{N}^k \mapsto [1, n]$, the Cartesian product of k feature sets can be computed much more efficiently, compared to using a dictionary.

3.2 Position Based Feature Definitions

For in-sentence cue and scope prediction we make use of the same token level feature templates as for sentence level detection. An additional level of expressivity is added in that each token level template is associated with a token position. A template is addressed either relative to the token currently being decoded, or by the dependency arc of a token, which in turn is addressed by a relative position. The addressing can be either to a single position, or a range of positions. Feature templates may further be defined with respect to features of the input pattern, the token level labels predicted so far, or with respect to combinations of input and label features. Joint features, just as complex feature combinations, are created by forming the Cartesian product of an input feature set and a label feature set.

The feature templates are instantiated by prefixing the template name to each member of the feature set. To exemplify, the single position template TOKEN$_i$, given that the token currently being decoded at position i is *suggests*, is instantiated as the singleton set $\{\text{TOKEN}_i = \text{suggests}\}$. The range template TOKEN$_{i,i+1}$, given that the current token is *suggests* and the next token is *that*, is instantiated as the set $\{\text{TOKEN}_{i,i+1} = \text{suggests}, \text{TOKEN}_{i,i+1} = \text{that}\}$; i.e. each member of the set is prefixed by the range template name.

In addition to the token level templates used for sentence level prediction, the following templates were explored:

LABEL Label predicted so far at the addressed position(s).

HEAD.X An arbitrary feature, X, addressed by following the dependency arc(s) from the addressed position(s). For example, HEAD.LEMMA$_i$ corresponds to the lemma found by looking at the dependency head of the current token.

CUE, CUESCOPE Whether the token(s) addressed is respectively, a cue marker, or within the syntactic scope of the current cue, following the definition of scope provided by Vincze et al. (2008).

3.3 Feature Template Selection

Just as with sentence level detection, we used a greedy forward selection strategy when searching for the optimal subset of feature templates. The cue and scope detection subtasks were optimised separately.

The scoring measures used in the search for cue and scope detection features differ. In order to match the official scoring measure for cue detection, we optimise the F_1-score of labels corresponding to cue tags, i.e. we treat the BEGIN and INSIDE cue tags as an equivalence class. The official scoring measure for scope prediction, on the other hand, corresponds to the exact match of scope boundaries. Unfortunately using exact match performance turned out to be not very well suited for use in greedy forward selection. This is because before a sufficient per token accuracy has been reached, and even when it has, the exact match score may fluctuate wildly. Therefore, as a substitute, we instead guide the search by token level accuracy. This discrepancy between the search criterion and the official scoring metric is unfortunate.

Again, when taking into account position addressing, joint features and combined features, the complete set of explored templates is too large to fit in the current experiment. The selected features together with their corresponding scores are found in Table 2.

Task	Template set	Dev F_1	Test F_1
Cue	TOKEN_i	74.0 (1.5)	-
	$\cup\ \text{TOKEN}_{i-1}$	81.0 (.30)	68.78
	$\cup\ \text{MORPH}_i$	83.6 (.10)	74.06
	$\cup\ \text{LEMMA}_i \otimes \text{LEMMA}_{i+1}$	85.6 (.20)	78.41
	$\cup\ \text{SYN}_i$	86.5 (.41)	78.28
	$\cup\ \text{LEMMA}_{i-1} \otimes \text{LEMMA}_i$	86.7 (.42)	78.52
Scope	CueScope_i	66.9 (.92)	-
	$\cup\ \text{LABEL}_{i-2,i-1}$	79.5 (.67)	34.80
	$\cup\ \text{LEMMA}_i$	82.4 (1.1)	33.18
	$\cup\ \text{MORPH}_i$	83.1 (.35)	35.70
	$\cup\ \text{CUE}_{i-2,i-1}$	83.4 (.13)	40.14
	$\cup\ \text{CUE}_{i,i+1,i+2}$	83.6 (.11)	41.15
	$\cup\ \text{LEMMA}_{i-1}$	84.1 (.16)	40.04
	$\cup\ \text{MORPH}_i$	84.4 (.33)	40.04
	$\cup\ \text{TOKEN}_{i+1}$	84.5 (.09)	39.64

Table 2: Top feature templates for in-sentence detection of hedge cues and scopes.

4 Discussion

Our final F_1-score results for the corrected system are, in Task 1 for the biological domain 85.97, for the Wikipedia domain 58.25; for Task 2, our results are 39.64 for the entire task with a score of 78.52 for cue detection.

Any gold standard-based shared experiment unavoidably invites discussion on the reliability of the gold standard. It is easy to find borderline examples in the evaluation corpus, e.g. sentences that may just as well be labeled "certain" rather than "uncertain". This gives an indication of the true complexity of assessing the hidden variable of uncertainty and coercing it to a binary judgment rather than a dimensional one. It is unlikely that everyone will agree on a binary judgment every time.

To improve experimental results and the generalisability of the results for the task of detecting uncertain information on a sentence level, we would need to break reliance on the purely lexical cues. For instance, we now have identified *possible* and *putative* as markers for uncertainty, but in many instances they are not (*Finally, we wish to ensure that others can use and evaluate the GREC as simply as possible*). This would be avoidable through either a deeper analysis of the sentence to note that *possible* in this case does not modify anything of substance in the sentence, or alternatively through a multi-word term preprocessor to identify *as simply as possible* as an analysis unit.

In the Wikipedia experiment, where the objective is to identify *weasel* phrases, the judicious encoding of quantifiers such as "some of the most well-known researchers say that X" would be likely to identify the sought-for sentences when the quantified NP is in subject position. In our experiment we find that our dependency analysis did not distinguish between the various syntactic roles of quantified NPs. As a result, we marked several sentences with a quantifier as a "weasel" sentence, even where the quantified NP was in a non-subject role – leading to overly many weasel sentences. An example is given in Table 3.

If certainty can be identified separately, not as absence of overt uncertainty, identifying uncertainty can potentially be aided through the identification of explicit certainty together with negation, as found by Kilicoglu and Bergler (2008). In keeping with their results, we found negations in a sizeable proportion of the annotated training material. Currently we capture negation as a lexical cue in immediate bigrams, but with longer range negations, we will miss some clear cases: Table 3 gives two examples. To avoid these misses, we will both need to identify overt expressions of certainty and to identify and track the scope of negation – the first challenge is unexplored but would not seem to be overly complex; the second is a well-known and established challenge for NLP systems in general.

In the task of detecting in-sentence uncertainty – identification of hedge cues and their scopes – we find that an evaluation method based on exact match of a token sequence is overly unforgiving. There are many cases where the marginal tokens of a sequence are less than central or irrelevant for the understanding of the hedge cue and its scope: moving the boundary by one position over an uninteresting token may completely invalidate an otherwise arguably correct analysis. A token-by-token scoring would be a more functional evaluation criterion, or perhaps a fuzzy match, allowing for a certain amount of erroneous characters.

For our experiments, this has posed some challenges. While we model the in-sentence uncertainty detection as a sequence labelling problem in the BIO-representation (BEGIN, INSIDE, OUTSIDE), the provided corpus uses an XML-representation. Moreover, the official scoring tool requires that the predictions are well formed XML, necessitating a conversion from XML to BIO prior to training and from BIO to XML after prediction. Consistent tokenisation is important, but the syntactic analysis components used by us distorted the original tokenisation and restoring the exact same token sequence proved problematic.

Conversion from BIO to XML is straightforward for cues, while some care must be taken when annotating scopes, since erroneous scope predictions may result in malformed XML. When adding the scope annotation, we use a stack based algorithm. For each sentence, we simultaneously traverse the scope-sequence corresponding to each cue, left to right, token by token. The stack is used to ensure that scopes are either separated or nested and an additional restriction ensures that scopes may never start or end inside a cue. In case the algorithm fails to place a scope according to these restrictions, we fall back and let the scope cover the whole sentence. Several of the more frequent errors in our analyses are scoping errors, many likely to do with the fallback solution. Our analysis quite frequently fails also to assign the subject of a sentence to the scope of a hedging verb. Table 3 shows one example each of these errors – overextended scope and missing subject.

Unfortunately, the tokenisation output by our analysis components is not always consistent with the tokenisation assumed by the BioScope annotation. A post-processing step was therefore added in which each, possibly complex, token in the predicted BIO-sequence is heuristically mapped to its corresponding position in the XML structure. This post-processing is not perfect and scopes and cues at non-word token boundaries, such as parentheses, are quite often misplaced with respect to the BioScope annotation. Table 3 gives one example which is scored "erroneous" since the token "(63)" is in scope, where the "correct" solution has it outside the scope. These errors are not important to address, but are quite frequent in our results – approximately 80 errors are of this type.

To achieve more general and effective methods to detect uncertainty in an argument, we should note that uncertainty is signalled in a text through many mechanisms, and that the purely lexical and explicit signal found through the present experiments in hedge identification is effective and useful, but will not catch everything we might want to find. Lexical approaches are also domain dependent. For instance, Szarvas (2008) and Morante and Daelemans (2009) report loss in performance, when applying the same methods developed on biological data, on clinical text. Using the systems developed for scientific text elsewhere poses a migration challenge. It would be desirable both to automatically learn a hedging lexicon from a general seed set and to have features on a higher level of abstraction.

Our main result is that casting this task as a sequence labelling problem affords us the possibility to combine linguistic analyses with a highly efficient implementation of a max-margin prediction algorithm. Our framework processes the data sets in minutes for training and seconds for prediction on a standard personal computer.

5 Acknowledgements

The authors would like to thank Joakim Nivre for feedback in earlier stages of this work. This work was funded by The Swedish National Graduate School of Language Technology and by the Swedish Research Council.

References

Rong-En Fan, Kai-Wei Chang, Cho-Jui Hsieh, Xiang-Rui Wang, and Chih-Jen Lin. 2008. LIBLINEAR: A library for large linear classification. *Journal of Machine Learning Research*, 9:1871–1874.

Richárd Farkas, Veronika Vincze, György Móra, János

Neg + certain	However, how IFN-γ and IL-4 inhibit IL-17 production is **not** yet **known**.
Neg + certain	The mechanism by which Tregs preserve peripheral tolerance is still **not** entirely **clear**.
"some": not weasel	Tourist folks usually visit this peaceful paradise to enjoy **some leisure**$_{nonsubj}$.
"some": weasel	**Some**$_{subj}$ suggest that the origin of music likely stems from naturally occurring sounds and rhythms.
Prediction	dRas85DV12 <xcope _.1><cue _.1>may</cue> be more potent than dEGFRλ because dRas85DV12 can activate endogenous PI3K signaling [16]</xcope>.
Gold standard	dRas85DV12 <xcope _.1><cue _.1>may</cue> be more potent than dEGFRλ</xcope> because dRas85DV12 can activate endogenous PI3K signaling [16].
Prediction	However, the precise molecular mechanisms of Stat3-mediated expression of RORγt <xcope _.1>are still <cue _.1>unclear</cue></xcope>.
Gold standard	However, <xcope _.1>the precise molecular mechanisms of Stat3-mediated expression of RORγt are still <cue _.1>unclear</cue></xcope>.
Prediction	Interestingly, Foxp3 <xcope _.1><cue _.1>may</cue> inhibit RORγt activity on its target genes, at least in par,t through direct interaction with RORγt (63)</xcope>.
Gold standard	Interestingly, Foxp3 <xcope _.1><cue _.1>may</cue> inhibit RORt activity on its target genes, at least in par,t through direct interaction with RORt</xcope> (63).

Table 3: Examples of erroneous analyses.

Csirik, and György Szarvas. 2010. The CoNLL-2010 Shared Task: Learning to Detect Hedges and their Scope in Natural Language Text. In *Proceedings of the 14th Conference on Computational Natural Language Learning (CoNLL-2010): Shared Task*, pages 1–12, Uppsala, Sweden, July. Association for Computational Linguistics.

Viola Ganter and Michael Strube. 2009. Finding hedges by chasing weasels: hedge detection using Wikipedia tags and shallow linguistic features. In *ACL-IJCNLP '09: Proceedings of the ACL-IJCNLP 2009 Conference Short Papers*, Morristown, NJ, USA. Association for Computational Linguistics.

Halil Kilicoglu and Sabine Bergler. 2008. Recognizing speculative language in biomedical research articles: a linguistically motivated perspective. *BMC Bioinformatics*, 9.

John D. Lafferty, Andrew McCallum, and Fernando C. N. Pereira. 2001. Conditional random fields: Probabilistic models for segmenting and labeling sequence data. In *Proc. 18th Int. Conf. on Machine Learning*. Morgan Kaufmann Publishers.

Marc Light, Xin Ying Qiu, and Padmini Srinivasan. 2004. The language of bioscience: Facts, speculations, and statements in between. In Lynette Hirschman and James Pustejovsky, editors, *HLT-NAACL 2004 Workshop: BioLINK 2004, Linking Biological Literature, Ontologies and Databases*, Boston, USA. ACL.

Ben Medlock and Ted Briscoe. 2007. Weakly supervised learning for hedge classification in scientific literature. In *Proceedings of the 45th Annual Meeting of the Association of Computational Linguistics*, Prague, Czech Republic. Association for Computational Linguistics.

Ben Medlock. 2008. Exploring hedge identification in biomedical literature. *Journal of Biomedical Informatics*, 41(4):636–654.

Roser Morante and Walter Daelemans. 2009. Learning the scope of hedge cues in biomedical texts. In *BioNLP '09: Proceedings of Workshop on BioNLP*, Morristown, NJ, USA. ACL.

Andrew Y. Ng. 2004. Feature selection, l1 vs. l2 regularization, and rotational invariance. In *ICML '04: Proceedings of the 21st International Conference on Machine learning*, page 78, New York, NY, USA. ACM.

Arzucan Özgür and Dragomir R. Radev. 2009. Detecting speculations and their scopes in scientific text. In *Proceedings of 2009 Conference on Empirical Methods in Natural Language Processing*, Singapore. ACL.

Randolph Quirk, Sidney Greenbaum, Geoffrey Leech, and Jan Svartvik. 1985. *A comprehensive grammar of the English language*. Longman.

Nathan D. Ratliff, Andrew J. Bagnell, and Martin A. Zinkevich. 2007. (Online) subgradient methods for structured prediction. In *Eleventh International Conference on Artificial Intelligence and Statistics (AIStats)*.

György Szarvas. 2008. Hedge classification in biomedical texts with a weakly supervised selection of keywords. In *Proceedings of ACL-08: HLT*, Columbus, Ohio. ACL.

Pasi Tapanainen and Timo Järvinen. 1997. A non-projective dependency parser. In *Proceedings of the 5th Conference on Applied Natural Language Processing*.

Benjamin Taskar, Carlos Guestrin, and Daphne Koller. 2003. Max-margin Markov networks. In Sebastian Thrun, Lawrence K. Saul, and Bernhard Schölkopf, editors, *NIPS*. MIT Press.

Ioannis Tsochantaridis, Thorsten Joachims, Thomas Hofmann, and Yasemin Altun. 2005. Large margin methods for structured and interdependent output variables. *Journal of Machine Learning Research*, 6:1453–1484.

Veronika Vincze, György Szarvas, Richárd Farkas, György Móra, and János Csirik. 2008. The BioScope corpus: biomedical texts annotated for uncertainty, negation and their scopes. *BMC Bioinformatics*, 9(S-11).

Kilian Weinberger, Anirban Dasgupta, John Langford, Alex Smola, and Josh Attenberg. 2009. Feature hashing for large scale multitask learning. In *ICML '09: Proceedings of the 26th Annual International Conference on Machine Learning*, New York, NY, USA. ACM.

Hedge Detection and Scope Finding by Sequence Labeling with Normalized Feature Selection*

Shaodian Zhang[12], **Hai Zhao**[123]†, **Guodong Zhou**[3] and **Bao-Liang Lu**[12]
[1]Center for Brain-Like Computing and Machine Intelligence
Dept of Computer Science and Engineering, Shanghai Jiao Tong University
[2]MOE-Microsoft Key Laboratory for Intelligent Computing and Intelligent Systems
Shanghai Jiao Tong University
[3]School of Computer Science and Technology, Soochow University
zhangsd.sjtu@gmail.com, zhaohai@cs.sjtu.edu.cn
gdzhou@suda.edu.cn, blu@cs.sjtu.edu.cn

Abstract

This paper presents a system which adopts a standard sequence labeling technique for hedge detection and scope finding. For the first task, hedge detection, we formulate it as a hedge labeling problem, while for the second task, we use a two-step labeling strategy, one for hedge cue labeling and the other for scope finding. In particular, various kinds of syntactic features are systemically exploited and effectively integrated using a large-scale normalized feature selection method. Evaluation on the CoNLL-2010 shared task shows that our system achieves stable and competitive results for all the closed tasks. Furthermore, post-deadline experiments show that the performance can be much further improved using a sufficient feature selection.

1 Introduction

Hedges are linguistic devices representing speculative parts of articles. Previous works such as (Hyland, 1996; Marco and Mercer, 2004; Light et al., 2004; Thompson et al., 2008) present research on hedge mainly as a linguistic phenomenon. Meanwhile, detecting hedges and their scopes automatically are increasingly important tasks in natural language processing and information extraction, especially in biomedical community. The shared task of CoNLL-2010 described in Farkas et al. (2010) aims at detecting hedges (task 1) and finding their scopes (task 2) for the literature from BioScope corpus (Szarvas et al., 2008) and Wikipedia. This paper describes a system adopting sequence labeling which performs competitive in the official evaluation, as well as further test. In addition, a large-scale feature selection procedure is applied in training and development. Considering that BioScope corpus is annotated by two independent linguists according to a formal guideline (Szarvas, 2008), while Wikipedia weasels are tagged by netizens who are diverse in background and various in evaluation criterion, it is needed to handle them separately. Our system selects features for Wikipedia and BioScope corpus independently and evaluate them respectively, leading to fine performances for all of them.

The rest of the paper is organized as follows. The next section presents the technical details of our system of hedge detection and scope finding. Section 3 gives information of features. Section 4 shows the evaluation results, including official results and further ones after official outputs collection. Section 5 concludes the paper.

2 Methods

Basically, the tasks are formulated as sequence labeling in our approach. The available label set differs between task 1 and 2. In addition, it is needed to introduce an indicator in order to find scopes for the multi-hedge sentences properly.

2.1 Hedge detection

The valid label set of task 1, hedge detection, contains only two labels: "Hedge" and "_", which represent that a word is in a hedge cue or not respectively. Since results of hedge detection in this shared task are evaluated at sentence level, a sentence will be classified as "uncertain" in the post-process if it has one or more words labeled "Hedge" in it and otherwise "certain".

* This work is partially supported by the National Natural Science Foundation of China (Grants 60903119, 60773090, 90820018 and 90920004), the National Basic Research Program of China (Grant No. 2009CB320901), and the National High-Tech Research Program of China (Grant No.2008AA02Z315).

† corresponding author

Proceedings of the Fourteenth Conference on Computational Natural Language Learning: Shared Task, pages 92–99,
Uppsala, Sweden, 15-16 July 2010.

2.2 Scope finding

The second task is divided into two steps in our system. The first step is quite the same as what the system does in task 1: labeling the words as in hedge cues or not. Then the scope of each hedge will be labeled by taking advantage of the result of the first step. A scope can be denoted by a beginning word and an ending word to represent the first and the last element. In scope finding the available label set contains "Begin", "End", "Middle" and "_", representing the first and last word in the scope, in-scope and out-of-scope. As an example, a sentence with hedge cue and scope labeling is given in Table 1. Hedge cue "indicating" with its scope from "indicating" itself to "transcription" are labeled. While evaluating outputs, only "Begin"s and "End"s will be taken into consideration and be treated as the head and tail tokens of the scopes of specific hedge cues.

Furthermore	...	_	_
,	...	_	_
inhibition	...	_	_
can	...	_	_
be	...	_	_
blocked	...	_	_
by	...	_	_
actinomycin	...	_	_
D	...	_	_
,	...	_	_
indicating	...	Hedge	Begin
a	...	_	Middle
requirement	...	_	Middle
for	...	_	Middle
de	...	_	Middle
novo	...	_	Middle
transcription	...	_	End
.	...	_	_

Table 1: A sentence with hedge cue and scope labeling

It seems that the best labeling result of task 1 can be used directly to be the proper intermediate representation of task 2. However, the complexity of scope finding for multi-hedge sentences forces us to modify the intermediate result of task 2 for the sake of handling the sentences with more than one hedge cue correctly. Besides, since task 1 is a sentence classification task essentially, while the goal of the first step of task 2 is to label the words as accurately as possible, it is easy to find that the optimal labeling results of task 1 may not be optimal to be the intermediate representations for task 2. This problem can be solved if sentence-level hedge detection and intermediate representation finding are treated as two separate tasks with independent feature selection procedures. The details of feature selection will be given in section 3.

2.3 Scope finding for multi-hedge cases

Sentences with more than one hedge cue are quite common in both datasets of BioScope corpus and Wikipedia. By counting hedges in every sentence, we find that about one fourth of the sentences with hedges have more than one hedge cue in all three data sources (Table 2). In Morante and Daelemans (2009), three classifiers predict whether each token is Begin, End or None and a postprocessing is needed to associate Begins and Ends with their corresponding hedge cues. In our approach, in order to decrease ambiguous or illegal outputs e.g. inequivalent numbers of Begins and Ends, a pair of Begin and End without their corresponding hedge cue between them, etc., sentences with more than one hedge cue will be preprocessed by making copies as many as the number of hedges and be handled separately.

The sentence which is selected as a sample has two hedge cues: "suggesting" and "may", so our system preprocesses the sentence into two single-hedge ones, which is illustrated in Table 3. Now it comes to the problem of finding scope for single-hedge sentence. The two copies are labeled separately, getting one scope from "suggesting" to "mitogenesis" for the hedge cue "suggesting" and the other from "IFN-alpha" to "mitogenesis" for "may". Merging the two results will give the final scope resolution of the sentence.

However, compared with matching Begins and Ends in postprocessing given by Morante and Daelemans (2009), the above method gives rise to out of control of projections of the scopes, i.e. scopes of hedges may partially overlap after copies are merged. Since scopes should be intact constituents of sentences, namely, subtrees in syntax tree which never partly overlap with each other, results like this are linguistically illegal and should be discarded. We solve this problem by introducing an instructional feature called "Indicator". For sentences with more than one hedge cue, namely more than one copy while finding scopes, words inside the union of existing (labeled) scopes will be tagged as "Indicator" in unhandled copies before every labeling. For example, after finding scope for the first copy in Table 3 and words from

Dataset	# Sentence	# No-hedge	ratio	# One-hedge	ratio	# Multi-hedge	ratio
Biomedical Abstracts	11871	9770	82.3%	1603	13.5%	498	4.2%
Biomedical Fulltexts	2670	2151	80.6%	385	14.4%	134	5.0%
Wikipedia	11111	8627	77.6%	1936	17.4%	548	4.9%

Table 2: Statistics of hedge amount

IFN-alpha	_	IFN-alpha	_
also	_	also	_
sensitized	_	sensitized	_
T	_	T	_
cells	_	cells	_
to	_	to	_
IL-2-induced	_	IL-2-induced	_
proliferation	_	proliferation	_
,	_	,	_
further	_	further	_
suggesting	Hedge	suggesting	_
that	_	that	_
IFN-alpha	_	IFN-alpha	_
may	_	may	Hedge
be	_	be	_
involved	_	involved	_
in	_	in	_
the	_	the	_
regulation	_	regulation	_
of	_	of	_
T-cell	_	T-cell	_
mitogenesis	_	mitogenesis	_
.	_	.	_

Table 3: An example of 2-hedge sentence before scope finding

IFN-alpha	...	_	_	_
also	...	_	_	_
sensitized	...	_	_	_
T	...	_	_	_
cells	...	_	_	_
to	...	_	_	_
IL-2-induced	...	_	_	_
proliferation	...	_	_	_
,	...	_	_	_
further	...	_	_	_
suggesting	...	Indicator	_	_
that	...	Indicator	_	_
IFN-alpha	...	Indicator	_	Begin
may	...	Indicator	Hedge	Middle
be	...	Indicator	_	Middle
involved	...	Indicator	_	Middle
in	...	Indicator	_	Middle
the	...	Indicator	_	Middle
regulation	...	Indicator	_	Middle
of	...	Indicator	_	Middle
T-cell	...	Indicator	_	Middle
mitogenesis	...	Indicator	_	End
.	...	_	_	_

Table 4: Scope resolution with instructional feature: "Indicator"

"suggesting" to "mitogenesis" are put in the scope of cue "suggesting", these words should be tagged "Indicator" in the second copy, whose result is illustrated in Table 4. If not in a scope, any word is tagged "_" as the indicator. The "Indicator"s tagging from "suggesting" to "mitogenesis" in Table 4 mean that no other than the situations of a) "Begin" is after or at "suggesting" and "End" is before or at "mitogenesis" b) Both "Begin" and "End" are before "suggesting" c) Both next "Begin" and next "End" are after "mitogenesis" can be accepted. In other words, new labeling should keep the projections of scopes in the result. Although it is only an instructional indicator and does not have any coerciveness, the evaluation result of experiment shows it effective.

3 Feature selection

Since hedge and scope finding are quite novel tasks and it is not easy to determine the effective features by experience, a greedy feature selection is conducted. As it mentioned in section 2, our system divides scope finding into two sub-tasks:

a) Hedge cue labeling

b) Scope labeling

The first one is the same as hedge detection task in strategy, but quite distinct in target of feature set, because hedge detection is a task of sentence classification while the first step of scope finding aims at high accuracy of labeling hedge cues. Therefore, three independent procedures of feature selection are conducted for BioScope corpus dataset. As Wikipedia is not involved in the task of scope finding, it only needs one final feature set.

About 200 feature templates are initially considered for each task. We mainly borrow ideas and are enlightened by following sources while initializing feature template sets:

a) Previous papers on hedge detection and scope finding (Light et al., 2004; Medlock, 2008; Medlock and Briscoe, 2008; Kilicoglu and Bergler, 2008; Szarvas, 2008; Ganter and Strube, 2009; Morante and Daelemans, 2009);

b) Related works such as named entity recognition (Collins, 1999) and text chunking (Zhang et al., 2001);

c) Some literature on dependency parsing (Nivre and Scholz, 2004; McDonald et al., 2005; Nivre, 2009; Zhao et al., 2009c; Zhao et al., 2009a);

3.1 Notations of Feature Template

A large amount of advanced syntactic features including syntactic connections, paths, families and their concatenations are introduced. Many of these features come from dependency parsing, which aims at building syntactic tree expressed by dependencies between words. More details about dependency parsing are given in Nivre and Scholz (2004) and McDonald et al. (2005). The parser in Zhao et al. (2009a) is used to construct dependency structures in our system, and some of the notations in this paper adopt those presented in Zhao et al. (2009c). Feature templates are from various combinations or integrations of the following basic elements.

Word Property. This part of features includes word form (*form*), lemma (*lemma*), part-of-speech tag (*pos*), syntactic dependency (*dp*) , syntactic dependency label (*dprel*).

Syntactic Connection. This includes syntactic head (*h*), left(right) farthest(nearest) child (*lm, ln, rm* and *rn*) and high (low) support verb, noun or preposition. Here we specify the last one as an example, support verb(noun/preposition). From a given word to the syntactic root along the syntactic tree, the first verb/noun/preposition that is met is called its low support verb/noun/preposition, and the nearest one to the root(farthest to the given word) is called as its high support verb/noun/preposition. The concept of support verb was broadly used (Toutanova et al., 2005; Xue, 2006; Jiang and Ng, 2006), and it is extended to nouns and prepositions in Zhao et al. (2009b). In addition, a slightly modified syntactic head, *pphead*, is introduced, it returns the left most sibling of a given word if the word is headed by a preposition, otherwise it returns the original head.

Path. There are two basic types of path. One is the linear path (*linePath*) in the sequence, the other is the path in the syntactic parsing tree (*dpPath*). For example, $m{:}n|$*dpPath* represents the dependency path from word *m* to *n*. Assuming that the two paths from *m* and *n* to the root are p_m and p_n, $m{:}n|$*dpPathShare*, $m{:}n|$*dpPathPred* and $m{:}n|$*dpPathArgu* represent the common part of p_m and p_n, part of p_m which does not belong to p_n and part of p_n which does not belong to p_m, respectively.

Family. A children set includes all syntactic children(*children*) are used in the template notations.

Concatenation of Elements. For all collected elements according to *dpPath*, *children* and so on, we use three strategies to concatenate all those strings to produce the feature value. The first is *seq*, which concatenates all collected strings without doing anything. The second is *bag*, which removes all duplicated strings and sort the rest. The third is *noDup*, which removes all duplicated neighbored strings.

Hedge Cue Dictionary and Scope Indicator. Hedge cues in the training set are collected and put in a dictionary. Whether a word in the training or testing set is in the dictionary (*dic*) is introduced into feature templates. As the evaluation is non-open, we do not put in any additional hedge cues from other resources. An indicator (*indicator*) is given for multi-hedge scope finding, as specified in section 2.At last, in feature set for scope labeling, *hedge* represents that the word is in a hedge cue.

At last, we take x as current token to be labeled, and x_m to denote neighbor words. $m > 0$ represents that it is a word goes m_{th} after current word and $m < 0$ for word $-m_{th}$ before current word.

3.2 Feature template sets for each task

As optimal feature template subsets cannot be expected to be extracted from so large sets by hand, greedy feature selections according to Zhao et al. (2009b) are applied. The normalized feature selection has been proved to be effective in quite a lot of NLP tasks and can often successfully select an optimal or very close to optimal feature set from a large-scale superset. Although usually it needs 3 to 4 loops denoted by "While" in the Algorithm 1 of Zhao et al. (2009b) to get the best template set, we only complete one before official outputs collection because of time limitation, which to a large extent hinders the performance of the system.

Three template sets are selected for BioScope corpus. One with the highest accuracy for sentence-level hedge detection (Set B), one with the best performance for word-level hedge cue labeling (Set H) and another one with the maximal F-score for scope finding (Set S). In addition, one set is discovered for sentence-level hedge detection of Wikipedia (Set W)[1] . Table 5[2] lists some selected feature templates which are basic word or hedging properties for the three sets of BioScope corpus and Wikipedia. From the table we can see it is clear that the combinations of lemma, POS and word form of words in context, which are usually basic and common elements in NLP, are also effective for hedge detection. And as we expected, the feature that represents whether the word is in the hedge list or not is very useful especially in hedge cue finding, indicating that methods based on a hedge cue lists (Light et al., 2004) or keyword selection (Szarvas, 2008) are quite significant way to accomplish such tasks.

Some a little complicated syntactic features based on dependencies are systemically exploited as features for tasks. Table 6 enumerates some of the syntactic features which proves to be highly effective. We noticed that *lowSupportNoun*, *highSupportNoun* and features derived from *dpPath* is notably useful. It can be explained by the awareness that hedge labeling and scope finding are to process literatures in the level of semantics where syntactic features are often helpful.

We continue our feature selection procedures for BioScope corpus after official outputs collection and obtain feature template sets that bring better performance. Table 7 gives some of the features in the optimized sets for BioScope corpus resolution. One difference between the new sets and the old ones is the former contain more syntactic elements, indicating that exploiting syntactic feature is a correct choice. Another difference is the new sets assemble more information of words before or after the current word, especially words linearly far away but close in syntax tree. Appearance of combination of these two factors such as $x_{-1}.lm.form$ seems to provide an evidence of the insufficiency training and development of our system submitted to some extent.

-	$x.lemma + x_1.lemma + x_{-1}.lemma + x.dic + x_1.dic + x_{-1}.dic$
-	$x.lemma + x_1.pos + x_{-1}.pos + x.pos + x_1.lemma + x_{-1}.lemma$
-	$x.form$
Set B	$x.pos + x_1.pos + x_{-1}.pos + x_2.pos + x_{-2}.pos$
-	$x.dic + x_1.dic + x_{-1}.dic$
-	$x_1.pos$
-	$x.dic + x_1.dic + x_{-1}.dic + x_2.dic + x_{-2}.dic$
-	$x.pos + x_{-1}.pos$
-	$x.dic$
Set H	$x.dic + x.lemma + x.pos + x.form$
-	$x.pos + x_1.pos + x_{-1}.pos + x_2.pos + x_{-2}.pos$
-	$x_{-2}.form + x_{-2}.lemma$
-	$x_{-1}.form + x.form$
-	$x.dic + x_1.dic + x_{-1}.dic$
-	$x.dic + x_1.dic + x_{-1}.dic + x_2.dic + x_{-2}.dic + x_3.dic + x_{-3}.dic$
-	$x.indicator$
-	$x.hedge + x_1.hedge + x_{-1}.hedge$
Set S	$x.lemma + x_1.pos + x_{-1}.pos + x.pos + x_1.lemma + x_{-1}.lemma$
-	$x.pos + x.hedge + x.dp + x.dprel$
-	$x_1.pos$
-	$x.pos + x_1.pos + x_{-1}.pos + x_2.pos + x_{-2}.pos$
-	$x.lemma + x_1.lemma + x_{-1}.lemma + x.dic + x_1.dic + x_{-1}.dic$
-	$x.lemma + x_1.lemma + x_{-1}.lemma + x_2.lemma + x_{-2}.lemma + x.dic + x_1.dic + x_{-1}.dic + x_2.dic + x_{-2}.dic$
-	$x.lemma + x_1.lemma$
Set W	$x.hedge + x_1.hedge + x_{-1}.hedge + x_2.hedge + x_{-2}.hedge + x_3.hedge + x_{-3}.hedge$
-	$x.pos + x_1.pos + x_{-1}.pos + x_2.pos + x_{-2}.pos + x.dic + x_1.dic + x_{-1}.dic + x_2.dic + x_{-2}.dic$
-	$x.pos + x.dic$
-	$x.num + x.dic$

Table 5: Selected feature template sets

4 Evaluation results

Two tracks (closed and open challenges) are provided for CoNLL-2010 shared task. We participated in the closed challenge, select features based

[1] *num* in the set of Wikipedia represents the sequential number of word in the sentence

[2] Contact the authors to get the full feature lists, as well as entire optimized sets in post-deadline experiment

-	x.lowSupportNoun:x | dpPathArgu.dprel.seq
-	x.lowSupportNoun:x|dpPathArgu.dprel.seq + x.lowSupportProp:x|dpPathArgu.dprel.seq
-	x.lowSupoortNoun.pos
-	x.pos + x.children.dprel.bag
-	x.rm.dprel + x.form
Set B	x.pphead.lemma
-	x.form + x.children.dprel.bag
-	x.lowSupportNoun:x—dpTreeRelation
-	x.lowSupportProp.lemma
-	x.form + x.children.dprel.noDup
-	x.highSupportNoun:x|dpTreeRelation + x.form
-	x.lowSupportVerb.form
-	x.lowSupportProp:x|dpPathShared.dprel.seq
-	x.lowSupportProp:x|dpPathShared.pos.seq
-	x.highSupportNoun.pos
-	x.highSupportNoun:x|dpTreeRelation
-	x.highSupportNoun:x|dpPathArgu.dprel.seq + x.highSupportProp:x|dpPathArgu.dprel.seq
Set H	$x$lowSupportProp.lemma
-	x.rm.dprel
-	x.lm.form
-	x.lemma + x.pphead.form
-	x.lowSupportVerb.form
-	x.rm.lemma + x.rm.form
-	x.children.dprel.noDup
-	x.children.dprel.bag
-	x.highSupportNoun:x|dpTreeRelation
-	x.lemma + x.pphead.form
Set S	x.highSupportNoun:x|dpTreeRelation + x.form
-	x.lowSupportVerb.form
-	x.lowSupportVerb.lemma
-	x.h.children.dprel.bag
-	x.highSupportVerb.form
-	x.lm.form
-	x.lemma + x.pphead.form
-	x.lm.dprel + x.pos
-	x.lowSupportProp:x|dpPathPred.dprel.seq
-	x.pphead.lemma
Set W	x.rm.lemma
-	x.lowSupportProp:x|dpTreeRelation
-	x.lowSupportVerb:x|dpPathPred.dprel.seq
-	x.lowSupportVerb:x|dpPathPred.pos.seq
-	x.lowSupportVerb:x|dpPathShared.pos.seq
-	x.lowSupportProp:x|dpPathShared.pos.seq
-	x.lowSupportProp.form

Table 6: Syntactic features

-	x_{-1}.lemma
-	x.dic + x_1.dic + x_{-1}.dic + x_2.dic + x_{-2}.dic + x_3.dic + x_{-3}.dic
-	x_{-1}.pos + x_1.pos
Set H	x.rm.lemma
-	x.rm.dprel
-	x.lm.dprel + x.pos
-	x.lowSupportNoun:x | dpPathArgu.dprel.seq
-	x.lowSupportNoun:x|dpPathArgu.dprel.seq + x.lowSupportProp:x|dpPathArgu.dprel.seq
-	x_{-1}.lemma
-	x.lemma + x_1.lemma + x_{-1}.lemma + x.dic + x_1.dic + x_{-1}.dic
-	x.form + x.lemma + x.pos + x.dic
Set B	x_{-2}.form + x_{-1}.form
-	x.highSupportNoun:x|dpTreeRelation
-	x.highSupportNoun:x|dpPathArgu.dprel.seq
-	x.lowSupportProp:x|dpPathShared.dprel.seq
-	x_{-1}.lm.form
-	x_1.form
-	x.pos + x.dic
-	x.hedge + x_1.hedge + x_{-1}.hedge
-	x.pos + x_1.pos + x_{-1}.pos + x_2.pos + x_{-2}.pos
Set S	x.children.dprel.bag
-	x.lemma + x.pphead.form
-	x.highSupportVerb.form
-	x.highSupportNoun:x|dpTreeRelation + x.form
-	x.lowSupportNoun:x|dpTreeRelation + x.form

Table 7: Selected improved feature template sets for BioScope corpus

on the in-domain data and evaluated our system on the in-domain and cross-domain evaluation set. All the experiments are implemented and run by Maximum Entropy Markov Models (McCallum, 2000).

4.1 Official results

The official results for tasks are in Table 8, in which three in-domain tests and cue matching result for biomedical texts are listed. For the first task for BioCorpus, our system gives F-score 0.8363 in in-domain test and for Wikipedia we give F-score 0.5618 in closed evaluation. For the second task, our system gives results in closed and open test, with F-score 0.4425 and 0.4441 respectively.

We compare the F-score of our system with the best in the final result in Table 9. We rank pretty high in Wikipedia hedge detection, while other three are quite steady but not prominent. This is mainly due to two reasons:

1. Feature selection procedures are not perfectly conducted.

2. Abstracts and fulltexts in BioScope are mixed to be the training set, which proves quite inappropriate when the evaluation set contains

only fulltext literature, since abstract and fulltext are quite different in terms of hedging.

Dataset		F-score	Best
BioScope	Task1-closed	0.8363	0.8636
	Task2-closed	0.4425	0.5732
	Cue-matching	0.7853	0.8134
Wikipedia	Task1-closed	0.5618	0.6017

Table 9: Comparing results with the best

4.2 Further results

Intact feature selection procedures for BioScope corpus are conducted after official outputs collections. The results of evaluation with completely selected features compared with the incomplete one are given in Table 7. The system performs a higher score on evaluation data (Table 10), which is more competitive in both tasks on BioScope corpus. The improvement for task 2 is significant, but the increase of performance of hedge cue detection is less remarkable. We believe that a larger fulltext training set and a more considerate training plan will help us to do better job in the future work.

Dataset		Complete	Incomplete
BioScope	Task1-closed	0.8522	0.8363
	Task2-closed	**0.5151**	0.4425
	Cue-matching	0.7990	0.7853

Table 10: Comparing improved outputs with the best

5 Conclusion

We describe the system that uses sequence labeling with normalized feature selection and rich features to detect hedges and find scopes for hedge cues. Syntactic features which are derived from dependencies are exploited, which prove to be quite favorable. The evaluation results show that our system is steady in performance and does pretty good hedging and scope finding in both BioScope corpus and Wikipedia, especially when the feature selection procedure is carefully and totally conducted. The results suggest that sequence labeling and a feature-oriented method are effective in such NLP tasks.

References

Michael Collins. 1999. *Head-Driven Statistical Models for Natural Language Parsing*. Ph.D. thesis, University of Pennsylvania.

Richárd Farkas, Veronika Vincze, György Móra, János Csirik, and György Szarvas. 2010. The CoNLL-2010 Shared Task: Learning to Detect Hedges and their Scope in Natural Language Text. In *Proceedings of the Fourteenth Conference on Computational Natural Language Learning (CoNLL-2010): Shared Task*, pages 1–12, Uppsala, Sweden, July. Association for Computational Linguistics.

Viola Ganter and Michael Strube. 2009. Finding hedges by chasing weasels: Hedge detection using Wikipedia tags and shallow linguistic features. In *Proceedings of the ACL-IJCNLP 2009 Conference Short Papers*, pages 173–176, Suntec, Singapore, 4, August.

Ken Hyland. 1996. Writing without conviction: Hedging in science research articles. *Applied Linguistics*, 17:433–54.

Zheng Ping Jiang and Hwee Tou Ng. 2006. Semantic role labeling of NomBank: A maximum entropy approach. In *Proceedings of the EMNLP-2006*, pages 138–145, Sydney, Australia.

Halil Kilicoglu and Sabine Bergler. 2008. Recognizing speculative language in biomedical research articles: a linguistically motivated perspective. *BMC Bioinformatics*, 9.

Marc Light, Xin Ying Qiu, and Padimini Srinivasan. 2004. The language of bioscience: Facts, speculations, and statements in between. In *Proc. of the BioLINK 2004*, pages 17–24.

Chrysanne Di Marco and Robert E. Mercer. 2004. Hedging in scientific articles as a means of classifying citations. In *Working Notes of the AAAI Spring Symposium on Exploring Attitude and Affect in Text: Theories and Applications*, pages 50–54.

Andrew McCallum. 2000. Maximum entropy markov models for information extraction and segmentation. In *Proceedings of ICML 2000*, pages 591–598, Stanford, California.

Ryan McDonald, Fernando Pereira, Kiril Ribarov, and Jan Hajic. 2005. Non-projective dependency parsing using spanning tree algorithms. In *Proceedings of HLT/EMNLP 05*, pages 523–530, Vancouver, Canada, October.

Ben Medlock and Ted Briscoe. 2008. Weakly supervised learning for hedge classification in scientific literature. In *Proceedings of 45th Annual Meeting of the ACL*, pages 992–999, Prague, Czech Republic, June.

Ben Medlock. 2008. Exploring hedge identification in biomedical literature. *Journal of Biomedical Informatics*, 41:636–654.

Dataset		TP	FP	FN	precision	recall	F-score
BioScope	Task1-closed	669	141	121	0.8259	0.8468	0.8363
	Task2-closed	441	519	592	0.4594	0.4269	0.4425
	Cue-matching	788	172	259	0.8208	0.7526	0.7853
Wikipedia	Task1-closed	991	303	1243	0.7658	0.4436	0.5618

Table 8: Official results of our submission for in-domain tasks

Roser Morante and Walter Daelemans. 2009. Learning the scope of hedge cues in biomedical texts. In *Proceedings of the Workshop on BioNLP*, pages 28–36, Boulder, Colorado, June.

Joakim Nivre and Mario Scholz. 2004. Deterministic dependency parsing of English text. In *Proceedings of COLING-2004*, pages 64–70, Geneva, Switzerland, August 23rd-27th.

Joakim Nivre. 2009. Non-projective dependency parsing in expected linear time. In *Proceedings of ACL-IJCNLP 2009*, pages 351–359, Suntec, Singapore, 2-7 August.

György Szarvas, Veronika Vincze, Richárd Farkas, and János Csirik. 2008. The BioScope corpus: annotation for negation, uncertainty and their scope in biomedical texts. In *Proceedings of BioNLP 2008*, pages 38–45, Columbus, Ohio, USA, June.

György Szarvas. 2008. Hedge classification in biomedical texts with a weakly supervised selection of keywords. In *Proceedings of ACL-08*, pages 281–289, Columbus, Ohio, USA, June.

Paul Thompson, Giulia Venturi, John McNaught, Simonetta Montemagni, and Sophia Ananiadou. 2008. Categorising modality in biomedical texts. In *Proc. of the LREC 2008 Workshop on Building and Evaluating Resources for Biomedical Text Mining*, pages 27–34, Marrakech.

Kristina Toutanova, Aria Haghighi, and Christopher D. Manning. 2005. Joint learning improves semantic role labeling. In *Proceedings of ACL-2005*, pages 589–596, Ann Arbor, USA.

Nianwen Xue. 2006. Semantic role labeling of nominalized predicates in Chinese. In *Proceedings of the Human Language Technology Conference of the NAACL (NAACL-2006)*, pages 431–438, New York City, USA, June.

Tong Zhang, Fred Damerau, and David Johnson. 2001. Text chunking using regularized winnow. In *Proceedings of the 39th Annual Meeting on Association for Computational Linguistics*, pages 539–546, Toulouse, France.

Hai Zhao, Wenliang Chen, Jun'ichi Kazama, Kiyotaka Uchimoto, and Kentaro Torisawa. 2009a. Multilingual dependency learning: Exploiting rich features for tagging syntactic and semantic dependencies. In *Proceedings of CoNLL-2009, June 4-5*, Boulder, Colorado, USA.

Hai Zhao, Wenliang Chen, and Chunyu Kit. 2009b. Semantic dependency parsing of NomBank and PropBank: An efficient integrated approach via a large-scale feature selection. In *Proceedings of EMNLP-2009*, pages 30–39, Singapore.

Hai Zhao, Wenliang Chen, Chunyu Kit, and Guodong Zhou. 2009c. Multilingual dependency learning: A huge feature engineering method to semantic dependency parsing. In *Proceedings of CoNLL-2009, June 4-5*, Boulder, Colorado, USA.

Learning to Detect Hedges and their Scope Using CRF

Qi Zhao, Chengjie Sun, Bingquan Liu, Yong Cheng
Harbin Institute of Technology, HIT
Harbin, PR China
{qzhao, cjsun, liubq, ycheng}@insun.hit.edu.cn

Abstract

Detecting speculative assertions is essential to distinguish the facts from uncertain information for biomedical text. This paper describes a system to detect hedge cues and their scope using CRF model. HCDic feature is presented to improve the system performance of detecting hedge cues on BioScope corpus. The feature can make use of cross-domain resources.

1 Introduction

George Lakoff (1972) first introduced linguistic hedges which indicate that speakers do not back up their opinions with facts. Later other linguists followed the social functions of hedges closely. Interestingly, Robin Lakoff (1975) introduces that hedges might be one of the "women's language features" as they have higher frequency in women's languages than in men's.

In the natural language processing domain, hedges are very important, too. Along with the rapid development of computational and biological technology, information extraction from huge amount of biomedical resource becomes more and more important. While the uncertain information can be a noisy factor sometimes, affecting the performance of information extraction. Biomedical articles are rich in speculative, while 17.70% of the sentences in the abstracts section of the BioScope corpus and 19.44% of the sentences in the full papers section contain hedge cues (Vincze et al., 2008). In order to distinguish facts from uncertain information, detecting speculative assertions is essential in biomedical text.

Hedge detection is paid attention to in the biomedical NLP field. Some researchers regard the problem as a text classification problem (a sentence is speculative or not) using simple machine learning techniques. Light et al. (2004) use substring matching to annotate speculation in biomedical text. Medlock and Briscoe (2007) create a hedging dataset and use an SVM classifier and get to a recall/precision Break-Even Point (BEP) of 0.76. They report that the POS feature performs badly, while lemma feature works well. Szarvas (2008) extends the work of Medlock and Briscoe with feature selection, and further improves the result to a BEP of 0.85 by using an external dictionary. Szarvas concludes that scientific articles contain multiword hedging cues more commonly, and the portability of hedge classifiers is limited. Halil Kilicoglu and Sabine Bergler (2008) propose an algorithm to weight hedge cues, which are used to evaluate the speculative strength of sentences. Roser Morante and Walter Daelemans (2009) introduce a metalearning approach to process the scope of negation, and they identify the hedge cues and their scope with a CRF classifier based on the original work. They extract a hedge cues dictionary as well, but do not combine it with the CRF model.

In the CoNLL-2010 shared task (Farkas et al., 2010), there are two subtasks for worldwide participants to choose:

- Task 1: learning to detect sentences contain-ing uncertainty.
- Task 2: learning to resolve the in-sentence scope of hedge cues.

This paper describes a system using CRF model for the task, which is partly based on Roser Morante and Walter Daelemans' work.

2 Hedges in the training dataset of BioScope and Wikipedia Corpus

Two training datasets, the BioScope and Wikipedia corpus are provided in the CoNLL-2010 shared task. BioScope consists of two parts, full articles and abstracts collected from biomedical papers. The latter is analyzed for having larger scale and more information of hedges.

In Table 1, the percentage of the speculative sentences in the abstracts section of BioScope corpus is the same as Vincze et al. (2008) reported. We can estimate 1.28 cue words per sentence, meaning that each sentence usually just has one hedge cue. The statistics in Table 1 also

Proceedings of the Fourteenth Conference on Computational Natural Language Learning: Shared Task, pages 100–105,
Uppsala, Sweden, 15-16 July 2010.

indicate that a hedge cue appears 26.7 times on average.

Dataset	ITEM	#
Abstracts of BioScope	Sentences	11871
	Certain sentences	9770
	Uncertain sentences	2101 (17.7%)
	Hedge cues	2694
	cues# per sentence	1.28
	Different hedge cues	143
	Max length of the cues	4
Wikipedia	Sentences	11111
	Certain sentences	8627
	Uncertain sentences	2484 (22.4%)
	weasel cues	3133
	Different weasel cues	1984
	Max length of the cues	13 words

Table 1: Statistics about the abstracts section of the BioScope corpus and Wikipedia corpus.

We extract all the hedge cues from the abstracts section of BioScope corpus, getting 143 different hedge cues and 101 cues with ignoring morphological changes. The maximum length of the cues is 4, with 1.44 words per hedge cue. This suggests that most hedge cues happen to be a single word. We assume that hedge cues set is a limited one in BioScope corpus. Most hedge cues could be identified if the known dataset of hedge cues is large enough. The cue words collected from the BioScope corpus play an important role in the speculative sentences detection.

In contrast to the biomedical abstracts, the weasel cues on Wikipedia corpus make a little difference. Most weasel cues consist of more than one word, and usually appear once. This leads to different results in our test.

A hedge cue word may appear in the non-speculative sentences. Occurrences of the four typical words in speculative and non-speculative sentences are counted.

As shown in Table 2, the cue words can be divided into two classes generally. The hedge cue words "feel" and "suggesting", which are grouped as one class, only act as hedge cues with never appearing in the non-speculative sentences. While "may" and "or" appear both in the speculative and non-speculative sentences, which are regard as the other one. Moreover, we treat the words "may" and "or" in the same class differently, while "may" is more likely to be a hedge cue than "or". The treatment is also unequal between "feel" and "suggesting". In the training datasets, the non-S#/S# ratio can give a weight to distinguish the words in each class. After all, we can divide the hedge cues into 4 groups.

word	S#	non-S#
feel	1	0
suggesting	150	0
may	516	1
or	118	6218

Table 2: Statistics of cue words. (S# short for the occurrence times in speculative sentences, non-S# for the count in non-speculative ones)

3 Methods

Conditional random fields (CRF) model was firstly introduced by Lafferty et al. (2001). CRF model can avoid the label bias problem of HMMs and other learning approaches. It was applied to solve sequence-labeling problems, and has shown good performance in NER task. We consider hedge cues detection as some kind of sequence-labeling problem, and the model will contribute to a good result.

We use CRF++ (version 0.51) to implement the CRF model. Cheng Yong, one of our team members has evaluated the several widespread used CRF tool kits, and he points out that CRF++ has better precision and recall but longer training time. Fortunately, the training time cost of BioScope corpus is acceptable. In our system, all the data training and testing processing step can be completed within 8 minutes (Intel Xeon 2.0GHz CPU, 6GB RAM). It is likely due to the small scale of the training dataset and the limited types of the annotation.

To identify sentences in the biomedical texts that contain unreliable or uncertain information (CoNLL-2010 shared task1), we start with hedge cues detection:

- If one or more than one hedge cues are detected in the sentence, then it will be annotated "uncertain"
- If not, the sentence will be tagged as "certain".

3.1 Detecting hedge cues

The BioScope corpus annotation guidelines [1] show that most typical instances of keywords can be grouped into 4 types as Auxiliaries, Verbs of hedging or verbs with speculative content, Adjectives or adverbs, and Conjunctions. So the POS (part-of-speech) is thought to be the feature reasonably. Lemma feature of the word and chunk features are also considered to improve system performance. Chunk features may help to the recognition of biomedical entity boundaries. GENIA Tagger (Tsuruoka et al., 2005) is employed to obtain part-of-speech (POS) features, chunk features and lemma features. It works well for biomedical documents.

In the biomedical abstracts section of BioScope corpus, the hedge cues are collected into a dictionary (HCDic, short for the Hedge Cues Dictionary). As mentioned in section 2, one hedge cue appears 26.7 times on average, and we assume the set of hedge cues is limited. The HCDic consist of 143 different hedge cues extracted from the abstracts. The dictionary (HCDic) extracted from the corpus is very valuable for the system. We can focus on whether the word such as "or" listed in table 2 is a hedge cue or not. The cue words in HCDic are divided into 4 different levels with the non-S#/S# ratio.

The four types are described as "L", "H", "FL" and "FH". "L" shows low confidence of the cue word being a hedge cue, while "H" indicates high confidence about it. The prefix 'F' for "FL"/"FH" shows false negatives may happen to the cue word in HCDic. The threshold for the non-S#/S# ratio to distinguish "FL" type from "FH" is set 1.0. As the non-S#/S# ratio of "L" and "H" is always zero, we set the hedge cue whose S# is more than 5 as "H" type as shown in table 3. The four types are added into the HCDic along with the hedge cues,

In our experiment, HCDic types of word sequence are tagged as follows:

- If words are found in HCDic using maximum matching method, label them with their types in HCDic. For hedges of multi-word, label them with *BI* scheme which will be described later.
- If not, tag the words as 'O' type.

[1] http://www.inf.u-szeged.hu/rgai/bioscope

The processing assigns each token of a sentence with an HCDic type. The *BIO* types for each token are involved as features for the CRF.

The HCDic can be expanded to a larger scale. Hedge cues extracted from different corpora can be added into HCDic, and regular expression of hedge cues can be used, too. This will be helpful to the usage of cross-domain resources.

word	S#	non-S#	type
feel	1	0	L
suggesting	150	0	H
may	516	1	FH
or	118	6218	FL

Table 3: Types of the HCDic words. (S# and non-S# have the same meaning as in Table 2)

The features F (F stands for all the Features) including unigram, bigram, and trigram types is used for CRF as follows:

F(n)(n=-2,-1,0,+1,+2)
F(n-1)F(n)(n=-1,0,+1,+2)
F(n-2)F(n-1)F(n) (n=0,+1,+2)
Where F(0) is the current feature, F(-1) is the previous one, F(1) is the following one, etc.

We regard each word in a sentence as a token and each token is tagged with a cue-label. The *BIO* scheme is used for tagging multiword hedge cues, such as "whether or not" in our HCDic. where B-cue (tag for "whether") represents that the token is the start of a hedge cue, I-cue (tag for "or", "not") stands for the inside of a hedge cue, and O (tag for the other words in the sentence) indicates that the token does not belong to any hedge cue.

We also have the method tested on Wikipedia corpus with a preprocessing of the HCDic.

Section 2 reports that most weasel cues in Wikipedia corpus are multiword, and usually appear once. Different from our assumption in BioScope corpus, the set of weasel cues seems numerous. The HCDic of Wikipedia would be not so valuable if it tags few tokens for a new given text. To prevent these from happening, a preprocessing of the HCDic is taken.

Most of the hedge cues in Wikipedia corpus accord with the structure of "adjective + noun" e.g. "many persons". Although most cue words appear just once, the adjective usually happens to be the same, and we call them core words. Therefore, the hedge cue dictionary (HCDic) can be simplified with the core words. It helps to reduce the scale of the hedges cues from 1984 cues down to 170. Then, we process the Wikipedia text the same way as the BioScope corpus.

3.2 Detecting scope of hedge cues

This phase (for CoNLL-2010 shared task 2) is based on Roser Morante and Walter Daelemans' scope detection system.

CRF model is applied in this part, too. The word, POS, lemma, chunk and HCDic tags are also applied to be the features as in the step of hedge cues detection. In section 3.1, we can obtain the hedge cues in a sentence. The scope relies on its cue vary much. We make the *BIO* schema of detected hedge cues to be the important features of this part. Besides, the sentences tagged as "certain" type are neglected in this step.

Here is an example of golden standard of scope label.

<sentence id="S5.149"> We <xcope id="X5.149. 3"><cue ref="X5.149.3" type= "specula-tion"> propose </cue> that IL-10-producing Th1 cells <xcope id="X5.149.2"> <cue ref="X5.149.2" type= "speculation" >may</cue> be the essential regulators of acute infection-induced inflammation </xcope> and that such "self-regulating" Th1 cells <xcope id= "X5.149.1"> <cue ref= "X5.149.1" type= "speculation" >may</cue> be essential for the infection to be cleared without inducing immune-mediated pathology </xcope> </xcope>.

As shown, each scope is a block with a beginning and an end, and we refer to the beginning of scope as scope head (*<xcope...>*), and the end of the scope as scope tail (*</xcope>*).

The types of the scope are labeled as:

1. Label the token next to scope head as "xcope-H" (e.g. *propose, may*)
2. Tag the token before scope tail as "xcope-T"(e.g. *pathology* for both scopes)
3. The other words tag 'O' , including the words inside the scope and out of it. This is very different from the *BIO* scheme.

The template for each feature is the same as in section 3.1.

Following are our rules to form the scope of a hedge:

1. Most hedge cues have only one scope tag, meaning there is one-to-one relationship between hedge cue and its scope.
2. The scope labels may be nested.
3. The scope head of the cue words appears nearest before hedge cue.
4. The scope tail appears far from the cue word.
5. The most frequent head/tail positions of the scope are shown in Table 4.
   a) The scope head usually is just before the cue words.
   b) The scope tail appears in the end of the sentence frequently.

Scopes of hedge cues in BioScope corpus should be found for the shared task. The training dataset of abstract part is analyzed for its larger scale

item	Following strings with high frequency	%
1 scope head	*<cue...>*(cue words)	0.861
2 scope tail	'.'(sentence end)	0.695
	</xcope> (another scope tail)	0.144
	',' ';' ':'	0.078

Table 4: Statistics of the strings nearby the scope head and tail. Item 1 shows the word follow scope head, and item 2 shows the frequent words next to the scope tail.

We analyze the words around the scope head and the scope tail. The item 1 in Table 4 shows that 86.1% of the following words of the scope head are hedge cues. Other following words not listed are less than 1%, according to our statistics. The item 2 lists the strings with high frequency next to the scope tail as well. The first 2 words in item 2 can be combined sometimes, so the percentage of scope tail at the end of the sentence can be more than 80%. The strings ahead of scope head and tail not listed are also counted, but they do not give such valuable information as the two items listed in Table 4.

Therefore, when the CRF model gives low confidence, we just set the most probable positions of scope head and tail.

For the one-to-one relationship between hedge cues and their scopes, we make rules to insure each cue has only one scope, including the scope head and scope tail.

Rule 1: if more than one scope heads or tails are predicted, we get rid of the farther head or nearer tail.

Rule 2: if none of scope head or tail is predicted, the head is set to the word just before the cue words; the tail is set at the end of the sentence.

Rule 3: if one scope head and one tail are predicted, we consider them the result of scope detection.

4 Results

Our experiments are based on the CoNLL-2010 shared task's datasets, including BioScope and Wikipedia corpus. All the experiments for BioScope use abstracts and full papers for training data and the provided evaluation for testing.

We employ CRF model to detect the hedge cues in the BioScope. The experiments are carried out on different feature sets: words sequence with the chunk feature only, lemma feature only and POS feature only. The effect of the HCDic feature is also evaluated.

Features	prec.	recall	F-score
Chunk only	0.7236	0.6275	0.6721
Lemma only	0.7278	0.6103	0.6639
POS only	0.7320	0.6208	0.6718
Without HCDic	0.7150	0.6447	0.6781
ALL	0.7671	0.7393	0.7529

Table 5: Results at hedge cue-level

As described in section 1 of this paper, the feature of POS may be not so significant as the lemma, but we do not agree with this point of view for given POS feature's better performance in F-score (in Table 5). The interesting cue-level result does not go into for time limitations. The F-score of the three features, chunk, lemma and POS are approximately equal. When all of the three features are used for CRF model, the performance is not improved so significantly. The recall rate is a bit low in the experiment without HCDic features. As shown in Table 5, the feature of HCDic is effective to get a better score both in precision rate and in recall rate. As our assumption, hedges in the evaluation dataset are limited, too. Most of them along with some non-hedges can be tagged with HCDic. Then the tag could contribute to a good recall. It also helps the classifier to focus on whether the words with "L", "FL", and "FH" are hedge cues or not, which will be good for a better precision.

With detected hedge cues, we can get sentences containing uncertainty for the shared task 1. A sentence is tagged as "uncertain" type if any hedge cue is found in it.

	precision	recall	F-score
Without HCDic	0.8965	0.7898	0.8398
ALL	0.8344	0.8481	0.8412

Table 6: Evaluation result of task 1

Statistics in Table 6 show that even poor performance in cue-level test can get a satisfactory F-score of speculative sentences detection as well. It seems that hedges detection at cue-level is not proportionate to the sentence-level. Think about instance of more than one cues in a sentence such as the example of golden standard in section 3.2, the sentence will be tagged even if only one hedge cue has been identified (lower recall at cue-level). Moreover, in the speculative sentence with one hedge cue, false positives (lower precision at cue-level) can also lead to the correct result at sentence-level.

The method is also tested on Wikipedia corpus, using provided training dataset and evaluation data. The method has a bad performance in our close test. The results are listed in Table 7.

As talked in section 2, hedges in Wikipedia corpus are very different from in BioScope corpus. Besides, the string matching method for simplified HCDic is not so effective. The usefulness of HCDic is not so significant for a good recall in Wikipedia corpus.

dataset	precision	recall	F-score
Wikipedia	0.7075	0.2001	0.3120
BioScope	0.7671	0.7393	0.7529

Table 7: Results of weasel/hedge detection in Wikipedia and BioScope corpus.

In CoNLL-2010 shared task 2, the evaluation result shows our precision, recall and F-score are 34.8%, 41% and 37.6%. The performance of identifying the scope relies on the cue-level detection. Therefore, the false positive and false negatives of hedge cues can lead to recognition errors. The result shows that our lexical-level method for the semantic problem is limited. For the time constraints, we do not probe deeply.

5 Conclusions

This paper presents an approach for extracting the hedge cues and their scopes in BioScope corpus using two CRF models for CoNLL-2010 shared task. In the first task, the HCDic feature is proposed to improve the system performances, getting better performance (84.1% in F-score) than the baseline. The HCDic feature is also helpful to make use of cross-domain resources. The comparison of our methods based on between BioScope and Wikipedia corpus is given, which shows that ours are good at hedge cues detection in BioScope corpus but short at the in Wikipedia corpus. To detect the scope of hedge cues, we make rules to post process the text. For future work, we will look forward to constructing regulations for the HCDic to improve our system.

References

Richárd Farkas, Veronika Vincze, György Móra, János Csirik, and György Szarvas. 2010. The CoNLL-2010 Shared Task: Learning to Detect Hedges and their Scope in Natural Language Text. In *Proceedings of the Fourteenth Conference on Computational Natural Language Learning (CoNLL-2010): Shared Task*, pages 1–12, Uppsala, Sweden, July. Association for Computational Linguistics.

Halil Kilicoglu, and Sabine Bergler. 2008. Recognizing speculative language in biomedical research articles: a linguistically motivated perspective. *BMC Bioinformatics*, 9(Suppl 11):S10.

John Lafferty, Andrew K. McCallum, and Fernando Pereira. 2001. Conditional random fields: probabilistic models for segmenting and labeling sequence data. In *ICML*, pages 282–289.

George Lakoff. 1972. Hedges: a study in meaning criteria and the logic of fuzzy concepts. *Chicago Linguistics Society Papers*, 8:183–228.

Marc Light, Xin Y. Qiu, and Padmini Srinivasan. 2004 The language of bioscience: facts,speculations, and statements in between. In *BioLINK 2004: Linking Biological Literature, Ontologies and Databases*, pages 17–24.

Ben Medlock, and Ted Briscoe. 2007. Weakly supervised learning for hedge classification in scientific literature. In *Proceedings of ACL 2007*, pages 992–999.

Roser Morante, and Walter Daelemans. 2009. Learning the scope of hedge cues in biomedical texts. In *Proceedings of the BioNLP 2009 Workshop*, pages 28-36, Boulder, Colorado, June 2009. Association for Computational Linguistics.

Roser Morante, and Walter Daelemans. 2009. A metalearning approach to processing the scope of negation. In *Proceedings of CoNLL-2009*. Boulder, Colorado.

György Szarvas. 2008. Hedge classification in biomedical texts with a weakly supervised selection of keywords. In *Proceedings of ACL 2008*, pages 281–289, Columbus, Ohio, USA. ACL.

Yoshimasa Tsuruoka, Yuka Tateishi, Jin-Dong Kim, Tomoko Ohta, John McNaught, Sophia Ananiadou, and Jun'ichi Tsujii. 2005. Developing a robust part-of-speech tagger for biomedical text. In: *Advances in Informatics, PCI 2005*, pages 382–392.

Veronika Vincze, György Szarvas, Richárd Farkas, György Móra, and János Csirik. 2008. The BioScope corpus: biomedical texts annotated for uncertainty, negation and their scopes. *BMC Bioinformatics*, 9(Suppl 11):S9.

Exploiting Multi-Features to Detect Hedges and Their Scope in Biomedical Texts

Huiwei Zhou[1], Xiaoyan Li[2], Degen Huang[3], Zezhong Li[4], Yuansheng Yang[5]
Dalian University of Technology
Dalian, Liaoning, China
{[1]zhouhuiwei, [3]huangdg, [5]yangys}@dlut.edu.cn
[2]lixiaoyan@mail.dlut.edu.cn
[4]lizezhonglaile@163.com

Abstract

In this paper, we present a machine learning approach that detects hedge cues and their scope in biomedical texts. Identifying hedged information in texts is a kind of semantic filtering of texts and it is important since it could extract speculative information from factual information. In order to deal with the semantic analysis problem, various evidential features are proposed and integrated through a Conditional Random Fields (CRFs) model. Hedge cues that appear in the training dataset are regarded as keywords and employed as an important feature in hedge cue identification system. For the scope finding, we construct a CRF-based system and a syntactic pattern-based system, and compare their performances. Experiments using test data from CoNLL-2010 shared task show that our proposed method is robust. F-score of the biological hedge detection task and scope finding task achieves 86.32% and 54.18% in in-domain evaluations respectively.

1. Introduction

Identifying sentences in natural language texts which contain unreliable or uncertain information is an increasingly important task of information extraction since the extracted information that falls in the scope of hedge cues cannot be presented as factual information. Szarvas et al. (2008) report that 17.69% of the sentences in the abstracts section of the BioScope corpus and 22.29% of the sentences in the full papers section contain hedge cues. Light et al. (2004) estimate that 11% of sentences in MEDLINE abstracts contain speculative fragments. Szarvas (2008) reports that 32.41% of gene names mentioned in the hedge classification dataset described in Medlock and Briscoe (2007) appear in a speculative sentence. Many Wikipedia articles contain a specific *weasel tag* which mark sentences as non-factual (Ganter and Strube, 2009).

There are some Natural Language Processing (NLP) researches that demonstrate the benefit of hedge detection experimentally in several subjects, such as the ICD-9-CM coding of radiology reports and gene named Entity Extraction (Szarvas, 2008), question answering systems (Riloff et al., 2003), information extraction from biomedical texts (Medlock and Briscoe, 2007).

The CoNLL-2010 Shared Task (Farkas et al., 2010) "Learning to detect hedges and their scope in natural language text" proposed two tasks related to speculation research. Task 1 aimed to identify sentences containing uncertainty and Task 2 aimed to resolve the in-sentence scope of hedge cues. We participated in both tasks.

In this paper, a machine learning system is constructed to detect sentences in texts which contain uncertain or unreliable information and to find the scope of hedge cues. The system works in two phases: in the first phase uncertain sentences are detected, and in the second phase in-sentence scopes of hedge cues are found. In the uncertain information detecting phase, hedge cues play an important role. The sentences that contain at least one hedge cue are considered as uncertain, while sentences without cues are considered as factual. Therefore, the task of uncertain information detection can be converted into the task of hedge cue identification. Hedge cues that appear in the training dataset are collected and used as keywords to find hedges. Furthermore, the detected keywords are employed as an important feature in hedge cue identification system. In addition to keywords, various evidential features are proposed and integrated through a machine learning model. Finding the scope of a hedge cue is to determine at sentence level which words are affected by the

Proceedings of the Fourteenth Conference on Computational Natural Language Learning: Shared Task, pages 106–113,
Uppsala, Sweden, 15-16 July 2010.

hedge cue. In the scope finding phase, we construct a machine learning-based system and a syntactic pattern-based system, and compare their performances.

For the learning algorithm, Conditional random fields (CRFs) is adopted relying on its flexible feature designs and good performance in sequence labeling problems as described in Lafferty et al. (2001). The main idea of CRFs is to estimate a conditional probability distribution over label sequences, rather than over local directed label sequences as with Hidden Markov Models (Baum and Petrie, 1966) and Maximum Entropy Markov Models (McCallum et al., 2000).

Evaluation is carried out on the CoNLL-2010 shared task (Farkas et al., 2010) dataset in which sentences containing uncertain information are annotated. For the task of detecting uncertain information, uncertain cues are annotated. And for the task of finding scopes of hedge cues, hedge cues and their scope are annotated as shown in sentence (a): hedge cue *indicate that*, and its scope *indicate that dhtt is widely expressed at low levels during all stages of Drosophila development* are annotated.

(a)*Together, these data <xcope id="X8.74.1"><cue ref="X8.74.1" type="speculation">indicate that</cue> dhtt is widely expressed at low levels during all stages of Drosophila development</xcope>.*

2. Related Work

In the past few years, a number of studies on hedge detection from NLP perspective have been proposed. Elkin et al. (2005) exploited handcrafted rule-based negation/uncertainty detection modules to detect the negation or uncertainty information. However, their detection modules were hard to develop due to the lack of standard corpora that used for evaluating the automatic detection and scope resolution. Szarvas et al. (2008) constructed a corpus annotated for negations, speculations and their linguistic scopes. It provides a common resource for the training, testing and comparison of biomedical NLP systems.

Medlock and Briscoe (2007) proposed an automatic classification of hedging in biomedical texts using weakly supervised machine learning. They started with a very limited amount of annotator-labeled seed data. Then they iterated and acquired more training seeds without much manual intervention. The best classifier using their model achieved 0.76 precision/recall break-even-point (BEP). Further, Medlock (2008) illuminated the hedge identification task including annotation guidelines, theoretical analysis and discussion. He argued for separation of the acquisition and classification phases in semi-supervised machine learning method and presented a probabilistic acquisition model. In probabilistic model he assumed bigrams and single terms as features based on the intuition that many hedge cues are bigrams and single terms and achieves a peak performance of around 0.82 BEP.

Morante and Daelemans (2009) presented a meta-learning system that finds the scope of hedge cues in biomedical texts. The system worked in two phases: in the first phase hedge cues are identified, and in the second phase the full scopes of these hedge cues are found. The performance of the system is tested on three subcorpora of the BioScope corpus. In the hedge finding phase, the system achieves an F-score of 84.77% in the abstracts subcorpus. In the scope finding phase, the system with predicted hedge cues achieves an F-score of 78.54% in the abstracts subcorpus.

The research on detecting uncertain information is not restricted to analyze biomedical documents. Ganter and Strube (2009) investigated Wikipedia as a source of training data for the automatic hedge detection using word frequency measures and syntactic patterns. They showed that the syntactic patterns worked better when using the manually annotated test data, word frequency and distance to the weasel tag was sufficient when using Wikipedia weasel tags themselves.

3. Identifying Hedge Cues

Previous studies (Light et al., 2004) showed that the detection of hedging could be solved effectively by looking for specific keywords which were useful for deciding whether a sentence was speculative. Szarvas (2008) reduces the number of keyword candidates without excluding helpful keywords for hedge classification. Here we also use a simple keyword-based hedge cue detection method.

3.1 Keyword-based Hedge Cue Detection

In order to recall as many hedge cues as possible,

all hedge cues that appear in the training dataset are used as keywords. Hedge cues are represented by one or more tokens. The list of all hedge cues in the training dataset is comprised of 143 cues. 90 hedge cues are unigrams, 24 hedge cues are bigrams, and the others are trigrams, four-grams and five-grams. Besides, hedge cues that appear in the training dataset and their synonyms in WordNet[1] are also selected as keywords for hedge cue detection. The complete list of them contains 438 keywords, 359 of which are unigrams. Many tokens appear in different grams cues, such as *possibility* appears in five-grams cue *cannot rule out the possibility*, four-gram cue *cannot exclude the possibility*, trigrams cue *raise the possibility* and unigram cue *possibility*. To find the complete cues, keywords are matched through a maximum matching method (MM) (Liu et al., 1994). For example, though *indicate* and *indicate that* are both in keywords list, *indicate that* is extracted as a keyword in sentence (a) through MM.

3.2 CRF-based Hedge Cue Detection

Candidate cues are extracted based on keywords list in keyword-based hedge cue detection stage. But the hedge cue is extremely ambiguous, so CRFs are applied to correct the false identification results that occurred in the keyword-based hedge cue detection stage. The extracted hedge cues are used as one feature for CRFs-based hedge cue detection.

A CRF identifying model is generated by applying a CRF tool to hedge cue labeled sequences. Firstly, hedge cue labeled sentences are transformed into a set of tokenized word sequences with IOB2 labels:

B-cue Current token is the beginning of a hedge cue

I-cue Current token is inside of a hedge cue

O Current token is outside of any hedge cue

For sentence (a) the system assigns the B-cue tag to *indicate*, the I-cue tag to *that* and the O tag to the rest of tokens as shown in Figure1.

The hedge cues that are found by keyword-based method is also given IOB2 labels feature as shown in Figure1.

[1] Available at http://wordnet.princeton.edu/

Text	Keyword Labels Feature	Cue Labels
...	...	...
these	O	O
data	O	O
indicate	B	B-cue
that	I	I-cue
dhtt	O	O
is	O	O
...	...	...

Figure 1: Example of Cues labels and Keywords labels Feature

Diverse features including keyword feature are employed to our CRF-based hedge cue detection system.

(1) Word Features

• *Word (i) (i=-n, ..., −2, −1, 0, +1, +2, ..., +n)*

Where *Word (0)* is the current word, *Word (-1)* is the first word to the left, *Word (1)* is the first word to the right, etc.

(2) Stem Features

The motivation for stemming in hedge identification is that distinct morphological forms of hedge cues are used to convey the same semantics (Medlock, 2008). In our method, GENIA Tagger[2] (Tsuruoka et al., 2005) is applied to get stem features.

• *Stem (i) (i=-n, ..., −2, −1, 0, +1, +2, ..., +n)*

where *Stem (0)* is the stem for the current word, *Stem(-1)* is the first stem to the left, *Stem (1)* is the first stem to the right, etc.

(3) Part-Of-Speech Features

Since most of hedge cues in the training dataset are verbs, auxiliaries, adjectives and adverbs. Therefore, Part-of-Speech (POS) may provide useful evidence about the hedge cues and their boundaries. GENIA Tagger is also used to generate this feature.

• *POS (i) (i=-n, ..., −2, −1, 0, +1, +2, ..., +n)*

where *POS (0)* is the current POS, *POS (-1)* is the first POS to the left, *POS (1)* is the first POS to the right, etc.

(4) Chunk Features

Some hedge cues are chunks consisting of more than one token. Chunk features may contribute to the hedge cue boundaries. We use GENIA Tagger to get chunk features for each token. The

[2] Available at http://www-tsujii.is.s.u-tokyo.ac.jp/GENIA/tagger/

chunk features include unigram, bigram, and trigram types, listed as follows:

• *Chunk (i) (i=-n, ..., −2, −1, 0, +1, +2, ..., +n)*

• *Chunk (i−1)+Chunk(i) (i =−1,0,+1,+2)*

• *Chunk (i−2) + Chunk (i−1)+Chunk (i) (i= 0,+1,+2)*

where *Chunk (0)* is the chunk label for the current word, *Chunk (−1)* is the chunk label for the first word to the left , *Chunk (1)* is the chunk label for the first word to the right, etc.

(5) Keyword Features

Keyword labels feature is an important feature.

• *Keyword (i) (i=-n, ..., −2, −1, 0, +1, +2, ..., +n)*

where *Keyword (0)* is the current keyword label, *Keywords (-1)* is the keyword label for the first keyword to the left, *Keywords (1)* is the keyword label for the first keyword to the right, etc.

Feature sets can be easily redefined by changing the window size *n*. The relationship of the window size and the F-score observed in our experiments will be reported in Section 5.

4. Hedge Scope Finding

In this task, a CRFs classifier is applied to predict for all the tokens in the sentence whether a token is the first token of the scope sequence (F-scope), the last token of the scope sequence (L-scope), or neither (None). For sentence (a) in Section 1, the classifier assigns F-scope to *indicate*, L-scope to *benchmarks*, and None to the rest of the tokens. Only sentences that assigned cues in the first phase are selected for hedge scope finding. Besides, a syntactic pattern-based system is constructed, and compared with the CRF-based system.

4.1 CRF-based System

The features that used in CRF-based hedge cue detection systems are also used for scope finding except for the keyword features. The features are:

(1) Word Features

• *Word (i) (i=-n, ..., −2, −1, 0, +1, +2, ..., +n)*

(2) Stem Features

• *Stem (i) (i=-n, ..., −2, −1, 0, +1, +2, ..., +n)*

(3) Part-Of-Speech Features

• *POS (i) (i=-n, ..., −2, −1, 0, +1, +2, ..., +n)*

(4) Chunk Features

The chunk features include unigram, bigram, and trigram types, listed as follows:

• *Chunk (i) (i=-n, ..., −2, −1, 0, +1, +2, ..., +n)*

• *Chunk (i−1)+Chunk(i) (i =−1,0,+1,+2)*

• *Chunk (i−2) + Chunk (i−1)+Chunk (i) (i= 0,+1,+2)*

(5) Hedge cues Features

Hedge cues labels that are doped out in Task 1 are selected as an important feature.

• *Hedge cues (i) (i=-n, ..., −2, −1, 0, +1, +2, ..., +n)*

where *Hedge cues (0)* is the cue label for the current word, *Hedge cues (−1)* is the cue label for the first word to the left , *Hedge cues (1)* is the cue label for the first word to the right, etc.

The scope of the sequence must be consistent with the hedge cues. That means that the number of the F-scope and L-scope must be the same with the hedge cues. However, sometimes their number predicted by classifier is not same. Therefore, we need to process the output of the classifier to get the complete sequence of the scope. The following post processing rules are adapted.

• If the number of F-scope, L-scope and hedge cue is the same, the sequence will start at the token predicted as F-scope, and end at the token predicted as L-scope.

• If one token has been predicted as F-scope and none has been predicted as L-scope, the sequence will start at the token predicted as F-scope and end at the end of the sentence. Since when marking the scopes of keywords, linguists always extend the scope to the biggest syntactic unit possible.

• If one token has been predicted as L-scope and none has been predicted as F-scope, the sequence will start at the hedge cue and end at the token predicted as L-scope. Since scopes must contain their cues.

• If one token has been predicted as F-scope and more than one has been predicted as L-scope, the sequence will end at the first token predicted as L-scope. Statistics from prediction on CoNLL-2010 Shared Task evaluation data show that 20 sentences are in this case. And the scope of 6 sentences extends to the first L-scope, and the scope of 3 sentences end at the last L-scope, the others are predicted mistakenly. Our system prediction and gold-standard annotation are shown in sentence (b1) and (b2) respectively.

(b1) our system annotation:
dRas85DV12 <xcope id="X3.64.1"><cue ref="X3.64.1" type="speculation">may</cue> be more potent than dEGFRλ</xcope> because dRas85DV12 can activate endogenous PI3K signaling</xcope> [16].

(b2) gold-standard annotation:
dRas85DV12 <xcope id="X3.64.1"><cue ref="X3.64.1" type="speculation">may</cue> be more potent than dEGFRλ</xcope> because dRas85DV12 can activate endogenous PI3K signaling [16].

• If one token has been predicted as L-scope and more than one has been predicted as F-scope, the sequence will start at the first token predicted as F-scope.
• If an L-scope is predicted before an F-scope, the sequence will start at the token predicted as F-scope, and finished at the end of the sentence.

4.2 Syntactic Pattern-based System

Hedge scopes usually can be determined on the basis of syntactic patterns dependent on the cue. Therefore, a syntactic pattern-based system is also implemented for hedge scope finding. When the sentence is predicted as uncertain, the toolkit of Stanford Parser[3] (Klein and Manning, 2003) is utilized to parse the sentence into a syntactic tree, which can release a lot of information about the grammatical structure of sentences that is beneficial for the finding of hedge scope. For sentence (c) the Stanford Parser gives the syntactic tree as showed in Figure 2.

(c) *This <xcope id="X*.*.*"><cue ref="X*.*.*" type="speculation"> may </cue> represent a viral illness</xcope>.*

It is obvious to see from the syntactic tree, all the words of the parsed sentence concentrate at the places of leaves. We use the following rules to find the scope.

• If the tag of the word is "B-cue", it is predicted as F-scope.
• If the POS of the hedge cue is verbs and auxiliaries, the L-scope is signed at the end of the clause.
• If the POS of the hedge cue is attributive adjectives, the L-scope is signed at the following noun phrase.
• If the POS of the hedge cue is prepositions, the L-scope is signed at the following noun phrase.
• If none of the above rules apply, the scope of a hedge cue starts with the hedge cue and ends at the following clause.

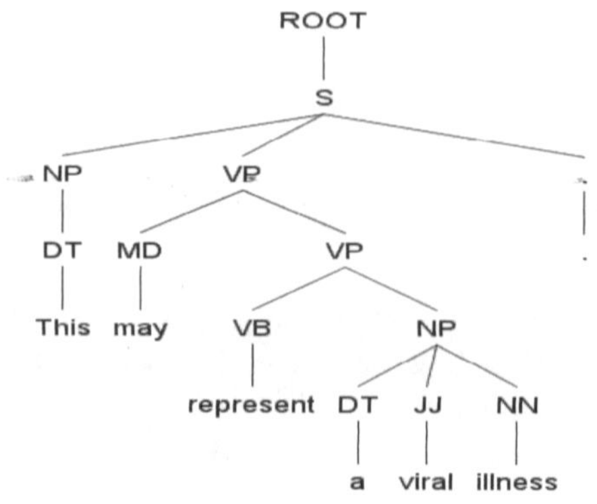

Figure 2: Syntactic tree parsed by Stanford Parser

5. Experiments and Discussion

We evaluate our method using CoNLL-2010 shared task dataset. The evaluation of uncertain information detection task is carried out using the sentence-level F-score of the uncertainty class. As mentioned in Section 1, Task 1 is converted into the task of hedge cues identification. Sentences can be classified as certain or uncertain according to the presence or absence of a few hedge cues within the sentences. In task of finding in-sentence scopes of hedge cues, a scope is correct if all the tokens in the sentence have been assigned the correct scope class for a specific hedge signal.

5.1 Detecting Uncertain Information

In the CoNLL-2010 Shared Task 1, our in-domain system obtained the F-score of 85.77%. Sentence-level results of in-domain systems under the condition *n=3* (window size) are summarized in Table 1.

System	Prec.	Recall	F-score
Keyword-based	41.15	99.24	58.18
CRF-based system (without keyword features)	88.66	80.13	84.18
CRF-based system + keyword features	86.21	84.68	85.44
CRF-based system	86.49	85.06	85.77

[3] Available at http://nlp.stanford.edu/software/lex-parser.shtml

+ keyword features + MM			

Table 1: Official in-domain results for Task 1 (*n=3*)

The keyword-based system extracts hedge cues through maximum matching method (MM). As can be seen in Table 1, the system achieves a high recall (99.24%). This can be explained that almost all of the hedge cues in the test dataset are in the keywords list. However, it also brings about the low precision since not all potential speculative keywords convey real speculation. So the keyword-based method can be combined with our CRF-based method to get better performance.

All the CRF-based systems in Table 1 significantly outperform the keyword-based system, since the multi-features achieve a high precision. And the result with keyword features is better than the result without it. The keyword features improve the performance by recalling 39 true positives. In addition, further improvement is achieved by using Maximum Matching method (MM).

In the test dataset, there should be a few hedge cues not in the training dataset. And the additional resources besides the manually labeled data are allowed for in-domain predictions. Therefore, the synonyms of the keywords can be used for in-domain systems. The synonyms of the keywords are added to the keywords list, and are expected to improve detecting performance. The synonyms are obtained from WordNet.

Table 2 shows the relationship between the window size and the sentence-level results. This table shows the results with and without synonyms. Generally, the results with synonyms are better than the results without them. With respect to window size, the wider the window size, the better precision can be achieved. However, large window size leads to low recall which is probably because of data sparse. The best F-score 86.32 is obtained when the window size is +/-4.

Window size	**Synonyms**	**Prec.**	**Recall**	**F-score**
1	without synonyms	85.27	86.46	85.86
	with synonyms	85.66	86.20	85.93
2	without synonyms	86.35	85.70	86.02
	with synonyms	86.14	84.94	85.53
3	without synonyms	86.49	85.06	85.77
	with synonyms	86.69	84.94	85.81
4	without synonyms	86.34	84.81	85.57
	with synonyms	87.21	85.44	**86.32**

Table 2: Sentence-level results relative to synonyms and window size for speculation detection

5.2 Finding Hedge Scope

In the CoNLL-2010 Shared Task 2, our in-domain system obtained the F-score of 44.42%. Table 3 shows the scope finding results. For in-domain scope finding system, we use the hedge cues extracted by the submitted CRF-based in-domain system (the best result 85.77 in Table 1). The result of the syntactic pattern-based system is not ideal probably due to the syntactic parsing errors and limited annotation rules.

System	**Prec.**	**Recall**	**F-score**
syntactic pattern-based	44.31	42.59	43.45
CRF-based	45.32	43.56	44.42

Table 3: Official in-domain results for Task 2

Through analyzing the false of our scope finding system, we found that many of our false scope were caused by such scope as sentence (d1) shows. Our CRF-based system signed the L-scope to the end of sentence mistakenly. The incorrectly annotation of our system and gold-standard annotation are shown in sentence (d1) and (d2) respectively. So an additional rule is added to our CRF-based system to correct the L-scope. The rule is:

- If one token has been predicted as L-scope, and if the previous token is ")", or "]", the L-scope will be modified just before the paired token "(" or "[".

(d1) The incorrectly predicted version:
These factors were <cue ref="X1.178.1" type="speculation">presumed</cue> to be pathogenic</xcope> (85).
(d2) Gold-standard annotation:
These factors were <cue ref="X1.178.1" type="speculation">presumed</cue> to be pathogenic (85) </xcope>.

F-score is reached to 51.83 by combining this additional rule with the submitted CRF-based in-domain system as shown in Table 4.

TP	FP	FN	Prec.	Recall	F-score
525	468	508	52.87	50.82	51.83

Table 4: Official in-domain results for Task 2

Several best results of Task 1 are exploited to investigate the relationship between the window size and the scope finding results. From the results of Table 5, we can see that the case of *n=4* gives the best precision, recall and F-score. And the case of *n=2* and the case of *n=3* based on the same task 1 system have a very similar score. With respect to the different systems of Task 1, in principle, the higher the F-score of Task 1, the better the performance of Task 2 can be expected. However, the result is somewhat different from the expectation. The best F-score of Task 2 is obtained under the case *F-score (task 1) =86.02*. This indicates that it is not certain that Task 2 system based on the best Task 1 result gives the best scope finding performance.

F-score (Task 1)	Window size	Prec.	Recall	F-score
86.32	4	54.32	51.69	52.98
	3	52.59	50.05	51.29
	2	52.90	50.34	51.59
86.02	4	54.85	52.57	**53.68**
	3	53.13	50.92	52.00
	2	53.13	50.92	52.00
85.86	4	54.19	52.57	53.37
	3	52.50	50.92	51.70
	2	52.50	50.92	51.70

Table 5: Scope finding results relative to the results of task 1 and window size

In the case that scopes longer than *n* (window size) words, the relevant cue will thus not fall into the +/-n word window of the L-scope and all hedge cue features will be O tag. The hedge cue features will be useless for detecting L-scopes. Taking into account the importance of hedge cue features, the following additional features are also incorporated to capture hedge cue features.

- *Distance to the closest preceding hedge cue*
- *Distance to the closest following hedge cue*
- *Stem of the closest preceding hedge cue*
- *Stem of the closest following hedge cue*
- *POS of the closest preceding hedge cue*
- *POS of the closest following hedge cue*

Table 6 shows the results when the additional hedge cue features are used. The results with additional hedge cue feature set are constantly better than the results without them. In most of cases, the improvement is significant. The best F-score 54.18% is achieved under the case *F-score (task 1) =86.02* and *n=4*.

F-score (Task 1)	Window size	Prec.	Recall	F-score
86.32	4	54.73	52.08	53.37
	3	54.22	51.60	52.88
	2	53.41	50.82	52.08
86.02	4	55.35	53.05	**54.18**
	3	54.75	52.47	53.58
	2	53.94	51.69	52.79
85.86	4	54.49	52.86	53.66
	3	53.79	52.18	52.97
	2	53.09	51.50	52.29

Table 6: Scope finding results relative to the results of Task 1 and window size with additional cue features

The upper-bound results of CRF-based system assuming gold-standard annotation of hedge cues are show in Table 7.

TP	FP	FN	Prec.	Recall	F-score
618	427	415	59.14	59.83	59.48

Table 7: Scope finding result with gold-standard hedge signals

A comparative character analysis of syntactic pattern-based method and CRF-based method will be interesting, which can provide insights leading to better methods in the future.

6. Conclusion

In this paper, we have exploited various useful features evident to detect hedge cues and their scope in biomedical texts. For hedge detection task, keyword-based system is integrated with CRF-based system by introducing keyword features to CRF-based system. Our experimental results show that the proposed method improves the performance of CRF-based system by the additional keyword features. Our system has achieved a state of the art F-score 86.32% on the sentence-level evaluation. For scope finding task, two different systems are established: CRF-based and syntactic pattern-based system. CRF-based system outperforms syntactic pattern-based system due to its evidential features.

In the near future, we will improve the hedge cue detection performance by investigating more implicit information of potential keywords. On the other hand, we will study on how to improve scope finding performance by integrating CRF-based and syntactic pattern-based scope finding systems.

References

Leonard E. Baum, and Ted Petrie. 1966. Statistical inference for probabilistic functions of finite state Markov chains. *Annals of Mathematical Statistics*, 37(6):1554–1563.

Peter L. Elkin, Steven H. Brown, Brent A. Bauer, Casey S. Husser, William Carruth, Larry R. Bergstrom, and Dietlind L. Wahner-Roedler. 2005. A controlled trial of automated classification of negation from clinical notes. *BMC Medical Informatics and Decision Making*, 5(13).

Richárd Farkas, Veronika Vincze, György Móra, János Csirik, and György Szarvas. 2010. The CoNLL-2010 Shared Task: Learning to Detect Hedges and their Scope in Natural Language Text. In *Proceedings of CoNLL-2010: Shared Task, 2010*, pages 1–12.

Viola Ganter, and Michael Strube. 2009. Finding hedges by chasing weasels: Hedge detection using wikipedia tags and shallow linguistic features. In *Proceedings of the ACL-IJCNLP 2009 Conference Short Papers*, pages 173–176.

Dan Klein, and Christopher D. Manning. 2003. Accurate unlexicalized parsing. In *Proceedings of the 41st Meeting of the Association for Computational Linguistics*, pages 423–430.

John Lafferty, Andrew McCallum, and Fernando Pereira. 2001. Conditional random fields: Probabilistic models for segmenting and labeling sequence data. In *Proceedings of the Eighteenth International Conference on Machine Learning*, pages 282–289.

Marc Light, Xin Ying Qiu, and Padmini Srinivasan. 2004. The language of bioscience: facts, speculations, and statements in between. In *HLT-NAACL 2004 Workshop: BioLINK 2004, Linking Biological Literature, Ontologies and Databases*, pages 17–24.

Yuan Liu, Qiang Tan, and Kunxu Shen. 1994. *The word segmentation rules and automatic word segmentation methods for Chinese information processing*. QingHua University Press and GuangXi Science and Technology Press.

Andrew McCallum, Dayne Freitag, and Fernando Pereira. 2000. Maximum entropy Markov models for information extraction and segmentation. In *Proceedings of ICML 2000*, pages 591–598.

Ben Medlock. 2008. Exploring hedge identification in biomedical literature. *Journal of Biomedical Informatics*, 41(4):636–654.

Ben Medlock, and Ted Briscoe. 2007. Weakly supervised learning for hedge classification in scientific literature. In *Proceedings of ACL-07,* pages 992–999.

Roser Morante, and Walter Daelemans. 2009. Learning the scope of hedge cues in biomedical texts. In *Proceedings of the Workshop on BioNLP, ACL 2009*, pages 28–36.

Ellen Riloff, Janyce Wiebe, and Theresa Wilson. 2003. Learning subjective nouns using extraction pattern bootstrapping. In *Proceedings of the 7th Conference on Computational Natural Language Learning,* pages 25–32.

György Szarvas. 2008. Hedge classification in biomedical texts with a weakly supervised selection of keywords. In *Proceedings of ACL: HLT*, pages 281–289.

György Szarvas, Veronika Vincze, Richárd Farkas, and János Csirik. 2008. The BioScope corpus: biomedical texts annotated for uncertainty, negation and their scopes. In *Proceedings of BioNLP 2008: Current Trends in Biomedical Natural Language*, pages 38–45.

Yoshimasa Tsuruoka, Yuka Tateishi, Jin-Dong Kim, Tomoko Ohta, John McNaught, Sophia Ananiadou, Jun'ichi Tsujii. 2005. Developing a robust part-of-speech tagger for biomedical text. In *Advances in Informatics 2005*, pages 382–392.

A Lucene and Maximum Entropy Model Based Hedge Detection System

Lin Chen
University of Illinois at Chicago
Chicago, IL, USA
lin@chenlin.net

Barbara Di Eugenio
University of Illinois at Chicago
Chicago, IL, USA
bdieugen@uic.edu

Abstract

This paper describes the approach to hedge detection we developed, in order to participate in the shared task at CoNLL-2010. A supervised learning approach is employed in our implementation. Hedge cue annotations in the training data are used as the seed to build a reliable hedge cue set. Maximum Entropy (MaxEnt) model is used as the learning technique to determine uncertainty. By making use of Apache Lucene, we are able to do fuzzy string match to extract hedge cues, and to incorporate part-of-speech (POS) tags in hedge cues. Not only can our system determine the certainty of the sentence, but is also able to find all the contained hedges. Our system was ranked third on the Wikipedia dataset. In later experiments with different parameters, we further improved our results, with a 0.612 F-score on the Wikipedia dataset, and a 0.802 F-score on the biological dataset.

1 Introduction

A hedge is a mitigating device used to lessen the impact of an utterance[1]. As a very important way to precisely express the degree of accuracy and truth assessment in human communication, hedging is widely used in both spoken and written languages. Detecting hedges in natural language text can be very useful for areas like text mining and information extraction. For example, in opinion mining, hedges can be used to assess the degree of sentiment, and refine sentiment classes from {positive, negative, objective} to {positive, somehow positive, objective, somehow objective, negative, somehow negative}.

Hedge detection related work has been conducted by several people. Light et al. (2004) started to do annotations on biomedicine article abstracts, and conducted the preliminary work of automatic classification for uncertainty. Medlock and Briscoe (2007) devised detailed guidelines for hedge annotations, and used a probabilistic weakly supervised learning approach to classify hedges. Ganter and Strube (2009) took Wikipedia articles as training corpus, used weasel words' frequency and syntactic patterns as features to classify uncertainty.

The rest of the paper is organized as follows. Section 2 shows the architecture of our system. Section 3 explains how we make use of Apache Lucene to do fuzzy string match and incorporate POS tag in hedge cues and our method to generate hedge cue candidates. Section 4 describes the details of using MaxEnt model to classify uncertainty. We present and discuss experiments and results in section 5, and conclude in section 6.

2 System Architecture

Our system is divided into training and testing modules. The architecture of our system is shown in Figure 1.

In the training module, we use the training corpus to learn a reliable hedge cue set with balanced support and confidence, then train a MaxEnt model for each hedge cue to classify the uncertainty for sentences matched by that hedge cue.

In the testing module, the learned hedge cues are used to match the sentences to classify, then each matched sentence is classified using the corresponding MaxEnt model. A sentence will be classified as uncertain if the MaxEnt model determines it is. Because of this design, our system is not only able to check if a sentence is uncertain, but also can detect the contained hedges.

[1] http://en.wikipedia.org/wiki/Hedge(linguistics)

Proceedings of the Fourteenth Conference on Computational Natural Language Learning: Shared Task, pages 114–119, Uppsala, Sweden, 15-16 July 2010.

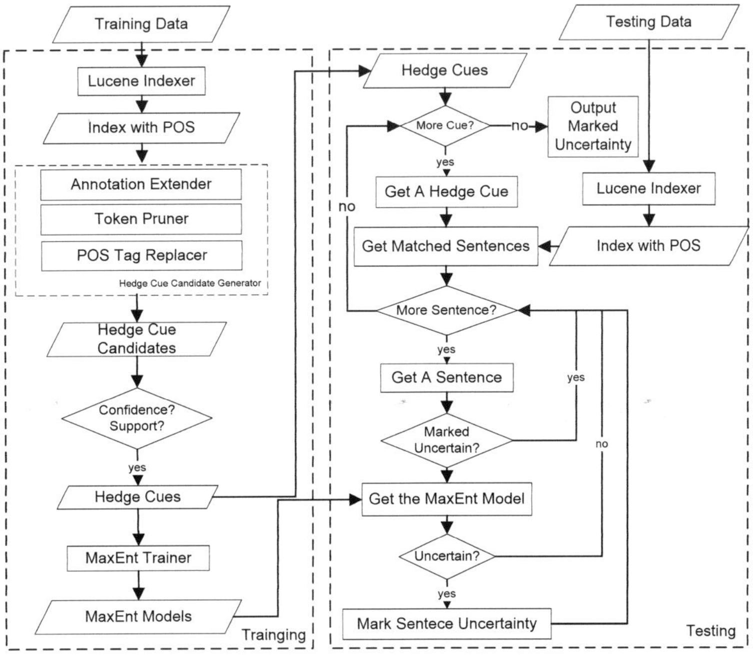

Figure 1: System Architecture

3 Learn Hedge Cues

The training data provided by CoNLL-2010 shared task contain "<ccue></ccue>" annotations for uncertain sentences. Most of the annotations are either too strict, which makes them hard to use to match other sentences, or too general, which means that most of the matched sentences are not uncertain.

Similar to how Liu (2007) measures the usefulness of association rules, we use support and confidence to measure the usefulness of a hedge cue.

Support is the ratio of sentences containing a hedge cue to all sentences. Because in a training dataset, the number of all the sentences is a fixed constant, we only use the number of sentences containing the hedge cue as support, see formula 1. In the other part of this paper, sentences matched by hedge cues means sentences contains hedge cues. We use support to measure the degree of generality of a hedge cue.

$$sup = count\,of\,matched\,sentences \qquad (1)$$

Confidence is the ratio of sentences which contain a hedge cue and are uncertain to all the sentences containing the hedge cue, as formula 2. We use confidence to measure the reliability for a word or phrase to be a hedge cue.

$$conf = \frac{count\,of\,matched\,and\,uncertain}{count\,of\,matched\,sentences} \qquad (2)$$

3.1 Usage of Apache Lucene

Apache Lucene[2] is a full text indexing Java library provided as an open source project of Apache Foundation. It provides flexible indexing and search capability for text documents, and it has very high performance. To explain the integration of Lucene into our implementation, we need to introduce several terms, some of which come from McCandless et al. (2010).

- Analyzer: Raw texts are preprocessed before being added to the index: text preprocessing components such as tokenization, stop words removal, and stemming are parts of an analyzer.
- Document: A document represents a collection of fields, it could be a web page, a text file, or only a paragraph of an article.
- Field: A field represents a document or the meta-data associated with that document, like the author, type, URL. A field has a name and a value, and a bunch of options to control how Lucene will index its value.
- Term: The very basic unit of a search. It contains a field name and a value to search.

[2] `http://lucene.apache.org`

- Query: The root class used to do search upon an index.

In our implementation, Lucene is used for the following 3 purposes:

- Enable quick counting for combinations of words and POS tags.
- Store the training and testing corpus for fast counting and retrieval.
- Allow gap between words or POS tags in hedge cues to match sentences.

Lucene provides the capability to build customized analyzers for complex linguistics analysis. Our customized Lucene analyzer employs tokenizer and POS tagger from OpenNLP tools[3] to do tokenization and POS tagging. For every word in the sentence, we put two Lucene tokens in the same position, by setting up the second token's PositionIncremental attribute to be 0.

For example, for sentence *it is believed to be very good*, our analyzer will make Lucene store it as Figure 2 in its index.

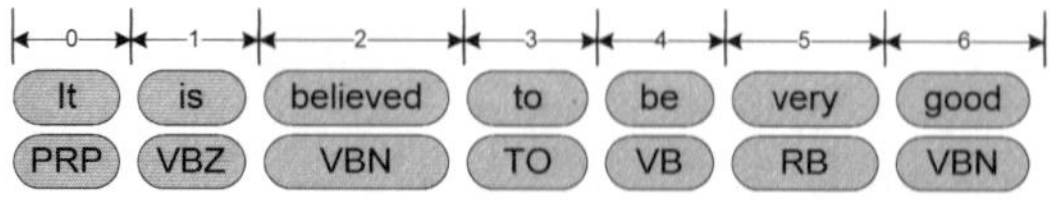

Figure 2: Customized Tokenizer Example

Indexing text in that way, we are able to match sentences cross words and POS tags. For example, the phrase *it is believed* will be matched by *it is believed*, *it is VBN*, *it VBZ believed*. This technique enables us to generalize a hedge cue.

In our implementation, all the data for training and testing are indexed. The indexing schema is: a sentence is treated as a Lucene document; the content of the sentence is analyzed by our customized analyzer; other information like sentence id, sentence position, uncertainty is stored as fields of the document. In this way, we can query all those fields, and when we find a match, we can easily get all the information out just from the index.

Lucene provides various types of queries to search the indexed content. We use SpanNearQuery and BooleanQuery to search the matched sentences for hedge cues. We rely on SpanNearQuery's feature of allowing positional restriction when matching sentences. When building a SpanNearQuery, we can specify the position gap allowed among the terms in the query. We build a SpanNearQuery from a hedge cue, put each token as a term of the query, and set the position gap to be 2. Take Figure 3 as an example, because the gap between token *is* and *said* is 1, is less than the specified gap setting 2, so *It is widely said to be good* will count as a match with hedge cue *is said*.

Figure 3: SpanNearQuery Matching Example

We use BooleanQuery with nested SpanNearQuery and TermQuery to count uncertain sentences, then to calculate the confidence of a hedge cue.

3.2 Hedge Cue Candidate Generation

We firstly tried to use the token as the basic unit for hedge cues. However, several pieces of evidence suggest it is not appropriate.

- Low Coverage. We only get 42 tokens in Wikipedia training data, using 20, 0.4 as the thresholds for support and confidence.
- Irrelevant words or stop words with lower thresholds. When we use 5, 0.3 as the thresholds for coverage and confidence, we get 279 tokens, however, words like *is*, *his*, *musical*, *voters*, *makers* appear in the list.

We noticed that many phrases with similar structures or fixed collocations appear very often in the annotations, like *it is believed*, *it is thought*, *many of them*, *many of these* and etc. Based on this observation, we calculated the support and confidence for some examples, see table 1.

Hedge Cue	Sup.	Conf.
it is believed	14	.93
by some	30	.87
many of	135	.65

Table 1: Hedge Cue Examples

We decided to use the phrase or collocation as the basic unit for hedge cues. There are two problems in using the original annotations as hedge cues:

[3]http://opennlp.sourceforge.net

- High confidence but low coverage: annotations that contain proper nouns always have very high confidence, usually 100%, however, they have very low support.
- High coverage but low confidence: annotations with only one token are very frequent, but only a few of them result in enough confidence.

To balance confidence and support, we built our hedge cue candidate generator. Its architecture is presented in Figure 4.

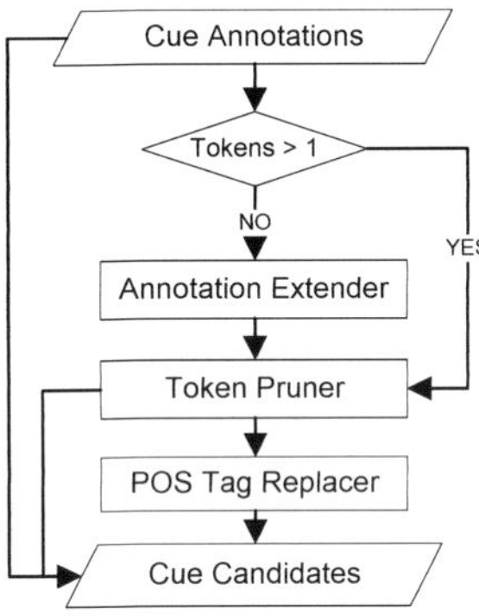

Figure 4: Hedge Cue Candidate Generator

The three main components of the hedge cue candidate generator are described below.

Annotation Extender: When the input hedge cue annotation contains only 1 token, this component will be used. It will generate 3 more hedge cue candidates by adding the surrounding tokens. We expect to discover candidates with higher confidence.

Token Pruner: According to our observations, proper nouns rarely contribute to the uncertainty of a sentence, and our Lucene based string matching method ensures that the matched sentences remain matched after we remove tokens from the original cue annotation. So we remove proper nouns in the original cue annotation to generate hedge cue candidates. By using this component, we expect to extract hedge cues with higher support.

POS Tag Replacer: This component is used to generalize similar phrases, by using POS tags to replace the concrete words. For example, we use the POS tag *VBN* to replace *believed* in *it is believed* to generate *it is VBN*. Hence, when a sentence contains *it is thought* in the testing dataset, even if *it is thought* never appeared in the training data set, we will still be able to match it and classify it against the trained MaxEnt model. We expect that this component will be able to increase support. Due to the O(2^n) time complexity, we did not try the brute force approach to replace every word, only the words with the POS tags in Table 2 are replaced in the process.

POS	**Description**	**Example**
VBN	past participle verb	it is **believed**
NNS	plural common noun	some **countries**
DT	determiner	some of **those**
CD	numeral, cardinal	**one** of the best

Table 2: POS Tag Replacer Examples

After hedge cue candidates are generated, we convert them to Lucene queries to calculate their confidence and support. We prune those that fall below the predefined confidence and support settings.

4 Learn Uncertainty

Not all the learned hedge cues have 100% uncertainty confidence, given a hedge cue, we need to learn how to classify whether a matched sentence is uncertain or not. The classification model is, given a tuple of (Sentence, Hedge Cue), in which the sentence contains the hedge cue, we classify it to the outcome set {Certain, Uncertain}.

MaxEnt is a general purpose machine learning technique, it makes no assumptions in addition to what we know from the data. MaxEnt has been widely used in Natural Language Processing (NLP) tasks like POS tagging, word sense disambiguation, and proved its efficiency. Due to MaxEnt's capability to combine multiple and dependent knowledge sources, we employed MaxEnt as our machine learning model. Features we used to train the model include meta information features and collocation features.

Meta Information Features include three features:

- Sentence Location: The location of the sentence in the article, whether in the title or in the content. We observed sentences in the title are rarely uncertain.
- Number of Tokens: The number of tokens in the sentence. Title of article is usually shorter, and more likely to be certain.

- Hedge Cue Location: The location of matched tokens in a sentence. We consider them to be in the beginning, if the first token of the matched part is the first token in the sentence; to be at the end, if the last token of the matched part is the last token of the sentence; otherwise, they are in the middle. We were trying to use this feature as a simplified version to model the syntactic role of hedge cues in sentences.

Collocation Features include the word and POS tag collocation features:

- Word Collocation: Using a window size of 5, extract all the word within that window, excluding punctuation.

- POS Tag Collocation: Using a window size of 5, extract all the POS tags of tokens within that window, excluding punctuation.

We use the OpenNLP MaxEnt[4] Java library as the MaxEnt trainer and classifier. For each hedge cue, the training is iterated 100 times, with no cut off threshold for events.

5 Experiments and Discussion

We first ran experiments to evaluate the performance of the entire system. We used official dataset as training and testing, with different confidence and support thresholds. The result on official Wikipedia dataset is presented in Table 3. Result on the biological dataset is listed in Table 4. In the result tables, the first 2 columns are the confidence and support threshold; "Cues" is the number of generated hedge cues; the last 3 columns are standard classifier evaluation measures.

Our submitted result used 0.35, 5 as the thresholds for confidence and support. We officially placed third on the Wikipedia dataset, with a 0.5741 F-score, and third from last on the biological dataset, with a 0.7692 F-score. In later experiments, we used different parameters, which resulted in a 0.03 F-score improvement. We believe the big difference of ranking on different datasets comes from the incomplete training. Due to incorrect estimation of running time, we only used the smaller training file in our submitted biological result.

From Table 3 and 4, we can see that a higher confidence threshold gives higher precision, and

[4]http://maxent.sourceforge.net

Conf.	Sup.	Cues	Prec.	Recall	F
0.4	10	360	0.658	0.561	0.606
	15	254	0.672	0.534	0.595
	20	186	0.682	0.508	0.582
0.45	10	293	0.7	0.534	0.606
	15	190	0.717	0.503	0.591
	20	137	0.732	0.476	0.577
0.5	5	480	0.712	0.536	**0.612**
	10	222	0.736	0.492	0.590
	15	149	0.746	0.468	0.575
	20	112	0.758	0.443	0.559

Table 3: Evaluation Result on Wikipedia Dataset

Conf.	Sup.	Cues	Prec.	Recall	F
0.4	10	330	0.68	0.884	0.769
	15	229	0.681	0.861	0.76
	20	187	0.679	0.842	0.752
0.45	10	317	0.689	0.878	0.772
	15	220	0.69	0.857	0.764
	20	179	0.688	0.838	0.756
0.5	5	586	0.724	0.899	**0.802**
	10	297	0.742	0.841	0.788
	15	206	0.742	0.819	0.779
	20	169	0.74	0.8	0.769

Table 4: Evaluation Result on Biological Dataset

a lower support threshold leads to higher recall. Since the lower support threshold could generate more hedge cues, it will generate less training instances for hedge cues with both low confidence and support, which affects the performance of the MaxEnt classifier. In both datasets, it appears that 0.5 and 5 are the best thresholds for confidence and support, respectively.

Beyond the performance of the entire system, our hedge cue generator yields very promising results. Using the best parameters we just noted above, our hedge cue generator generates 52 hedge cues with confidence 100% on the Wikipedia dataset, and 332 hedge cues in the biological dataset. Some hedge cue examples are shown in Table 5.

We also ran experiments to verify the performance of our MaxEnt classifier. We used the same setting of datasets as for the system performance evaluation. Given a hedge cue, we extracted all the matched sentences from the training set to train a MaxEnt classifier, and used it to classify the matched sentences by the hedge cue in testing set.

Hedge Cue	Sup.	Conf.	TestSize	Prec.	Recall	F
indicated that	63	0.984	6	1.0	1.0	1.0
by some	30	0.867	29	0.966	1.000	0.983
are considered	29	0.724	10	0.750	0.857	0.800
some of NNS	62	0.613	27	1.000	0.778	0.875
the most JJ	213	0.432	129	0.873	0.475	0.615

Table 6: MaxEnt Classifier Performance

Hedge Cue	Conf.	Sup.
probably VBN	1.0	21
DT probably	1.0	15
many NNS believe	1.0	10
NNS suggested DT	1.0	248
results suggest	1.0	122
has VBN widely VBN	1.0	10

Table 5: Generated Hedge Cue Examples

Table 6 shows the results, the hedge cues were manually chosen with relative higher support.

We can see that the performance of the MaxEnt classifier correlates tightly with confidence and support. Higher confidence means a more accurate detection for a phrase to be hedge cue, while higher support means more training instances for the classifier: the best strategy would be to find hedge cues with both high confidence and support.

While experimenting with the system, we found several potential improvements.

- Normalize words. Take the word *suggest* as an example. In the generated hedge cues, we found that its other forms are everywhere, like *it suggested*, *NNS suggests a*, and *DT suggesting that*. As we put POS tags into Lucene index, we can normalize words to their base forms using a morphology parser, and put base forms into index. After that, the query with *suggest* will match all the forms.

- Use more sophisticated features to train the MaxEnt classifier. Currently we only use shallow linguistics information as features, however we noticed that the role of the phrase could be very important to decide whether it indicates uncertainty. We can deep parse sentences, extract the role information, and add it to the feature list of classifier.

6 Conclusion

In this paper, we described the hedge detection system we developed to participate in the shared task of CoNLL-2010. Our system uses a heuristic learner to learn hedge cues, and uses MaxEnt as its machine learning model to classify uncertainty for sentences matched by hedge cues. Hedge cues in our system include both words and POS tags, which make them more general. Apache Lucene is integrated into our system to efficiently run complex linguistic queries on the corpus.

Acknowledgments

This work is supported by award IIS-0905593 from the National Science Foundation.

References

Viola Ganter and Michael Strube. 2009. Finding hedges by chasing weasels: Hedge detection using Wikipedia tags and shallow linguistic features. In *Proceedings of the ACL-IJCNLP 2009 Conference Short Papers*, pages 173–176, Suntec, Singapore, August. Association for Computational Linguistics.

Marc Light, Xin Ying Qiu, and Padmini Srinivasan. 2004. The language of bioscience: Facts, speculations, and statements in between. In *Proceedings of BioLink 2004 Workshop on Linking Biological Literature, Ontologies and Databases: Tools for Users*, pages 17–24, Boston, Mass, May.

Bing Liu. 2007. *Web data mining: exploring hyperlinks, contents, and usage data*. Springer.

Michael McCandless, Erik Hatcher, and Otis Gospodneti. 2010. *Lucene in action*. Manning Publications Co, 2nd edition.

Ben Medlock and Ted Briscoe. 2007. Weakly supervised learning for hedge classification in scientific literature. In *Proceedings of the 45th Annual Meeting of the Association of Computational Linguistics*, pages 992–999. Association for Computational Linguistics, June.

HedgeHunter: A System for Hedge Detection and Uncertainty Classification

David Clausen
Department of Linguistics
Stanford University
Stanford, CA 94305, USA.
clausend@stanford.edu

Abstract

With the dramatic growth of scientific publishing, Information Extraction (IE) systems are becoming an increasingly important tool for large scale data analysis. Hedge detection and uncertainty classification are important components of a high precision IE system. This paper describes a two part supervised system which classifies words as hedge or non-hedged and sentences as certain or uncertain in biomedical and Wikipedia data. In the first stage, our system trains a logistic regression classifier to detect hedges based on lexical and Part-of-Speech collocation features. In the second stage, we use the output of the hedge classifier to generate sentence level features based on the number of hedge cues, the identity of hedge cues, and a Bag-of-Words feature vector to train a logistic regression classifier for sentence level uncertainty. With the resulting classification, an IE system can then discard facts and relations extracted from these sentences or treat them as appropriately doubtful. We present results for in domain training and testing and cross domain training and testing based on a simple union of training sets.

1 Introduction

With the rapid increase in domain specific (biomedical) and domain general (WWW) text collections information extraction is an increasingly important tool for making use of these data sets. In order to maximize the usefulness of extracted relations an Information Extraction (IE) system needs the ability to separate the factual and reliable relationships from the uncertain and unreliable relationships. Most work on this problem has focused on the task of hedge detection where the goal is to classify a span of text as hedged or as non-hedged with the goal of facilitating sentence level classification of certain or uncertain. Much of the work was conducted within the framework of the BioNLP 2009 shared task sub task on uncertainty detection focusing on biomedical datasets (Kim et al., 2009) motivating further work in the biomedical NLP field (Aramaki et al., 2009; Conway et al., 2009). Other work has focused on creating annotated datasets from both a linguistically sophisticated perspective (Saurí and Pustejovsky, 2009) or from a language engineering perspective (Vincze et al., 2008).

Early work by Light et al. (2004) framed the task as determining the degree of speculation or uncertainty at the sentence level. The presence of a hedge cue, a phrase indicating that authors cannot back up their opinions or statements with facts, is a high precision feature of sentence level uncertainty. Other early work focused on semi-supervised learning due to a lack of annotated datasets (Medlock and Briscoe, 2007). Linguistically motivated approaches achieved a robust baseline on the sentence classification task (Kilicoglu and Bergler, 2008) although their training methods are hand tuned. Morante and Daelemans (2009) cast the problem as a sequence labeling task and show that performance is highly domain dependent and requires high precision hedge detection in order to perform the complex task of hedge scope labeling. Szarvas (2008) demonstrates that semi-supervised learning is even more effective with more labeled training data and sophisticated feature selection.

HedgeHunter is built to perform the CoNLL-2010 sentence uncertainty classification task. The task is a supervised learning task with training data drawn from Wikipedia and biomolecular articles and abstracts. Each training sentence is la-

Proceedings of the Fourteenth Conference on Computational Natural Language Learning: Shared Task, pages 120–125,
Uppsala, Sweden, 15-16 July 2010. ©2010 Association for Computational Linguistics

beled as certain or uncertain and every hedge cue is also labeled. HedgeHunter separates the task into two stages: hedge detection and uncertainty classification, with the goal of producing an independent high precision hedge detection system for use in other tasks such as hedge scope detection. The system is designed to be expanded using semi-supervised learning although this is not implemented at this time. This paper will describe the hedge detection stage in Section 2 and the sentence classification stage in Section 3. Section 4 describes the evaluation of the system and Section 5 discusses the results. Section 6 discusses the results in a larger context and suggest future areas for improvement. Section 7 summarizes the conclusions.

2 Hedge Detection

Hedge detection is largely based on the identification of lexical items like *suggest* and *might* which indicate sentence level uncertainty. As a result, reasonable hedge detection in English can be accomplished by collecting a list of all lexical items that convey hedging. These include epistemic verbs (*may, might, could, should, can, ought to*), psychological verbs of perception, knowing or concluding (*seems, guess, suppose, hope, assume, speculate, estimate*), adverbs (*possibly, unlikely, probably, approximately*), adjectives (*quite, rare, apparent*) and many nouns. While some of these, especially the epistemic verbs, are often applied across domains to indicate hedge cues, many are unique to a particular domain. Further complicating hedge detection in English is the fact that the same word types occasionally have different, non-hedging uses.

The form of a hedge cue often acts as a high precision feature, whenever one is present in a sentence it is highly likely to be labeled as a hedge cue in the training set. Lexical hedge cues often vary from domain to domain and contain multiple words so non-lexical features are required for recognizing hedge cues robustly across domains although they are unlikely to provide a large benefit due to the largely lexical nature of hedges. As a result HedgeHunter uses both lexical and POS features for classification. Some hedges like *ought to* span multiple words so we also use positional features in order to capture multi-word hedges.

The hedge detection stage labels each word in a sentence independently. Labeling is done by logistic regression using Quasi-Newton minimization to set feature weights. This is a classification method that is both fast and robust for binary classification tasks like the one at hand. Features are drawn from the target word to be labeled and its context, the three words to the left and right of the target word. For the target word we extract features based on the word form, the word lemma and its POS as determined by a maximum entropy POS tagger trained on the PennTreebank implemented in Stanford JavaNLP. For the 6 words in the context window we also extract features based on the word, its lemma and its POS.

3 Uncertainty Classification

Uncertainty classification involves partitioning the set of sentences in a dataset into certain and uncertain classes. In most scientific writing sentences are generally certain so uncertain sentences are the minority class. This holds even more so for the Wikipedia dataset due to the method by which annotations were obtained and the encyclopedic nature of the dataset. Wikipedia hedge cues were identified by the presence of the *weasel word* tag which editors are allowed to append to spans of text in a Wikipedia article. These are often applied in a manner similar to hedge cues in the annotated biomedical datasets but they also focus on identifying non universal statements like those quantified by some or few. Due to the collaborative nature of Wikipedia, what qualifies as a *weasel word* varies greatly contributing to the increased variation in hedge cues in this dataset. Weasel words often get edited quickly so there are not many examples in the training set creating further difficulties.

The presence of one or more hedge cues in a sentence is a good indication that the sentence should be classified as uncertain, although as we will see in the results section, non-hedge features are also useful for this task. To capture this we extract features from each sentence including the number of hedge cues found by the hedge detection stage and the string value of the first four lexical hedge cues found in each sentence. To capture any other non-hedge words which may contribute to sentence level uncertainty, we also include BOW features based on vocabulary items with frequencies above the mean frequency in the corpus. This is achieved by creating binary features for the presence of every word in the vocabulary.

Classification is again performed by a logistic regression using Quasi-Newton minimization. It should be stressed that all hedge related features used by the uncertainty classification stage are taken from the results of the hedge detection stage and not from the gold standard annotation data. This was done to allow the system to fold new unannotated sentences into the training set to perform semi-supervised learning. Time constraints and implementation difficulties prevented fully implementing this system component. Future work plans to extract high class conditional likelihood features from unannotated sentences, annotate the sentences based on treating these features as hedges, and retrain the hedge detection stage and uncertainty classification stage in an iterative manner to improve coverage.

4 Evaluation

The dataset provided for the CoNLL-2010 shared task consists of documents drawn from three separate domains. Two domains, biomedical abstracts and full articles, are relatively similar while the third, selected Wikipedia articles, differs considerably in both content and hedge cues for the reasons previously discussed. Overall the dataset contains 11,871 sentences from abstracts, 2,670 from full articles, and 11,111 from Wikipedia articles.

Performance for the hedge detection system was calculated at the word level while performance for the uncertainty classification stage was calculated at the sentence level using the classes of hedged and uncertain as the positive class for precision, recall and F1 statistics. We compare our hedge detection system to a state of the art system presented in Morante and Daelemans (2009) and trained on a dataset of 20,924 sentences drawn from clinical reports and biomedical abstracts and articles. The Morante system used 10 fold cross validation while our system randomly withholds 10 percent of the dataset for testing so our results may be viewed as less reliable. We do provide the first evaluation of one system on both domain specific and domain general datasets. Table 1 provides a breakdown of performance by system and dataset.

We evaluated the performance of the HedgeHunter system on the withheld training data including 5003 evaluation sentences from the biomedical domain and 9634 sentences from Wikipedia. For uncertainty classification we compare our system to the results from the CoNLL-2010 shared task comparing to the state of the art systems. For more details see the task description paper (Farkas et al., 2010). Table 2 summarizes the results for the closed domain training subtask. Table 3 summarizes the best performing systems in the Wikipedia and biomedical domain on the cross domain training subtask and compares to the HedgeHunter system.

System	Precision	Recall	F1
Morante			
Abstracts	.9081	.7984	.8477
Articles	.7535	.6818	.7159
Clinical	.8810	.2751	.41.92
HedgeHunter			
Abstracts	.8758	.5800	.6979
Articles	.8704	.4052	.5529
Wikipedia	.5453	.2434	.3369
All	.6289	.3464	.4467

Table 1: Hedge detection performance

System	Precision	Recall	F1
Tang			
Biomedical	.8503	.8777	.8636
Georgescul			
Wikipedia	.7204	.5166	.6017
HedgeHunter			
Biomedical	.7933	.8063	.7997
Wikipedia	.7512	.4203	.5390

Table 2: Uncertainty classification performance closed

System	Precision	Recall	F1
Li			
Biomedical	.9040	.8101	.8545
Ji			
Wikipedia	.6266	.5528	.5874
HedgeHunter			
Biomedical	.7323	.6405	.6833
Wikipedia	.7173	.4168	.5272

Table 3: Uncertainty classification performance cross

5 Results

The Hedge Detection stage performed slightly worse than the state of the art system. Although precision was comparable for biomedical articles and abstracts our system suffered from very low recall compared to the Morante system. The Morante system included chunk tagging as an approximation of syntactic constituency. Since many multi word hedge cues are constituents of high precision words and very frequent words (*ought to*) this constituency information likely boosts recall. Like the Morante system, HedgeHunter suffered a significant performance drop when tested across domains, although our system suffered more due to the greater difference in domains between biomedical and Wikipedia articles than between biomedical and clinical reports and due to the annotation standards for each dataset. HedgeHunter achieved better results on biomedical abstracts than the full articles due to higher recall based on the significantly larger dataset. Our system produced the worst performance on the Wikipedia data although this was mostly due to a drop in precision compared to the biomedical domain. This is in line with the drop in performance experienced by other systems outside of the biomedical domain and indicates that Wikipedia data is noisier than the peer reviewed articles that appear in the biomedical literature confirming our informal observations. Since the dataset has an overwhelming number of certain sentences and unhedged words, there is already a large bias towards those classes as evidenced by high overall classification accuracy (87% for certainty detection and 97% for hedge detection on all data) despite sometimes poor F1 scores for the minority classes. During development we experimented with SVMs for training but abandoned them due to longer training times and it is possible that we could improve the recall of our system by using a different classifier, a weaker prior or different parameters that allowed for more recall by paying less attention to class priors. We plan to expand our system using semi-supervised learning so it is not necessarily a bad thing to have high precision and low recall as this will allow us to expand our dataset with high quality sentences and by leveraging the vast amounts of unannotated data we should be able to overcome our low recall.

The uncertainty classification system performed robustly despite the relatively poor performance of the hedge detection classifier. The use of BOW features supplemented the low recall of the hedge detection stage while still relying on the hedge features when they were available as shown by feature analysis. We did not implement bi or trigram features although this would likely give a further boost in recall. Wikipedia data was still the worst performing domain although our cross domain system performed near the state of the art system with higher precision.

Overall our system produced a high precision hedge detection system for biomedical domain data which fed a high precision uncertainty classifier. Recall for the hedge detection stage was low overall but the use of BOW features for the uncertainty classification stage overcame this to a small degree. The amount of annotated training data has a significant impact on performance of the HedgeHunter system with more data increasing recall for the hedge detection task. For the sentence uncertainty task the system still performed acceptably on the Wikipedia data.

6 Discussion

HedgeHunter confirmed many of the findings of previous research. The most significant finding is that domain adaptation in the task of hedge detection is difficult. Most new domains contain different vocabulary and hedges tend to be highly lexicalized and subject to variation across domains. This is reinforced by feature analysis where the top weighted features for our hedge detection classifier were based on the word or its lemma and not on its POS. Once our system learns that a particular lexical item is a hedge it is easy enough to apply it precisely, the difficulty is getting the necessary training examples covering all the possible lexical hedge cues the system may encounter. The lexicon of hedge cues used in biomedical articles tends to be smaller so it is easier to get higher recall in this domain because the chance of seeing a particular hedge cue in training is increased. With the Wikipedia data, however, the set of hedge cues is more varied due to the informal nature of the articles. This makes it less likely that the hedge detection system will be exposed to a particular hedge in training.

One possible avenue for future work should consider using lexical resources like WordNet, measures of lexical similarity, or n-gram language models to provide backoff feature weights for unseen lexical items. This would increase the recall of the system despite the limited nature of annotated training sets by leveraging the lexical nature of hedges and their relatively closed class status.

We also found that the size of the training set matters significantly. Each domain employs a certain number of domain specific hedge cues along with domain general cues. While it is easy enough to learn the domain general cues, domain specific cues are difficult and can only be learned by seeing the specific lexical items to be learned. It is important that the training dataset include enough examples of all the lexical hedge cues for a specific domain if the system is to have decent recall. Even with thousands of sentences to train on, HedgeHunter had low recall presumably because there were still unseen lexical hedge cues in the test set. Future work should concentrate on methods of expanding the size of the training sets in order to cover a larger portion of the domain specific hedging vocabulary because it does not appear that there are good non-lexical features that are robust at detecting hedges across domains. This may include using lexical resources as described previously or by leveraging the high precision nature of hedge cues and the tendency for multiple cues to appear in the same sentence to perform semi-supervised learning.

This work also confirmed that hedge cues provide a very high precision feature for uncertainty classification. The highest weighed features for the classifier trained in the uncertainty classification stage were those that indicated the presence and number of lexical hedge cues. Contrary to some previous work which found that features counting the number of hedge cues did not improve performance, HedgeHunter found that the number of hedge cues was a strong feature with more hedge cues indicating an increased likelihood of being uncertain (Szarvas, 2008). It is largely a limitation of the task that we treat all uncertain sentences as equally uncertain. From a linguistic perspective a speaker uses multiple hedge cues to reinforce their uncertainty and our system seems to confirm that in terms of the likelihood of class membership even if the datasets do not encode the degree of uncertainty directly. Future work should focus on creating more sophisticated models of uncertainty that recognize the fact that it is at least a scalar phenomena and not a binary classification. Ideally a hedge detection and uncertainty quantification system would function to attach a probability to every fact or relation extracted from a sentence in an IE system determined in part by the hedging vocabulary used to express that fact or relation. This would yield a more nuanced view of how language conveys certainty and allow for interesting inference possibilities for systems leveraging the resulting IE system output.

One surprising finding was that uncertain sentences often contained multiple hedge cues, sometimes up to 4 or more. This is useful because it allows us to hypothesize that a sentence that is unannotated and has a high chance of being uncertain due to containing a hedge cue that we have seen in training, possibly contains other hedge cues that we have not seen. We can then use the large amounts of unannotated sentences that are available to extract n-gram features that have high uncertainty class conditional probability and add them to our training set with those features labeled as hedges as described in Medlock and Briscoe (2007). Because hedges are high precision features for uncertainty this should not hurt precision greatly. This allows us to increase the size of our training set substantially in order to expose our system to a greater variety of hedge cues in a semi-supervised manner. As with most semi-supervised systems we run the risk of drift resulting in a drop in precision. Future work will have to determine the correct balance between precision and recall, ideally by embedding this task within the larger IE framework to provide extrinsic evaluation

This work neglected to address the more difficult task of hedge scope detection. Determining hedge scope requires paring spans of sentences that fall within the hedge scope to a given hedge cue. Along with a move towards a scalar notion of uncertainty we should move towards a scope based instead of sentence based representation of uncertainty. Hedges take scope over subparts of a sentence so just because a relation occurs in the same sentence as a hedge cue does not mean that the given relation is hedged. It seems unnecessarily strict to ignore all relations or facts in a sentence just because it contains a hedge. Hedge detection is an important precursor to hedge scope detection. Without a high performing hedge detection system we cannot hope to link hedge cues with their respective scopes. This work hopes to produce a method for training such a hedge detection system for use as a component of a hedge scope finding system.

This work also failed to integrate constituency or dependency features into either stage of the system. Dependencies encode important information and we plan to include features based on dependency relationships into future versions of the system. At the hedge detection stage it should improve recall by allowing the system to detect which multi word hedge cues are part of the same cue. At the uncertainty classification stage it should allow the extraction of multiword features not just based on n-gram frequency. For semi-supervised learning it should allow the system to more accurately annotated multi word features that have a high class conditional probability. This should be even more important when performing the task of hedge scope detection where scope is often delimitated at the phrase level and determining the dependency relations between words can capture this observation.

7 Conclusion

This work described HedgeHunter, a two stage hedge detection and uncertainty classification system. It confirmed the lexical nature of the hedge detection task, the importance of hedge cues to uncertainty classification and sharpened the need for large amounts of training data in order to achieve broad coverage. It highlights the issues involved in developing an open domain system by evaluating across very disparate datasets. It provides a framework that can be extended to semi-supervised learning in order to leverage large amounts of unannotated data to improve both in domain and cross domain performance.

References

Eiji Aramaki, Yasuhide Miura, Masatsugu Tonoike, Tomoko Ohkuma, Hiroshi Mashuichi, and Kazuhiko Ohe. 2009. TEXT2TABLE: Medical Text Summarization System Based on Named Entity Recognition and Modality Identification. In *Proceedings of the BioNLP 2009 Workshop*, pages 185–192, Boulder, Colorado, June. Association for Computational Linguistics.

Mike Conway, Son Doan, and Nigel Collier. 2009. Using Hedges to Enhance a Disease Outbreak Report Text Mining System. In *Proceedings of the BioNLP 2009 Workshop*, pages 142–143, Boulder, Colorado, June. Association for Computational Linguistics.

Richárd Farkas, Veronika Vincze, György Móra, János Csirik, and György Szarvas. 2010. The CoNLL-2010 Shared Task: Learning to Detect Hedges and their Scope in Natural Language Text. In *Proceedings of the Fourteenth Conference on Computational Natural Language Learning (CoNLL-2010): Shared Task*, pages 1–12, Uppsala, Sweden, July. Association for Computational Linguistics.

Halil Kilicoglu and Sabine Bergler. 2008. Recognizing Speculative Language in Biomedical Research Articles: A Linguistically Motivated Perspective. In *Proceedings of the Workshop on Current Trends in Biomedical Natural Language Processing*, pages 46–53, Columbus, Ohio, June. Association for Computational Linguistics.

Jin-Dong Kim, Tomoko Ohta, Sampo Pyysalo, Yoshinobu Kano, and Jun'ichi Tsujii. 2009. Overview of BioNLP'09 Shared Task on Event Extraction. In *Proceedings of the BioNLP 2009 Workshop Companion Volume for Shared Task*, pages 1–9, Boulder, Colorado, June. Association for Computational Linguistics.

Marc Light, Xin Ying Qiu, and Padmini Srinivasan. 2004. The Language of Bioscience: Facts, Speculations, and Statements in Between. In *Proc. of the HLT-NAACL 2004 Workshop: Biolink 2004, Linking Biological Literature, Ontologies and Databases*, pages 17–24.

Ben Medlock and Ted Briscoe. 2007. Weakly Supervised Learning for Hedge Classification in Scientific Literature. In *Proceedings of the ACL*, pages 992–999, Prague, Czech Republic, June.

Roser Morante and Walter Daelemans. 2009. Learning the Scope of Hedge Cues in Biomedical Texts. In *Proceedings of the BioNLP 2009 Workshop*, pages 28–36, Boulder, Colorado, June. Association for Computational Linguistics.

Roser Saurí and James Pustejovsky. 2009. FactBank: a corpus annotated with event factuality. *Language Resources and Evaluation*, 43(3):227–268.

György Szarvas. 2008. Hedge Classification in Biomedical Texts with a Weakly Supervised Selection of Keywords. In *Proceedings of ACL-08: HLT*, pages 281–289, Columbus, Ohio, June. Association for Computational Linguistics.

Veronika Vincze, György Szarvas, Richárd Farkas, György Móra, and János Csirik. 2008. The BioScope Corpus: Biomedical Texts Annotated for Uncertainty, Negation and their Scopes. *BMC Bioinformatics*, 9(Suppl 11):S9.

Exploiting CCG Structures with Tree Kernels for Speculation Detection

Liliana Mamani Sánchez, Baoli Li, Carl Vogel
Computational Linguistics Group
Trinity College Dublin
Dublin 2, Ireland
{mamanisl,baoli.li,vogel}@tcd.ie

Abstract

Our CoNLL-2010 speculative sentence detector disambiguates putative keywords based on the following considerations: a speculative keyword may be composed of one or more word tokens; a speculative sentence may have one or more speculative keywords; and if a sentence contains at least one real speculative keyword, it is deemed speculative. A tree kernel classifier is used to assess whether a potential speculative keyword conveys speculation. We exploit information implicit in tree structures. For prediction efficiency, only a segment of the whole tree around a speculation keyword is considered, along with morphological features inside the segment and information about the containing document. A maximum entropy classifier is used for sentences not covered by the tree kernel classifier. Experiments on the Wikipedia data set show that our system achieves 0.55 F-measure (in-domain).

1 Introduction

Speculation and its impact on argumentation has been studied by linguists and logicians since at least as far back as Aristotle (trans 1991, 1407a, 1407b), and under the category of linguistic "hedges" since Lakoff (1973). Practical application of this research has emerged due to the efforts to create a biomedical database of sentences tagged with speculation information: BioScope (Szarvas et al., 2008) and because of the association of some kinds of Wikipedia data with the speculation phenomenon (Ganter and Strube, 2009). It is clear that specific words can be considered as clues that can qualify a sentence as speculative. However, the presence of a speculative keyword not always conveys a speculation assertion which makes the speculation detection a tough problem. For instance, the sentences below contain the speculative keyword "*may*", but only the sentence (a) is speculative.

(a) *These effects* ***may*** *be reversible.*

(b) *Members of an alliance* ***may*** *not attack each other.*

The CoNLL-2010 Shared Task (Farkas et al., 2010), "Learning to detect hedges and their scope in natural language text" proposed two tasks related to speculation research. Task 1 aims to detect sentences containing uncertainty and Task 2 aims to resolve the intra-sentential scope of hedge cues. We engaged in the first task in the biomedical and Wikipedia domains as proposed by the organizers, but eventually we got to submit only Wikipedia domain results. However, in this paper we include results in the biomedical domain as well.

The BioScope corpus is a linguistically hand annotated corpus of negation and speculation phenomena for medical free texts, biomedical article abstracts and full biomedical articles. The aforesaid phenomena have been annotated at sentence level with keyword tags and linguistic scope tags. Some previous research on speculation detection and boundary determination over biomedical data has been done by Medlock & Briscoe (2007) and Özgür & Radev (2009) from a computational view using machine learning methods.

The Wikipedia speculation dataset was generated by exploiting a weasel word marking. As weasel words convey vagueness and ambiguity by providing an unsupported opinion, they are discouraged by Wikipedia editors. Ganter & Strube (2009) proposed a system to detect hedges based on frequency measures and shallow information, achieving a F-score of 0.69[1].

We formulate the speculation detection problem as a word disambiguation problem and developed a system as a pipelined set of natural

[1]They used different Wikipedia data.

Proceedings of the Fourteenth Conference on Computational Natural Language Learning: Shared Task, pages 126–131,
Uppsala, Sweden, 15-16 July 2010.

language processing tools and procedures to pre-process the datasets. A Combinatory Categorial Grammar parsing (CCG) (Steedman, 2000) tool and a Tree Kernel (TK) classifier constitute the core of the system.

The Section 2 of this paper describes the overall architecture of our system. Section 3 depicts the dataset pre-processing. Section 4 shows how we built the speculation detection module, outlines the procedure of examples generation and the use of the Tree-kernel classifier. Section 5 presents the experiments and results, we show that sentence CCG derivation information helps to differentiate between apparent and real speculative words for speculation detection. Finally Section 6 gives our conclusions.

2 Speculation detection system

Our system for speculation detection is a machine learning (ML) based system (Figure 1). In the pre-processing module a dataset of speculative/non-speculative sentences goes through a process of information extraction of three kinds: speculative word or keyword extraction,[2] sentence extraction and document feature extraction (i.e document section). Later the extracted keywords are used to tag potential speculative sentences in the training/evaluation datasets and used as features by the classifiers. The sentences are submitted to the tokenization and parsing modules in order to provide a richer set of features necessary for creating the training/evaluation datasets, including the document features as well.

In the ML module two types of dataset are built: one used by a TK classifier and other one by a bag-of-features based maximum entropy classifier. As the first one processes only those sentences that contain speculative words, we use the second classifier, which is able to process samples of all the sentences.

The models built by these classifiers are combined in order to provide a better performance and coverage for the speculation problem in the classification module which finally outputs sentences labeled as speculative or non-speculative. Used tools are the GeniaTagger (Tsuruoka et al., 2005) for tokenization and lemmatization, and the C&C Parser (Clark and Curran, 2004). The next sections explain in detail the main system components.

[2]Extraction of keywords for the training stage.

3 Dataset pre-processing for rich feature extraction

The pre-processing module extracts keywords, sentences and document information.

All sentences are processed by the tokenizer/lemmatizer and at the same time specific information about the keywords is extracted.

Speculative keywords

Speculative sentences are evidenced by the presence of speculation keywords. We have the following observations:

- A hedge cue or speculative keyword [3] may be composed of one or more word tokens.
- In terms of major linguistic categories, the word tokens are heterogeneous: they may be verbs, adjectives, nouns, determiners, etc. A stop-word removing strategy was dismissed, since no linguistic category can be eliminated.
- A keyword may be covered by another longer one. For instance, the keyword *most* can be seen in keywords like *most of all the heroes* or *the most common*.

Considering these characteristics for each sentence, in the training stage, the keyword extraction module retrieves the speculative/non-speculative property of each sentence, the keyword occurrences, number of keywords in a sentence, the initial word token position and the number of word tokens in the keyword. We build a keyword lexicon with all the extracted keywords and their frequency in the training dataset, this speculative keyword lexicon is used to tag keyword occurrences in non-speculative training sentences and in all the evaluation dataset sentences.

The overlapping problem when tagging keywords is solved by maximal matching strategy. It is curious that speculation phrases come in degrees of specificity; the approach adopted here favors "specific" multi-word phrases over single-word expressions.

Sentence processing

Often, speculation keywords convey certain information that can not be successfully expressed by morphology or syntactic relations provided by phrase structure grammar parsers. On the other

[3]Or just "keyword" for sake of simplicity.

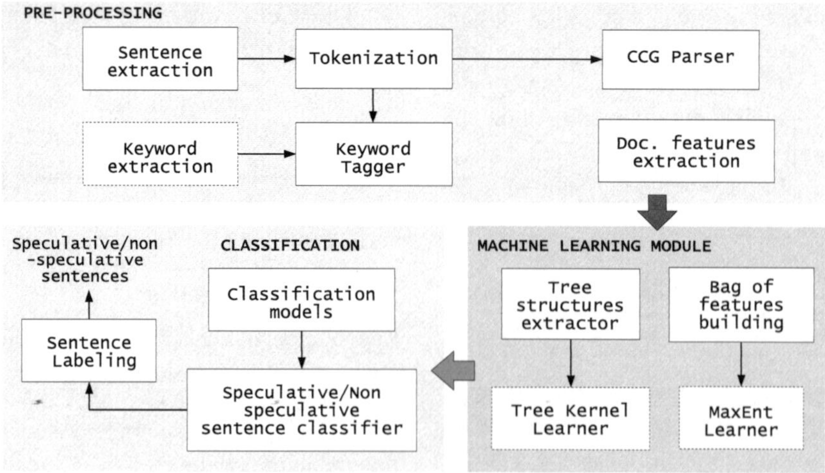

Figure 1: Block diagram for the speculation detection system.

hand, CCG derivations or dependencies provide deeper information, in form of predicate-argument relations. Previous works on semantic role labeling (Gildea and Hockenmaier, 2003; Boxwell et al., 2009) have used features derived from CCG parsings and obtained better results.

C&C parser provides CCG predicate-argument dependencies and Briscoe and Carroll (2006) style grammatical relations. We parsed the tokenized sentences to obtain CCG derivations which are binary trees as shown in the Figure 2. The CCG derivation trees contain function category and part-of-speech labels; this information is contained in the tree structures to be used in building a subtree dataset for the TK classifier.

4 Speculative sentence classifier

4.1 Tree Kernel classification

The subtree dataset is processed by a Tree Kernel classifier (Moschitti, 2006) based on Support Vector Machines. TK uses a kernel function between two trees, allowing a comparison between their substructures, which can be subtrees (ST) or subset trees (SST). We chose the comparison between subset trees since it expands the kernel calculation to those substructures with constituents that are not in the leaves. Our intuition is that real speculative sentences have deep semantic structures that are particularly different from those ones in apparent speculative sentences, and consequently the comparison between the structures of well identified and potential speculative sentences may enhance the identification of real speculative keywords.

4.2 Extracting tree structures

The depth of a CCG derivation tree is proportional to the number of word tokens in the sentence. Therefore, the processing of a whole derivation tree by the classifier is highly demanding and many subtrees are not relevant for the classification of speculative/non-speculative sentences, in particular when the scope of the speculation is a small proportion of a sentence.

In order to tackle this problem, a fragment of the CCG derivation tree is extracted. This fragment or subtree spans the keyword together with neighbors terms in a fixed-size window of n word tokens, (i.e. n word tokens to the left and n word tokens to the right of the keyword) and has as root the lower upper bound node of the first and last tokens of this span. After applying the subtree extraction, the subtree can contain more word tokens in addition to those contained in the n-span, which are replaced by a common symbol.

Potential speculative sentences are turned into training examples. However, as described in Section 3, a speculative sentence can contain one or more speculative keywords. This can produce an overlapping between their respective n-spans of individual keywords during the subtree extraction, producing subtrees with identical roots for both keywords. For instance, in the following sentence(c), the spans for the keywords *suggests* and *thought* will overlap if $n = 3$.

(c) *This* ***suggests*** *that diverse agents* ***thought*** *to activate NF-kappa B ...*

The overlapping interacts with the windows size and potential extraction of dependency relations

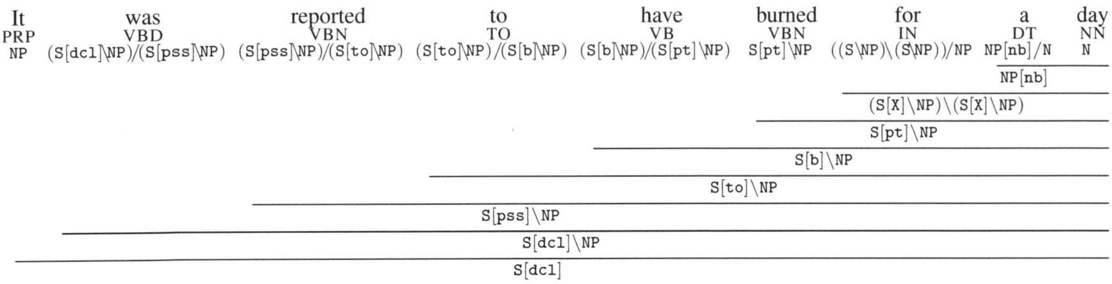

Figure 2: CCG derivations tree for *It was reported to have burned for a day.*

shared by terms belonging to the two different spans. We deal with this issue by extracting one training example if two spans have a common root and two different examples otherwise.

4.3 Bag of features model

By default, our system classifies the sentences not covered by the TK model using a baseline classifier that labels a sentence as speculative if this has at least one keyword. Alternatively, a bag of features classifier is used to complement the tree kernel, aimed to provide a more precise method that might detect even speculative sentences with new keywords in the evaluation dataset. The set of features used to build this model includes:

a) Word unigrams;
b) Lemma unigrams;
c) Word+POS unigrams;
d) Lemma+POS unigrams;
e) Word+Supertag unigrams;
f) Lemma+Supertag unigrams;
g) POS+Supertag unigrams;
h) Lemma bigrams;
i) POS bigrams;
j) Supertag bigrams;
k) Lemma+POS bigrams;
l) Lemma+Supertag bigrams;
m) POS+Supertag bigrams;
n) Lemma trigrams;
o) POS trigrams;
p) Supertag trigrams;
q) Lemma+POS trigrams;
r) Lemma+Supertag trigrams;
s) POS+Supertag trigrams;
t) Number of tokens;
u) Type of section in the document (Title, Text, Section);
v) Name of section in the document;
w) Position of the sentence in a section starting from beginning;
x) Position of the sentence in a section starting from end.

Dataset	Dev.	Train.	Eval.
Biomedical	39	14541	5003
Wikipedia	124	11111	9634

Table 1: Datasets sizes.

Position of the sentence information, composed by the last four features, represents the information about the sentence relative to a whole document. The bag of features model is generated using a Maximum Entropy algorithm (Zhang, 2004).

5 Experiments and results

5.1 Datasets

In the CoNLL-2010 Task 1, biomedical and Wikipedia datasets were provided for development, training and evaluation in the BioScope XML format. Development and training datasets are tagged with cue labels and a certainty feature.[4] The number of sentences for each dataset [5] is detailed in Table 1.

After manual revision of sentences not parsed by C&C parser, we found that they contain equations, numbering elements (e.g. (i), (ii).. 1), 2)), or long n-grams of named-entities, for instance: *...mannose-capped lipoarabinomannan (ManLAM) of Mycobacterium tuberculosis (M. tuberculosis)...* that out of a biomedical domain appear to be ungrammatical. Similarly, in the Wikipedia datasets, some sentences have many named entities. This suggests the need of a specific pre-processor or a parser for this kind of sentences like a named entity tagger.

In Table 2, we present the number of parsed sentences, processed sentences by the TK model and examples obtained in the tree structure extraction.

[4] certainty="uncertain" and certainty="certain".

[5] The biomedical abstracts and biomedical articles training datasets are processed as a single dataset.

Dataset	Parsed	Process.	Samples
Biomedical train.	14442	10852	23511
Biomedical eval.	4903	3395	7826
Wikipedia train.	10972	7793	13461
Wikipedia eval.	9559	4666	8467

Table 2: Count of processed sentences.

5.2 Experimental results

The CoNLL-2010 organizers proposed in-domain and cross-domain evaluations. In cross-domain experiments, test datasets of one domain can be used with classifiers trained on the other or on the union of both domains. We report here our results for the Wikipedia and biomedical datasets.

So far, we mentioned two settings for our classifier: a TK classifier complemented by a baseline classifier (BL) and TK classifier complemented by a bag of features classifier (TK+BF). Table 3 shows the scores of our submitted system (in-domain Task 1) on the Wikipedia dataset, whereas Table 4 gives the scores of the baseline system.

	TP	FP	FN	Precision	Recall	F
Our system	1033	480	1201	0.6828	0.4624	0.5514
Max.	1154	448	1080	0.7204	0.5166	0.6017
Min.	147	9	2087	0.9423	0.0658	0.123

Table 3: Comparative scores for our system with CoNLL official maximum and minimum scores in Task 1, Wikipedia dataset in-domain.

	TP	FP	FN	Precision	Recall	F
Biomedical	786	2690	4	0.2261	0.9949	0.3685
Wikipedia	1980	2747	254	0.4189	0.8863	0.5689

Table 4: Baseline results.

Additionally, we consider a bag of features classifier (BF) and a classifier that combines the baseline applied to the sentences that have at least one keyword plus the BF classifier for the remaining sentences (BL+BF). In Tables 5 to 10, results for the four classifiers (TK, TK+BF, BF, BL+BF) with evaluations in-domain and cross-domain are presented[6].

The baseline scores confirm that relying on just the keywords is not enough to identify speculative sentences. In the biomedical domain, the classifiers give high recall but too low precision resulting in low F-scores. Still, the TK, TK+BF and BF (in-domain configurations) gives much better results than BL and BL+BF which indicates that the information from CCG improves the performance of the classifiers when compared to the baseline classifier.

Even though in the Wikipedia domain the TK+BF score is less than the baseline score, still the performance of the classifiers do not fall much in any of the in-domain and cross-domain experiments. On the other hand, BF does not have a good performance in 5 of 6 the experiments. To make a more precise comparison between TK and BF, the TK and BL+BF scores show that BL+BF performs better than TK in only 2 of the 6 experiments but the better performances achieved by BL+BF are very small. This suggests that

[6]It is worth to note that the keyword lexicons have been not used in cross-domain way, so the TK and TK+BF models have not been tested in regards to keywords.

	TP	FP	FN	Precision	Recall	F
BL	1980	2747	254	0.4189	0.8863	0.5689
TK	1033	480	1201	0.6828	0.4624	0.5514
TK+BF	1059	516	1175	0.6729	0.4740	0.5560
BF	772	264	1462	0.7452	0.3456	0.4722
BL+BF	2028	2810	206	0.4192	0.9078	0.5735

Table 5: Results for Wikipedia dataset in-domain.

	TP	FP	FN	Precision	Recall	F
BL	1980	2747	254	0.4189	0.8863	0.5689
TK	1776	2192	458	0.4476	0.7950	**0.5727**
TK+BF	1763	2194	471	0.4455	0.7892	0.5695
BF	403	323	1831	0.5551	0.1804	0.2723
BL+BF	1988	2772	246	0.4176	0.8899	0.5685

Table 6: Wikipedia data classified with biomedical model scores (cross-domain).

	TP	FP	FN	Precision	Recall	F
BL	1980	2747	254	0.4189	0.8863	0.5689
TK	1081	624	1153	0.6340	0.4839	0.5489
TK+BF	1099	636	1135	0.6334	0.4919	0.5538
BF	770	271	1464	0.7397	0.3447	0.4702
BL+BF	2017	2786	217	0.4199	0.9029	0.5733

Table 7: Wikipedia data classified with biomedical + Wikipedia model scores (cross-domain).

	TP	FP	FN	Precision	Recall	F
BL	786	2690	4	0.2261	0.9949	0.3685
TK	759	777	31	0.4941	0.9606	0.6526
TK+BF	751	724	39	0.5092	0.9506	0.6631
BF	542	101	248	0.8429	0.6861	**0.7565**
BL+BF	786	2695	4	0.2258	0.9949	0.3681

Table 8: Biomedical data scores (in-domain).

	TP	FP	FN	Precision	Recall	F
BL	786	2690	4	0.2261	0.9949	0.3685
TK	786	2690	4	0.2261	0.9949	**0.3685**
TK+BF	771	2667	19	0.2243	0.9759	0.3647
BF	174	199	616	0.4665	0.2206	0.2992
BL+BF	787	2723	3	0.2242	0.9962	0.3660

Table 9: Biomedical data classified with Wikipedia model scores (cross-domain).

	TP	FP	FN	Precision	Recall	F
BL	786	2690	4	0.2261	0.9949	0.3685
TK	697	357	93	0.6613	0.8823	0.7560
TK+BF	685	305	105	0.6919	0.8671	**0.7697**
BF	494	136	296	0.7841	0.6253	0.6958
BL+BF	786	2696	4	0.2257	0.9949	0.3679

Table 10: Biomedical data classified with biomedical + Wikipedia model scores (cross-domain).

the complex processing made by tree kernels is more useful when disambiguating speculative keywords than BF. Nonetheless, the bag-of-features approach is also of importance for the task at hand when combined with TK. We observe that the TK classifer and BF classifier perform well making us believe that the CCG derivations provide relevant information for speculation detection. The use of tree kernels needs further investigations in order to evaluate the suitability of this approach.

6 Concluding remarks

Speculation detection is found to be a tough task given the high ambiguity of speculative keywords. We think these results can be improved by studying the influences of context on speculation assertions.

This paper presents a new approach for disambiguating apparent speculative keywords by using CCG information in the form of supertags and CCG derivations. We introduce the use of the tree kernel approach for CCG derivations trees. The inclusion of other features like grammatical relations provided by the parser needs to be studied before incorporating this information into the current classifier and possibly to resolve the boundary speculation detection problem.

Acknowledgments

This research is supported by the Trinity College Research Scholarship Program and the Science Foundation Ireland (Grant 07/CE/I1142) as part of the Centre for Next Generation Localisation (www.cngl.ie) at Trinity College of Dublin.

References

Aristotle. trans. 1991. *The Art of Rhetoric*. Penguin Classics, London. Translated with an Introduction and Notes by H.C. Lawson-Tancred.

Stephen Boxwell, Dennis Mehay, and Chris Brew. 2009. Brutus: A semantic role labeling system incorporating CCG, CFG, and dependency features. In *Proceedings of the Joint Conference of the 47th Annual Meeting of the ACL and the 4th International Joint Conference on Natural Language Processing of the AFNLP*, pages 37–45, Suntec, Singapore.

Ted Briscoe and John Carroll. 2006. Evaluating the accuracy of an unlexicalized statistical parser on the PARC DepBank. In *Proceedings of the COLING/ACL on Main conference poster sessions*, pages 41–48, Morristown, NJ, USA.

Stephen Clark and James R. Curran. 2004. Parsing the WSJ using CCG and log-linear models. In *ACL '04: Proceedings of the 42nd Annual Meeting on Association for Computational Linguistics*, page 103, Morristown, NJ, USA.

Richárd Farkas, Veronika Vincze, György Móra, János Csirik, and György Szarvas. 2010. The CoNLL-2010 Shared Task: Learning to Detect Hedges and their Scope in Natural Language Text. In *Proceedings of the Fourteenth Conference on Computational Natural Language Learning (CoNLL-2010): Shared Task*, pages 1–12, Uppsala, Sweden, July. Association for Computational Linguistics.

Viola Ganter and Michael Strube. 2009. Finding hedges by chasing weasels: Hedge detection using Wikipedia tags and shallow linguistic features. In *Proceedings of the ACL-IJCNLP 2009 Conference Short Papers*, pages 173–176, Suntec, Singapore.

Daniel Gildea and Julia Hockenmaier. 2003. Identifying semantic roles using combinatory categorial grammar. In *Proceedings of 2003 Conference on Empirical Methods in Natural Language Processing (EMNLP)*, Sapporo, Japan.

George Lakoff. 1973. Hedges: A study in meaning criteria and the logic of fuzzy concepts. *Journal of Philosophical Logic*, 2(4):458–508.

Ben Medlock and Ted Briscoe. 2007. Weakly supervised learning for hedge classification in scientific literature. In *Proceedings of the 45th Annual Meeting of the Association of Computational Linguistics*, pages 992–999, Prague, Czech Republic.

Alessandro Moschitti. 2006. Making tree kernels practical for natural language learning. In *Proceedings of the 11th Conference of the European Chapter of the Association for Computational Linguistics*.

Arzucan Özgür and Dragomir R. Radev. 2009. Detecting speculations and their scopes in scientific text. In *Proceedings of the 2009 Conference on Empirical Methods in Natural Language Processing*, pages 1398–1407, Singapore.

Mark Steedman. 2000. *The syntactic process*. MIT Press, Cambridge, MA, USA.

György Szarvas, Veronika Vincze, Richárd Farkas, and János Csirik. 2008. The BioScope corpus: annotation for negation, uncertainty and their scope in biomedical texts. In *Proceedings of the Workshop on Current Trends in Biomedical Natural Language Processing*, pages 38–45, Columbus, Ohio.

Yoshimasa Tsuruoka, Yuka Tateishi, Jin-Dong Kim, Tomoko Ohta, John McNaught, Sophia Ananiadou, and Jun'ichi Tsujii. 2005. Developing a robust part-of-speech tagger for biomedical text. In *Advances in Informatics*, pages 382–392.

Le Zhang. 2004. Maximum entropy modeling toolkit for Python and C++ (version 20041229). In *Natural Language Processing Lab, Northeastern*.

Uncertainty Learning Using SVMs and CRFs

Vinodkumar Prabhakaran
Computer Science Department
Columbia University, New York
vp2198@columbia.edu

Abstract

In this work, we explore the use of SVMs and CRFs in the problem of predicting certainty in sentences. We consider this as a task of tagging uncertainty cues in context, for which we used lexical, wordlist-based and deep-syntactic features. Results show that the syntactic context of the tokens in conjunction with the wordlist-based features turned out to be useful in predicting uncertainty cues.

1 Introduction

Extracting factual information from text is a critical NLP task which has important applications in Information Extraction, Textual Entailment etc. It is found that linguistic devices such as hedge phrases help to distinguish facts from uncertain information. Hedge phrases usually indicate that authors do not or cannot back up their opinions/statements with facts. As part of the CoNLL shared task 2010 (Farkas et al., 2010), we explored the applicability of different machine learning approaches and feature sets to learn to detect sentences containing uncertainty.

In Section 2, we present the task formally and describe the data used. Section 3 presents the system description and explains the features used in the task in detail. We investigated two different machine learning frameworks in this task and did experiments on various feature configurations. Section 4 presents those experiments and analyzes the results. Section 5 describes the system used for the shared task final submission and presents the results obtained in the evaluation. Section 6 concludes the paper and discusses a few future directions to extend this work.

2 Task Description and Data

We attempt only the Task 1 of the CoNLL shared task which was to identify sentences in texts which contain unreliable or uncertain information. In particular, the task is a binary classification problem, i.e. to distinguish factual versus uncertain sentences.

As training data, we use only the corpus of Wikipedia paragraphs with weasel cues manually annotated (Ganter and Strube, 2009). The annotation of weasel/hedge cues was carried out on the phrase level, and sentences containing at least one cue are considered as uncertain, while sentences with no cues are considered as factual. The corpus contained $11,110$ sentences out of which $2,484$ were tagged as uncertain. A sentence could have more than one cue phrases. There were 3143 cue phrases altogether.

3 System Description

3.1 Approach

We considered this task as a cue tagging task where in phrases suggesting uncertainty will be tagged in context. This is a 3-way classification problem at token level - B-cue, I-cue and O denoting beginning, inside and outside of a cue phrase. We applied a supervised learning framework for this task, for which We experimented with both SVMs and CRFs. For SVM, we used the Yamcha[1] system which is built on top of the tinySVM[2] package. Yamcha has been shown useful in similar tasks before. It was the best performing system in the CoNLL-2000 Shared task on chunking. In this task, Yamcha obtained the best performance for a quadratic kernel with a c value of 0.5. All results presented here use this setting. For CRF, we used the Mallet[3] software package. Experiments are done only with order-0 CRFs. CRFs proved to marginally improve the prediction accuracy while substantially improving the speed. For e.g, for a configuration of 10 features with context width of 2, Yamcha took around 5-6 hrs for 9-fold

[1] http://chasen.org/ taku/software/YamCha/
[2] http://chasen.org/ taku/software/TinySVM/
[3] http://mallet.cs.umass.edu/

Proceedings of the Fourteenth Conference on Computational Natural Language Learning: Shared Task, pages 132–137,
Uppsala, Sweden, 15-16 July 2010. ©2010 Association for Computational Linguistics

cross validation on the whole training set, where as Mallet took only around 30-40 minutes only.

3.2 Features

Our approach was to explore the use of deep syntactic features in this tagging task. Deep syntactic features had been proven useful in many similar tagging tasks before. We used the dependency parser MICA (Bangalore et al., 2009) based on Tree Adjoining Grammar (Joshi et al., 1975) to extract these deep syntactic features.

We classified the features into three classes - Lexical (L), Syntactic (S) and Wordlist-based (W). Lexical features are those which could be found at the token level without using any wordlists or dictionaries and can be extracted without any parsing with relatively high accuracy. For example, isNumeric, which denotes whether the word is a number or alphabetic, is a lexical feature. Under this definition, POS tag will be considered as a lexical feature.

Syntactic features of a token access its syntactic context in the dependency tree. For example, parentPOS, the POS tag of the parent word in the dependency parse tree, is a syntactic feature. The tree below shows the dependency parse tree output by MICA for the sentence *Republican leader Bill Frist said the Senate was hijacked.*

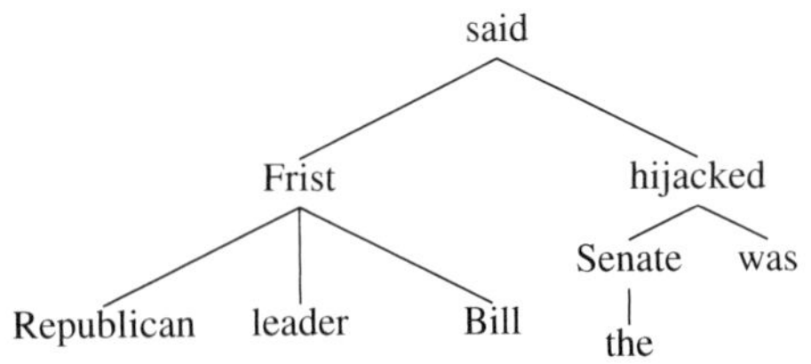

In this case, the feature haveReportingAncestor of the word *hijacked* is 'Y' because it is a verb with a parent verb *said*. Similarly, the feature haveDaughterAux would also be 'Y' because of daughter *was*, whereas whichAuxIsMyDaughter would get the value *was*.

Wordlist-based features utilized a list of words which occurred frequently as a cue word in the training corpus. We used two such lists – one which included adjectives like *many*, *most*, *some* etc. The other list contained adverbs like *probably*, *possibly* etc. The complete list of words in these wordlists are given in Table 1.

For finding the best performing feature set - context width configuration, we did an exhaustive search on the feature space, pruning away features which were proven not useful by results at stages.

The list of features we used in our experiments are summarized in Table 1 and Table 2. Table 1 contains features which were useful and are present in the results presented in section 4. Out of the syntactic features, parentPOS and isMyNNSparentGeneric turned out to be the most useful. It was noticed that in most cases in which a generic adjective (i.e., a quantifier such as *many, several, ...*) has a parent which is a plural noun, and this noun has only adjectival daughters, then it is part of a cue phrase. This distinction can be made clear by the below example.

- ⟨*ccue*⟩ *Many people* ⟨*/ccue*⟩ *enjoy having professionally made 'family portraits'*
- *Many departments, especially those in which students have research or teaching responsibilities ...*

In the first case, the noun *people* comes with the adjective *Many*, but is not qualified further. This makes it insufficiently defined and hence is tagged as a cue phrase. However in the second case, the clause which starts with *especially* is qualifying the noun *departments* further and hence the phrase is not tagged as a cue word despite the presence of *Many*. This scenario occurred often with other adjectives like *most*, *some* etc. This distinction was caught to a good extent by the combination of isMyNNSparentGeneric and isGenericAdj. Hence, the best performing configuration used features from both W and S categories.

The features which were found to be not useful is listed in Table 2. We used only two wordlist features, both of which were useful.

4 Experiments

To find the best configuration, we used 10% of the training data as the development set to tune parameters. Since even the development set was fairly large, we used 9-fold cross validation to evaluate each models. The development set was divided into 9 folds of which 8 folds were used to train a model which was tested on the 9th fold. All the reported results in this section are averaged over the 9 folds. We report $F_{\beta=1}$ (F)-measure as the harmonic mean between (P)recision and (R)ecall.

We categorized the experiments into three distinct classes as shown in Table 3. For each class, we did experiments with different feature sets and

No	Feature	Description
		Lexical Features
1	verbType	Modal/Aux/Reg (= 'nil' if the word is not a verb)
2	lemma	Lemma of the token
3	POS	Word's POS tag
4	whichModalAmI	If I am a modal, what am I? (= 'nil' if I am not a modal)
		Word List Features
1	isGenericAdj	Am I one of *some, many, certain, several*?
2	isUncertainAdv	Am I one of *generally, probably, usually, likely, typically, possibly, commonly, nearly, perhaps, often*?
3	levinClass	If I am a verb, which levin class do I belong to?
		Syntactic Features
1	parentPOS	What is my parent's POS tag?
2	leftSisPOS	What is my left sister's POS tag?
3	rightSisPOS	What is my right sister's POS tag?
4	whichModalIsMyDaughter	If I have a daughter which is a modal, what is it? (= 'nil' if I do not have a modal daughter)
5	Voice	Active/Passive (refer MICA documentation for details)
6	Mpos	MICA's mapping of POS tags (refer MICA documentation for details)
7	isMyNNSparentGeneric	If I am an adjective and if my parent is NNS and does not have a child other than adjectives
8	haveDaughterAux	Do I have a daughter which is an auxiliary.
9	whichAuxIsMyDaughter	If I have a daughter which is an auxiliary, what is it? (= 'nil' if I do not have an auxiliary daughter)

Table 1: Features used in the configurations listed in Table 4 and Table 6

Class	Description
L	Lexical features
LW	Lexical and Wordlist features
LS	Lexical and Syntactic features
LSW	Lexical, Syntactic and Wordlist features

Table 3: Experiment Sets

(linear) context widths. Here, context width denotes the window of tokens whose features are considered. For example, a context width of 2 means that the feature vector of any given token includes, in addition to its own features, those of 2 tokens before and after it as well as the prediction for 2 tokens before it. We varied the context widths from 1 to 5, and found that the best results were obtained for context width of 1 and 2.

4.1 Experimental Results

In this section, we present the results of experiments conducted on the development set as part of this task. The results for the system using Yamcha and Mallet are given in Table 4. CW stands for Context Width and P, R and F stands for Precision, Recall and F-measure, respectively. These results include the top performing 5 feature set - context width configurations using all three classes of features in both cases. It includes cue level prediction performance as well as sentence level prediction performance, where in a sentence is tagged as uncertain if it contains at least one cue phrase. In case of Mallet, it is observed that the best performing top 5 feature sets were all from the LSW category whereas in Yamcha, even configurations of LS category worked well.

We also present cue level results across feature categories for the Mallet experiments. Table 5 shows the best feature set - context width configuration for each class of experiments.

Class	Feature Set	CW
L	POS, verbType	2
LW	lemma, POS, modalMe, isGenericAdj, isUncertainAdj	2
LS	POS, parentPOS, modalDaughter, leftSisPOS, rightSisPOS, voice	2
LSW	POS, parentPOS, modalMe, isDaughterAux, leftSisPOS, mpos, isUncertainAdj, isGenericAdj, myNNSparentIsGeneric	1

Table 5: Best Feature sets - Across feature classes

Table 6 shows the cue level results of the best model for each class of experiments.

No	Feature	Description
		Lexical Features
1	Stem	Word stem (Using Porter Stemmer)
2	isNumeric	Word is Alphabet or Numeric?
		Syntactic Features
1	parentStem	Parent word stem (Using Porter Stemmer)
2	parentLemma	Parent word's Lemma
3	wordSupertag	Word's Super Tag (from Penn Treebank)
4	parentSupertag	Parent word's super tag (from Penn Treebank)
5	isRoot	Is the word the root of the MICA Parse tree?
6	pred	Is the word a predicate? (pred in MICA features)
7	drole	Deep role (drole in MICA features)
8	haveDaughterTo	Do I have a daughter 'to'?
9	haveDaughterPerfect	Do I have a daughter which is one of *has, have, had*?
10	haveDaughterShould	Do I have a daughter *should*?
11	haveDaughterWh	Do I have a daughter who is one of *where, when, while, who, why*?

Table 2: Features which turned out to be not useful

Class	Cue P	Cue R	Cue F
L	54.89	21.99	30.07
LW	51.14	20.70	28.81
LS	52.08	25.71	33.23
LSW	51.13	29.38	36.71

Table 6: Cue level Results - Across feature classes

4.2 Analysis

It is observed that the best results were observed on LSW category. The main constituent of this category was the combination of isMyNNSparentGeneric and isGenericAdj. Also, it was found that W features used without S features decreased the prediction performance. Out of the syntactic features, parentPOS, leftSisPOS and rightSisPOS proved to be the most useful in addition to isMyNNSparentGeneric.

Also, the highest cue level precision of 54.89% was obtained for L class, whereas it was lowered to 51.13% by the addition of S and W features. However, the performance improvement is due to the improved recall, which is as per the expectation that syntactic features would help identify new patterns, which lexical features alone cannot. It is also worth noting that addition of W features decreased the precision by 3.75 percentage points whereas addition of S features decreased the precision by 2.81 percentage points. Addition of S features improved the recall by 3.72 percentage points where as addition of both S and W features improved it by 7.39 percentage points. However, addition of W features alone decreased the recall by 1.29 percentage points. This suggests that the words in the wordlists were useful only when presented with the syntactic context in which they occurred.

Mallet proved to consistently over perform Yamcha in this task in terms of prediction performance as well as speed. For e.g, for a configuration of 10 features with context width of 2, Yamcha took around 5-6 hrs to perform the 9-fold cross validation on the entire training dataset, whereas Mallet took only around 30-40 minutes.

5 System used for Evaluation

In this section, we explain in detail the system which was used for the results submitted in the shared task evaluation.

For predicting the cue phrases on evaluation dataset for the shared task, we trained a model using the best performing configuration (feature set and machinery) from the experiments described in Section 4. The best configuration used the feature set <POS, parentPOS, modalMe, isDaughterAux, leftSisPOS, mpos, isUncertainAdj, isGenericAdj, myNNSparentIsGeneric> with a context width of 1 and it was trained using Mallet's CRF. The cross validation results of this configuration is reported in Table 4 (First feature set in the Mallet section). This model was trained on the entire Wikipedia training set provided for Task 1. We used this model to tag the evaluation dataset with uncertainty cues and any sentence where a cue phrase was tagged was classified as an uncertain sentence.

Feature Set	CW	Cue			Sent		
		P	R	F	P	R	F
Yamcha - Top 5 Configurations							
POS, parentPOS, modalDaughter, leftSisPOS, rightSisPOS, levinClass, myNNSparentIsGeneric	2	51.59	26.96	34.10	65.27	38.33	48.30
POS, parentPOS, amIuncertain	1	43.13	29.41	33.79	55.37	41.77	47.62
POS, parentPOS, modalDaughter, leftSisPOS, rightSisPOS, voice	2	52.08	25.71	33.23	66.52	37.10	47.63
POS, parentPOS, modalDaughter, leftSisPOS	2	54.25	25.16	33.20	69.38	35.63	47.08
POS, parentPOS, modalDaughter, leftSisPOS, rightSisPOS, mpos	2	51.82	25.56	33.01	65.62	36.12	46.59
Mallet - Top 5 Configurations							
POS, parentPOS, modalMe, isDaughterAux, leftSisPOS, mpos, isUncertainAdj, isGenericAdj, myNNSparentIsGeneric	1	51.13	29.38	36.71	66.29	42.71	51.95
POS, parentPOS, modalMe, isDaughterAux, leftSisPOS, mpos, voice, isUncertainAdj, isGenericAdj, myNNSparentIs-Generic	1	49.81	29.07	36.04	65.64	42.24	51.40
POS, parentPOS, modalMe, isUncertainAdj, isGenericAdj, myNNSparentIsGeneric	2	52.57	28.96	35.55	65.18	39.56	49.24
POS, parentPOS, modalMe, auxDaughter, leftSisPOS, mpos, voice, isUncertainAdj, isGenericAdj, myNNSparentIsGeneric	1	48.22	28.67	35.40	65.25	42.80	51.69
POS, parentPOS, modalMe, leftSisPOS, mpos, voice, isUncertainAdj, isGenericAdj, myNNSparentIsGeneric	1	52.26	28.12	35.34	65.99	40.05	49.85

Table 4: Overall Results

5.1 Evaluation Results

This section presents the results obtained on the shared task evaluation in detail. The sentence level results are given in Table 7. Our system obtained a high precision of 87.95% with a low recall of 28.42% and F-measure of 42.96% on the task. This was the 3rd best precision reported for the Wikipedia task 1.

System	Precision	Recall	F-Measure
Best System	72.04	51.66	60.17
...	...	...	...
This System	**87.95**	**28.42**	**42.96**
Last System	94.23	6.58	12.30

Table 7: Evaluation - Cue Level Results

Table 8 presents the cue level results for the task. Our system had a cue level prediction precision of 67.14% with a low recall of 16.70% and F-measure of 26.75%, which is the 3rd best F-measure result among the published cue level results[4].

We ran the best model trained on Wikipedia corpus on the biomedical evaluation dataset. As expected, the results were much lower. It obtained a precision of 67.54% with a low recall of 19.49% and F-measure of 30.26%.

[4]In the submitted result, cues were tagged in IOB format. Hence, cue level statistics were not computed and published in the CoNLL website.

System	Precision	Recall	F-Measure
X	63.01	25.94	36.55
X	76.06	21.64	33.69
This System	**67.14**	**16.70**	**26.75**
X	28.95	14.70	19.50
X	24.57	7.35	11.32

Table 8: Evaluation - Cue Level Results

6 Conclusion and Future Work

A simple bag of words approach at the sentence level could have given similar or even better performance for the sentence level prediction task. However, identifying cues in context is important to extend this task to application where we need to make semantic inferences or even identifying the scope of uncertainty (which was the task 2 of the shared task). Hence, we infer that this or a similar cue tagging approach with a more sophisticated feature set and machinery should be explored further.

Our experiments show that the addition of syntactic features helps in improving recall. However, the advantage given by syntactic features were surprisingly marginal. In detailed error analysis, it was found that the syntactic patterns that proved helpful for this task were fairly local. So, probably exploring shallow syntactic features instead of deep syntactic features might be helpful for this task. Also, we assume that using more sophisticated lexical features or custom made lexicons could also improve performance.

Acknowledgements

This work was supported by grants from the Human Language Technology Center of Excellence. Any opinions, findings, and conclusions or recommendations expressed in this material are those of the author and do not necessarily reflect the views of the sponsor.

I would also like to extend my heartfelt gratitude to Prof. Kathy McKeown and Yves Petinot for their vital encouragement and support throughout this project. I would also like to thank my advisors Dr. Mona Diab and Dr. Owen Rambow for their valuable suggestions and support.

References

Srinivas Bangalore, Pierre Boullier, Alexis Nasr, Owen Rambow, and Benoît Sagot. 2009. MICA: A probabilistic dependency parser based on tree insertion grammars. In *NAACL HLT 2009 (Short Papers)*.

Richárd Farkas, Veronika Vincze, György Móra, János Csirik, and György Szarvas. 2010. The CoNLL-2010 Shared Task: Learning to Detect Hedges and their Scope in Natural Language Text. In *Proceedings of the Fourteenth Conference on Computational Natural Language Learning (CoNLL-2010): Shared Task*, pages 1–12, Uppsala, Sweden, July. Association for Computational Linguistics.

Viola Ganter and Michael Strube. 2009. Finding Hedges by Chasing Weasels: Hedge Detection Using Wikipedia Tags and Shallow Linguistic Features. In *Proceedings of the ACL-IJCNLP 2009 Conference Short Papers*, pages 173–176, Suntec, Singapore, August. Association for Computational Linguistics.

Aravind K. Joshi, Leon Levy, and M Takahashi. 1975. Tree adjunct grammars. *Journal of the Computer and System Sciences*, 10:136–163.

Features for Detecting Hedge Cues

Nobuyuki Shimizu
Information Technology Center
The University of Tokyo
shimizu@r.dl.itc.u-tokyo.ac.jp

Hiroshi Nakagawa
Information Technology Center
The University of Tokyo
n3@dl.itc.u-tokyo.ac.jp

Abstract

We present a sequential labeling approach to hedge cue detection submitted to the biological portion of task 1 for the CoNLL-2010 shared task. Our main approach is as follows. We make use of partial syntactic information together with features obtained from the unlabeled corpus, and convert the task into one of sequential BIO-tagging. If a cue is found, a sentence is classified as uncertain and certain otherwise. To examine a large number of feature combinations, we employ a genetic algorithm. While some features obtained by this method are difficult to interpret, they were shown to improve the performance of the final system.

1 Introduction

Research on automatically extracting factual information from biomedical texts has become popular in recent years. Since these texts are abundant with hypotheses postulated by researchers, one hurdle that an information extraction system must overcome is to be able to determine whether or not the information is part of a hypothesis or a factual statement. Thus, detecting hedge cues that indicate the uncertainty of the statement is an important subtask of information extraction (IE). Hedge cues include words such as “may”, “might”, “appear”, “suggest”, “putative” and “or”. They also includes phrases such as “. . .raising an intriguing question that. . .” As these expressions are sparsely scattered throughout the texts, it is not easy to generalize results of machine learning from a training set to a test set. Furthermore, simply finding the expressions listed above does not guarantee that a sentence contains a hedge. Their function as a hedge cue depends on the surrounding context.

The primary objective of the CoNLL-2010 shared task (Farkas et al., 2010) is to detect hedge cues and their scopes as are present in biomedical texts. In this paper, we focus on the biological portion of task 1, and present a sequential labeling approach to hedge cue detection. The following summarizes the steps we took to achieve this goal. Similarly to previous work in hedge cue detection (Morante and Daelemans, 2009), we first convert the task into a sequential labeling task based on the BIO scheme, where each word in a hedge cue is labeled as B-CUE, I-CUE, or O, indicating respectively the labeled word is at the beginning of a cue, inside of a cue, or outside of a hedge cue; this is similar to the tagging scheme from the CoNLL-2001 shared task. We then prepared features, and fed the training data to a sequential labeling system, a discriminative Markov model much like Conditional Random Fields (CRF), with the difference being that the model parameters are tuned using Bayes Point Machines (BPM), and then compared our model against an equivalent CRF model. To convert the result of sequential labeling to sentence classification, we simply used the presence of a hedge cue, i.e. if a cue is found, a sentence is classified as uncertain and certain otherwise.

To prepare features, we ran the GENIA tagger to add partial syntactic parse and named entity information. We also applied Porter's stemmer (Jones and Willet, 1997) to each word in the corpus. For each stem, we acquired the distribution of surrounding words from the unlabeled corpus, and calculated the similarity between these distributions and the distribution of hedge cues in the training corpus. Given a stem and its similarities to different hedge cues, we took the maximum similarity and discretized it. All these features are passed on to a sequential labeling system. Using these base features, we then evaluated the effects of feature combinations by repeatedly training the system and selecting feature combinations that increased the performance on a heldout set. To au-

Proceedings of the Fourteenth Conference on Computational Natural Language Learning: Shared Task, pages 138–143,
Uppsala, Sweden, 15-16 July 2010.

tomate this process, we employed a genetic algorithm.

The contribution of this paper is two-fold. First, we describe our system, outlined above, that we submitted to the CoNLL-2010 shared task in more detail. Second, we analyze the effects of particular choices we made when building our system, especially the feature combinations and learning methods.

The rest of this paper is organized as follows. In Section 2, we detail how the task of sequential labeling is formalized in terms of linear classification, and explain the Viterbi algorithm required for prediction. We next present several algorithms for optimizing the weight vector in a linear classifier in Section 3. We then detail the complete list of feature templates we used for the task of hedge cue detection in Section 4. In order to evaluate the effects of feature templates, in Section 5, we remove each feature template and find that several feature templates overfit the training set. We finally conclude with Section 6.

2 Sequential Labeling

We discriminatively train a Markov model using Bayes Point Machines (BPM). We will first explain linear classification, and then apply a Markov assumption to the classification formalism. Then we will move on to BPM. Note that we assume all features are binary in this and upcoming sections as it is sufficient for the task at hand.

In the setting of sequential labeling, given the input sequence $\mathbf{x} = (x_1, x_2, x_3, ...x_n)$, a system is asked to produce the output sequence $\mathbf{y} = (y_1, y_2, y_3, ...y_n)$. Considering that $\mathbf{y}$ is a class, sequential labeling is simply a classification with a very large number of classes. Assuming that the problem is one of linear classification, we may create a binary feature vector $\phi(\mathbf{x})$ for an input $\mathbf{x}$ and have a weight vector $\mathbf{w_y}$ of the same dimension for each class $\mathbf{y}$. We choose a class $\mathbf{y}$ that has the highest dot product between the input vector and the weight vector for the class $\mathbf{y}$. For binary classification, this process is very simple: compare two dot product values. Learning is therefore reduced to specifying the weight vectors.

To follow the standard notations in sequential labeling, let weight vectors $\mathbf{w_y}$ be stacked into one large vector $\mathbf{w}$, and let $\phi(\mathbf{x}, \mathbf{y})$ be a binary feature vector such that $\mathbf{w}^\top \phi(\mathbf{x}, \mathbf{y})$ is equal to $\mathbf{w_y}^\top \phi(\mathbf{x})$. Classification is to choose $\mathbf{y}$ such that $\mathbf{y} = argmax_{\mathbf{y}'}(\mathbf{w}^\top \phi(\mathbf{x}, \mathbf{y}'))$.

Unfortunately, a large number of classes created out of sequences makes the problem intractable, so the Markov assumption factorizes $\mathbf{y}$ into a sequence of labels, such that a label y_i is affected only by the label before and after it (y_{i-1} and y_{i+1} respectively) in the sequence. Each structure, or label $\mathbf{y}$ is now associated with a set of the parts $parts(\mathbf{y})$ such that $\mathbf{y}$ can be recomposed from the parts. In the case of sequential labeling, parts consist of states y_i and transitions $y_i \rightarrow y_{i+1}$ between neighboring labels. We assume that the feature vector for an entire structure $\mathbf{y}$ decomposes into a sum over feature vectors for individual parts as follows: $\phi(\mathbf{x}, \mathbf{y}) = \sum_{r \in parts(\mathbf{y})} \phi(\mathbf{x}, r)$. Note that we have overloaded the symbol ϕ to apply to either a structure y or its parts r.

The Markov assumption for factoring labels lets us use the Viterbi algorithm (much like a Hidden Markov Model) in order to find

$$\begin{aligned} \mathbf{y} &= argmax_{\mathbf{y}'} \quad (\mathbf{w}^\top \phi(\mathbf{x}, \mathbf{y}')) \\ &= argmax_{\mathbf{y}'} \quad (\textstyle\sum_{j=1}^{n} \mathbf{w}^\top \phi(\mathbf{x}, y'_j) \\ &\qquad + \textstyle\sum_{j=1}^{n-1} \mathbf{w}^\top \phi(\mathbf{x}, y'_j \rightarrow y'_{j+1})). \end{aligned}$$

3 Optimization

We now turn to the optimization of the weight parameter $\mathbf{w}$. We compare three approaches – Perceptron, Bayes Point Machines and Conditional Random Fields, using our c++ library for structured output prediction [1].

Perceptron is an online update scheme that leaves the weights unchanged when the predicted output matches the target, and changes them when it does not. The update is:

$$\mathbf{w}_k := \mathbf{w}_k - \phi(\mathbf{x}^i, \mathbf{y}) + \phi(\mathbf{x}^i, \mathbf{y}^i).$$

Despite its seemingly simple update scheme, perceptron is known for its effectiveness and performance (Collins, 2002).

Conditional Random Fields (CRF) is a conditional model

$$P(\mathbf{y}|\mathbf{x}) = \frac{1}{Z_\mathbf{x}} exp(\mathbf{w}^\top \phi(\mathbf{x}, \mathbf{y}))$$

where w is the weight for each feature and $Z_\mathbf{x}$ is a normalization constant for each $\mathbf{x}$.

$$Z_\mathbf{x} = \sum_\mathbf{y} exp(\mathbf{w}^\top \phi(\mathbf{x}, \mathbf{y}))$$

[1] Available at http://soplib.sourceforge.net/

for structured output prediction. To fit the weight vector $\mathbf{w}$ using the training set $\{(\mathbf{x}^i, \mathbf{y}^i)\}_{i=1}^n$, we use a standard gradient-descent method to find the weight vector that maximizes the log likelihood $\sum_i^n logP(\mathbf{y}^i|x^i)$ (Sha and Pereira, 2003). To avoid overfitting, the log likelihood is often penalized with a spherical Gaussian weight prior: $\sum_i^n logP(\mathbf{y}^i|x^i) - \frac{C||\mathbf{w}||}{2}$. We also evaluated this penalized version, varying the trade-off parameter C.

Bayes Point Machines (BPM) for structured prediction (Corston-Oliver et al., 2006) is an ensemble learning algorithm that attempts to set the weight $\mathbf{w}$ to be the Bayes Point which approximates to Bayesian inference for linear classifiers. Assuming a uniform prior distribution over w, we revise our belief of w after observing the training data and produce a posterior distribution. We create the final w_{bpm} for classification using a posterior distribution as follows:

$$\mathbf{w}_{bpm} = E_{p(\mathbf{w}|D)}[\mathbf{w}] = \sum_{i=1}^{|V(D)|} p(\mathbf{w}_i|D)\mathbf{w}_i$$

where $p(\mathbf{w}|D)$ is the posterior distribution of the weights given the data D and $E_{p(\mathbf{w}|D)}$ is the expectation taken with respect to this distribution. $V(D)$ is the version space, which is the set of weights $\mathbf{w}_i$ that classify the training data correctly, and $|V(D)|$ is the size of the version space. In practice, to explore the version space of weights consistent with the training data, BPM trains a few different perceptrons (Collins, 2002) by shuffling the samples. The approximation of Bayes Point $\mathbf{w}_{bpm}$ is the average of these perceptron weights:

$$\mathbf{w}_{bpm} = E_{p(\mathbf{w}|D)}[\mathbf{w}] \approx \sum_{k=1}^{K} \frac{1}{K}\mathbf{w}_k.$$

The pseudocode of the algorithm is shown in Algorithm 3.1. We see that the inner loop is simply a perceptron algorithm.

Algorithm 3.1: BPM($K, T, \{(\mathbf{x}^i, \mathbf{y}^i)\}_{i=1}^n$)

```
w_bpm := 0;
for k := 1 to K
  Randomly shuffle the sequential order of
   samples {(x^i, y^i)}_{i=1}^n
  w_k := 0;
  for t := 1 to T   # Perceptron iterations
    for i := 1 to n   # Iterate shuffled samples
      y := argmax_y'(w_k^T φ(x^i, y'))
      if (y ≠ y^i)
        w_k := w_k − φ(x^i, y) + φ(x^i, y^i);
  w_bpm := w_bpm + (1/K) w_k;
return (w_bpm)
```

4 Features

4.1 Base Features

For each sentence $\mathbf{x}$, we have state features, represented by a binary vector $\phi(\mathbf{x}, y'_j)$ and transition features, again a binary vector $\phi(\mathbf{x}, y'_j \rightarrow y'_{j+1})$.

For transition features, we do not utilize lexicalized features. Thus, each dimension of $\phi(\mathbf{x}, y'_j \rightarrow y'_{j+1})$ is an indicator function that tests a combination of labels, for example, O→B-CUE, B-CUE→I-CUE or I-CUE→O.

For state features $\phi(\mathbf{x}, y'_j)$, the indicator function for each dimension tests a combination of y'_j and lexical features obtained from $\mathbf{x} = (x_1, x_2, x_3, ...x_n)$. We now list the base lexical features that were considered for this experiment.

F^0 a token, which is usually a word. As a part of preprocessing, words in each input sentence are tokenized using the GENIA tagger [2]. This tokenization coincides with Penn Treebank style tokenization [3].

We add a subscript to indicate the position. F_j^0 is exactly the input token x_j. From x_j, we also create other lexical features such as F_j^1, F_j^2, F_j^3, and so on.

F^1 the token in lower case, with digits replaced by the symbol #.

F^2 1 if the letters in the token are all capitalized, 0 otherwise.

F^3 1 if the token contains a digit, 0 otherwise.

F^4 1 if the token contains an uppercase letter, 0 otherwise.

F^5 1 if the token contains a hyphen, 0 otherwise.

[2]Available at: http:// www-tsujii.is.s.u-tokyo.ac.jp/ GENIA/ tagger/

[3]A tokenizer is available at: http:// www.cis.upenn.edu/ treebank/ tokenization.html

F^6 first letter in the token.

F^7 first two letters in the token.

F^8 first three letters in the token.

F^9 last letter in the token.

F^{10} last two letters in the token.

F^{11} last three letters in the token.

The features F^0 to F^{11} are known to be useful for POS tagging. We postulated that since most frequent hedge cues tend not to be nouns, these features might help identify them.

The following three features are obtained by running the GENIA tagger.

F^{12} a part of speech.

F^{13} a CoNLL-2000 style shallow parse. For example, B-NP or I-NP indicates that the token is a part of a base noun phrase, B-VP or I-VP indicates that it is part of a verb phrase.

F^{14} named entity, especially a protein name.

F^{15} a word stem by Porter's stemmer [4]. Porter's stemmer removes common morphological and inflectional endings from words in English. It is often used as part of an information retrieval system.

Upon later inspection, it seems that Porter's stemmer may be too aggressive in stemming words. The word *putative*, for example, after being processed by the stemmer, becomes simply *put* (which is clearly erroneous).

The last nine types of features utilize the unlabeled corpus for the biological portion of shared task 1, provided by the shared task organizers. For each stem, we acquire a histogram of surrounding words, with a window size of 3, from the unlabeled corpus. Each histogram is represented as a vector; the similarity between histograms was then computed. The similarity metric we used is called the Tanimoto coefficient, also called extended/vector-based Jaccard coefficient.

$$\frac{\mathbf{v}_i \cdot \mathbf{v}_j}{||\mathbf{v}_i|| + ||\mathbf{v}_j|| - \mathbf{v}_i \cdot \mathbf{v}_j}$$

It is based on the dot product of two vectors and reduces to Jaccard coefficient for binary features.

[4]Available at: http://tartarus.org/ martin/PorterStemmer/

This metric is known to perform quite well for near-synonym discovery (Hagiwara et al., 2008). Given a stem and its similarities to different hedge cues, we took the maximum similarity and discretized it.

F^{16} 1 if similarity is bigger than 0.9, 0 otherwise.

...

F^{19} 1 if similarity is bigger than 0.6, 0 otherwise.

...

F^{24} 1 if similarity is bigger than 0.1, 0 otherwise.

This concludes the base features we considered.

4.2 Combinations of Base Features

In order to discover combinations of base features, we implemented a genetic algorithm (Goldberg, 1989). It is an adaptive heuristic search algorithm based on the evolutionary ideas of natural selection and genetics. After splitting the training set into three partitions, given the first partition as the training set, the fitness is measured by the score of predicting the second partition. We removed the feature sets that did not score high, and introduced mutations – new feature sets – as replacements. After several generations, surviving feature sets performed quite well. To avoid over fitting, occasionally feature sets were evaluated on the third partition, and we finally chose the feature set according to this partition.

The features of the submitted system are listed in Table 1. Note that Table 1 shows the dimensions of the feature vector that evaluate to 1 given $\mathbf{x}$ and y'_j. The actual feature vector is created by instantiating all the combinations in the table using the training set.

Surprisingly, our genetic algorithm removed features F^{10} and F^{11}, the last two/three letters in a token. It also removed the POS information F^{12}, but kept the sequence of POS tags $F^{12}_{j-1}, F^{12}_{j}, F^{12}_{j+1}, F^{12}_{j+2}, F^{12}_{j+3}$. The reason for longer sequences is due to our heuristics for mutations. Occasionally, we allowed the genetic algorithm to insert a longer sequence of feature combinations at once. One other notable observation is that shallow parses and NEs are removed. Between the various thresholds from F^{16} to F^{24}, it only kept F^{19}, discovering 0.6 as a similarity threshold.

State $\phi(\mathbf{x}, y'_j)$
y'_j
y'_j, F^0_{j-2}
y'_j, F^0_{j-1}
y'_j, F^0_j
y'_j, F^0_j, F^{19}_j
$y'_j, F^0_{j-1}, F^0_j, F^0_{j+1}, F^0_{j+2}, F^0_{j+3}, F^0_{j+4}$ –(1)
y'_j, F^0_{j+1}
y'_j, F^0_{j+2}
y'_j, F^1_j
y'_j, F^2_j –(2)
y'_j, F^3_j
y'_j, F^4_j
$y'_j, F^4_{j-2}, F^4_{j-1}, F^4_j, F^4_{j+1}, F^4_{j+2}$
y'_j, F^5_j
y'_j, F^5_j, F^7_{j-1}
y'_j, F^6_j
y'_j, F^7_j
y'_j, F^8_j
$y'_j, F^9_{j-1}, F^9_j, F^9_{j+1}, F^9_{j+2}, F^9_{j+3}$
$y'_j, F^{12}_{j-1}, F^{12}_j, F^{12}_{j+1}, F^{12}_{j+2}, F^{12}_{j+3}$
$y'_j, F^{15}_j, F^{15}_{j+1}, F^{15}_{j+2}, F^{15}_{j+3}$
$y'_j, F^{19}_{j-2}, F^{19}_{j-1}, F^{19}_j, F^{19}_{j+1}, F^{19}_{j+2}$

Table 1: Features for Sequential Labeling

5 Experiments

In order to examine the effects of learning parameters, we conducted experiments on the test data after it was released to the participants of the shared task.

While BPM has two parameters, K and T, we fixed $T = 5$ and varied K, the number of perceptrons. As increasing the number of perceptrons results in more thorough exploration of the version space $V(D)$, we expect that the performance of the classifier would improve as K increases. Table 2 shows how the number of perceptrons affects the performance.

TP stands for True Positive, FP for False Positive, and FN for False Negative. The evaluation metrics were precision P (the number of true positives divided by the total number of elements labeled as belonging to the positive class) recall R (the number of true positives divided by the total number of elements that actually belong to the positive class) and their harmonic mean, the F_1 score ($F_1 = 2PR/(P + R)$). All figures in this paper measure hedge cue detection performance at the sentence classification level, not word/phrase classification level. From the results, once the number of perceptrons hits 20, the performance stabilizes and does not seem to show any improvement.

K	TP	FP	FN	P (%)	R (%)	F_1 (%)
10	641	80	149	88.90	81.14	84.84
20	644	79	146	89.07	81.52	85.13
30	644	80	146	88.95	81.52	85.07
40	645	81	145	88.84	81.65	85.09
50	645	80	145	88.97	81.65	85.15

Table 2: Effects of K in Bayes Point Machines

Next, in order to examine whether or not we have overfitted to the training/heldout set, we removed each row of Table 1 and reevaluated the performance of the system. Reevaluation was conducted on the labeled test set released by the shared task organizers after our system's output had been initially evaluated. Thus, these figures are comparable to the sentence classification results reported in Farkas et al. (2010).

	TP	FP	FN	P (%)	R (%)	F_1 (%)
1	647	79	143	89.12	81.90	85.36
2	647	80	143	89.00	81.90	85.30
1,2	647	81	143	88.87	81.90	85.24

Table 3: Effects of removing features (1) or (2), or both

Table 3 shows the effect of removing (1), (2), or both (1) and (2), showing that they overfit the training data. Removing any other rows in Table 1 resulted in decreased classification performance. While there are other large combination features such as ones involving F^4, F^9, F^{12}, F^{15} and F^{19}, we find that they do help improving the performance of the classifier. Since these features seem unintuitive to the authors, it is likely that they would not have been found without the genetic algorithm we employed. Error analysis shows that inclusion of features involving F^9 affects prediction of "believe", "possible", "putative", "assumed", "seemed", "if", "presumably", "perhaps", "suggestion", "suppose" and "intriguing". However, as this feature template is unfolded into a large number of features, we were unable to obtain further linguistic insights.

In the following experiments, we used the currently best performing features, that is, all features except (1) in Table 1, and trained the classifiers using the formalism of Perceptron and Conditional Random Fields besides Bayes Point Machines as we have been using. The results in Table 4 shows that BPM performs better than Perceptron or Conditional Random Fields. As the training time for BPM is better than CRF, our choice of BPM helped us to run the genetic algorithm repeatedly as well. After several runs of empirical tuning and tweaking, the hyper-parameters of the algorithms were set as follows. Perceptron was stopped at 40 iterations ($T = 40$). For BPM, we fixed $T = 5$ and $K = 20$. For Conditional Random Fields, we compared the penalized version with $C = 1$ and the unpenalized version ($C = 0$). The results in Table 4 is that of the unpenalized version, as it performed better than the penalized version.

Perceptron

TP	FP	FN	P (%)	R (%)	F_1 (%)
671	128	119	83.98	84.94	84.46

Conditional Random Fields

TP	FP	FN	P (%)	R (%)	F_1 (%)
643	78	147	89.18	81.39	85.11

Bayes Point Machines

TP	FP	FN	P (%)	R (%)	F_1 (%)
647	79	143	89.12	81.90	85.36

Table 4: Performance of different optimization strategies

6 Conclusion

To tackle the hedge cue detection problem posed by the CoNLL-2010 shared task, we utilized a classifier for sequential labeling following previous work (Morante and Daelemans, 2009). An essential part of this task is to discover the features that allow us to predict unseen hedge expressions. As hedge cue detection is semantic rather than syntactic in nature, useful features such as word stems tend to be specific to each word and hard to generalize. However, by using a genetic algorithm to examine a large number of feature combinations, we were able to find many features with a wide context window of up to 5 words. While some features are found to overfit, our analysis shows that a number of these features are successfully applied to the test data yielding good generalized performance. Furthermore, we compared different optimization schemes for structured output prediction using our c++ library, freely available for download and use. We find that Bayes Point Machines have a good trade-off between performance and training speed, justifying our repeated usage of BPM in the genetic algorithm for feature selection.

Acknowledgments

The authors would like to thank the reviewers for their comments. This research was supported by the Information Technology Center through their grant to the first author. We would also like to thank Mr. Ono, Mr. Yonetsuji and Mr. Yamada for their contributions to the library.

References

Michael Collins. 2002. Discriminative training methods for hidden Markov models: Theory and experiments with perceptron algorithms. In *Proceedings of Empirical Methods in Natural Language Processing (EMNLP)*.

Simon Corston-Oliver, Anthony Aue, Kevin Duh, and Eric Ringger. 2006. Multilingual dependency parsing using bayes point machines. In *Proceedings of the Human Language Technology Conference of the NAACL, Main Conference*, pages 160–167, June.

Richárd Farkas, Veronika Vincze, György Móra, János Csirik, and György Szarvas. 2010. The CoNLL-2010 Shared Task: Learning to Detect Hedges and their Scope in Natural Language Text. In *Proceedings of the Fourteenth Conference on Computational Natural Language Learning (CoNLL-2010): Shared Task*, pages 1–12, Uppsala, Sweden. ACL.

David E. Goldberg. 1989. *Genetic Algorithms in Search, Optimization, and Machine Learning*. Addison-Wesley Professional.

Masato Hagiwara, Yasuhiro Ogawa, and Katsuhiko Toyama. 2008. Context feature selection for distributional similarity. In *Proceedings of IJCNLP-08*.

Karen Spärk Jones and Peter Willet. 1997. *Readings in Information Retrieval*. Morgan Kaufmann.

Roser Morante and Walter Daelemans. 2009. Learning the scope of hedge cues in biomedical texts. In *BioNLP '09: Proceedings of the Workshop on BioNLP*, pages 28–36.

Fei Sha and Fernando Pereira. 2003. Shallow parsing with conditional random fields. In *Proceedings of the Human Language Technology Conference (HLT)*.

A Simple Ensemble Method for Hedge Identification

Ferenc P. Szidarovszky[1], **Illés Solt**[1], **Domonkos Tikk**[1,2]
[1] Budapest University of Technology and Economics, Budapest, Hungary
[2] Humboldt-Universität zu Berlin, Berlin, Germany
ferenc.szidarovszky@hotmail.com, {solt,tikk}@tmit.bme.hu

Abstract

We present in this paper a simple hedge identification method and its application on biomedical text. The problem at hand is a subtask of CoNLL-2010 shared task. Our solution consists of two classifiers, a statistical one and a CRF model, and a simple combination schema that combines their predictions. We report in detail on each component of our system and discuss the results. We also show that a more sophisticated combination schema could improve the F-score significantly.

1 Problem definition

The CoNLL-2010 Shared Task focused on the identification and localization of uncertain information and its scope in text. In the first task, a binary classification of sentences had to be performed, based on whether they are uncertain or not. The second task concentrated on the identification of the source of uncertainty – specifying the keyword/phrase that makes its context uncertain –, and the localization of its scope. The organizers provided training data from two application domains: biomedical texts and Wikipedia articles. For more details see the overview paper by the organizers (Farkas et al., 2010). We focused on task 1 and worked with biomedical texts exclusively.

The biomedical training corpus contains selected abstracts and full text articles from the BioScope corpus (Vincze et al., 2008). The corpus was manually annotated for *hedge cues* on the phrase level. Sentences containing at least one cue are considered as uncertain, while sentences with no cues are considered as factual. Though cue tagging was given in the training data, their marking in the submission was not mandatory.

The evaluation of systems at task 1 was performed on the sentence level with the F-measure of the uncertain class being the official evaluation metric. For evaluation, corpora also from both domains were provided that allowed for in-domain and cross-domain experiments as well. Nevertheless, we restricted the scope of our system to the in-domain biomedical subtask.

2 Background

Automatic information extraction methods may incorrectly extract facts that are mentioned in a negated or speculative context. If aiming at high accuracy, it is therefore crucial to be able to classify assertions to avoid such false positives. The importance of assertion classification has been recently recognized by the text mining community, which yielded several text-mining challenges covering this task. For example, the main task of Obesity Challenge (Uzuner, 2008) was to identify based on a free text medical record whether a patient is known to, speculated to or known not to have a disease; in the BioNLP '09 Shared Task (Kim et al., 2009), mentions of bio-molecular events had to be classified as either positive or negative statements or speculations.

Approaches to tackle assertion classification can be roughly organized into following classes: rule based models (Chapman et al., 2001), statistical models (Szarvas, 2008), machine learning (Medlock and Briscoe, 2007), though most contributions can be seen as a combination of these (Uzuner et al., 2009). Even when classifying sentences, the most common approach is to look for cues below the sentence-level (Özgür and Radev, 2009). The common in these approaches is that they use a text representation richer than bag-of-words, usually tokens from a fixed-width window with additional surface features.

Evaluation of assertion classification is mostly performed at the sentence level, where state-of-the-art systems have been reported to achieve an F-measure of 83–85% for hedge detection in

Proceedings of the Fourteenth Conference on Computational Natural Language Learning: Shared Task, pages 144–147,
Uppsala, Sweden, 15-16 July 2010.

biomedical literature (Medlock and Briscoe, 2007; Szarvas, 2008).

3 Methods

Although the problem itself is a binary categorization problem, we approach the problem at the token/phrase level. We search for hedge cues and used the decision model also applied by the annotators of the training corpus: when a sentence contains at least one uncertainty cue then it is uncertain, otherwise factual.

We applied two different models to identify hedge cues:

- a *statistical model* that creates a candidate list of cue words/phrases from the training samples, and cuts off the list based on the precision measured on the trial set;
- a sequence tagger *CRF model*, trained again with hedge cues using various feature sets.

Finally, we combined the outputs of the methods at the sentence level. Here we applied two very simple ways of combination: the aggressive one assigns a sentence to the uncertain class if any of the models finds a cue phrase therein (OR merger), while the conservative only if both models predict the sentence as uncertain (AND merger). We submitted the version which produced better result on the trial set. The overview of our system is depicted on Figure 1.

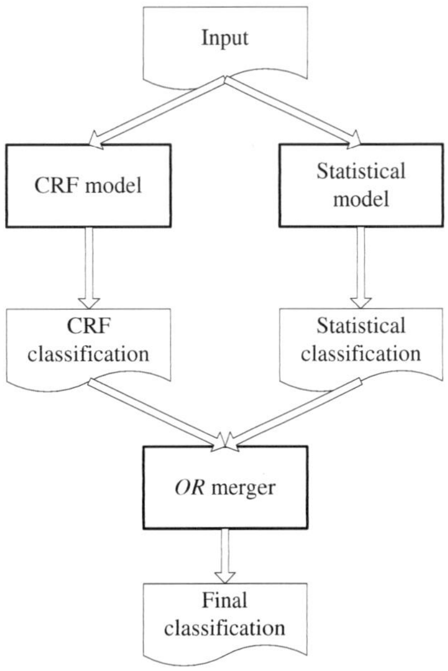

Figure 1: System overview

3.1 Preprocessing

The biomedical corpus was provided in two train/trial pairs (abstracts and full texts), see also Table 1. Because the ratio of uncertain sentences is similar in both train and trial sets, we merged the two train sets and the two trial sets, respectively, to obtain a single train/trial pair. Since the trial set was originally included also in the train set, we removed the elements of the merged trial set from the merged train set. In the following, we refer to them as *train* and *trial* sets. All data (train, trial, evaluation) were given as separate sentences; therefore no sentence segmentation had to be performed.

Merging train and trial sets was also motivated by the sparsity of data and the massively different train/trial ratio observed for the two types of biomedical texts (Table 1). Therefore building separate models for abstracts and full texts may only yield overfitting, particularly because such a distinction is not available for the evaluation set.

3.2 Statistical model

The statistical model considers a sentence uncertain, if it contains at least one cue from a validated set of cue phrases. To determine the set of cue phrases to be used, we first collected all annotated cues from the training data. From this candidate cue set we retained those ones that had a precision over a predefined threshold. To this end we measured on the training set the precision of each cue phrase. We depicted on Figure 2 the precision, recall and F-measure values obtained on the trial set with different cue phrase precision thresholds.

The candidate cue set contains 186 cue phrases, among which 83 has precision 1.0 and 141 has precision greater or equal 0.5. Best cue phrases include words/phrases like *cannot + verb phrase, hypothesis, indicate, may, no(t) + verb/noun, raise the + noun, seem, suggest, whether* etc., while low precision cues are, e.g., *assume, not fully understood, not, or, prediction, likelihood.*

3.3 CRF model

Identifying entities such as speculation cues can be efficiently solved by training conditional random field (CRF) models. As a general sequence tagger, a CRF can be naturally extended to incorporate token features and features of neighboring tokens. The trained CRF model is then applied to unseen

	Train set			Trial set			Evaluation set		
	sentences	uncertain	ratio	sentences	uncertain	ratio	sentences	uncertain	ratio
Abstract	11 832	2 091	17.7 %	39	10	25.6 %	–	–	–
Full text	2 442	468	19.2 %	228	51	22.4 %	–	–	–
Total	14 274	2 559	17.9 %	267	61	22.9 %	5 003	790	15.8 %

Table 1: Basic statistics of the provided train, trial, and evaluation sets

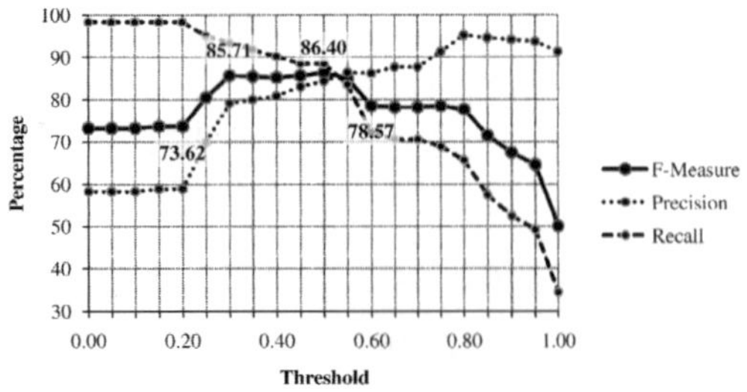

Figure 2: Cue phrase threshold selection

text, whenever a speculation cue is found the containing sentence is annotated as being speculative. In our experiments, we used MALLET (McCallum, 2002) to train CRF models using custom tokenization (Section 3.3.1) and feature sets (Section 3.3.2). We included features of 2–2 neighboring tokens in each direction, not surpassing the sentence limits.

3.3.1 Tokenization

We split text into tokens using punctuation and white-space tokenization, keeping punctuation symbols as separate tokens.

3.3.2 Feature sets

We experimented with the following binary surface features:

1. token text
2. token text in lowercase
3. stem of token in lowercase
4. indicator of the token being all lowercase
5. indicator whether the token is in sentence case (first character upper-, others lowercase)
6. indicator whether the token contains at least one digit
7. indicator of token being a punctuation symbol

These features were evaluated both in isolation and in combination on the trial set. The best performing combination was then used to train the final model.

3.3.3 Feature selection

Evaluating all combinations of the above features, we found that the combination of features 2 and 4 produced the best results on the trial set. For computational efficiency, when selecting the best performing feature subset, we considered lower feature count to overrule a slight increase in performance.

4 Results

Table 2 and Table 3 summarize the results for the statistical and CRF models and their AND and OR combinations on the trial and on the evaluation sets, respectively. For the latter, we used naturally all available labeled data (train and trial sets) for training. Numbers shown correspond to the output of the official evaluation tool. Results on the combination OR represent our official shared task evaluation.

5 Discussion

In the development scenario (Table 2), the main difference between the statistical and CRF model was that the former was superior in recall while the latter in precision. It was thus unclear which of the combinations OR and AND would perform better, we chose OR, the combination method which performed better on the trial set. Unfortunately, the rank of combination methods was different when measured on the evaluation set (Table 3). A possible explanation for this non-extrapolability is the different prior probability of speculative sentences in each set, e.g., 17.9% on the train set while 22.9% on the trial set and 15.8% on the evaluation set.

While using only a minimal amount of features, both of our models were on par with other participants' solutions. Overfitting was observed by the statistical model only (14% drop in precision on the evaluation set), the CRF model showed more consistent behavior across the datasets.

	Model			
	Statistical	CRF	Combination AND	Combination OR
Precision (%)	84.4	92.3	93.9	83.6
Recall (%)	88.6	78.7	75.4	91.8
F-measure (%)	**86.4**	**85.0**	**83.6**	**87.5**

Table 2: Results on trial set (development)

	Model			
	Statistical	CRF	Combination AND	Combination OR
Precision (%)	70.5	87.0	88.0	70.1
Recall (%)	89.4	82.7	81.0	91.0
F-measure (%)	**78.8**	**84.8**	**84.4**	**79.2**

Table 3: Results on evaluation set

6 Conclusion

We presented our method to identify hedging in biomedical literature, and its evaluation at the CoNLL-2010 shared task. We solved the sentence level assertion classification problem by using an ensemble of statistical and CRF models that identify speculation cue phrases. The non-extrapolability of the combination methods' performance observed emphasizes the sensitivity of ensemble methods to the distributions of the datasets they are applied to. While using only a minimal set of standard surface features, our CRF model was on par with participants' systems.

Acknowledgement

D. Tikk was supported by the Alexander-von-Humboldt Foundation.

References

Wendy W. Chapman, Will Bridewell, Paul Hanbury, Gregory F. Cooper, and Bruce G. Buchanan. 2001. A simple algorithm for identifying negated findings and diseases in discharge summaries. *Journal of Biomedical Informatics*, 2001:34–301.

Richárd Farkas, Veronika Vincze, György Móra, János Csirik, and György Szarvas. 2010. The CoNLL-2010 Shared Task: Learning to Detect Hedges and their Scope in Natural Language Text. In *Proceedings of the Fourteenth Conference on Computational Natural Language Learning (CoNLL-2010): Shared Task*, pages 1–12, Uppsala, Sweden. ACL.

Jin-Dong Kim, Tomoko Ohta, Sampo Pyysalo, Yoshinobu Kano, and Jun'ichi Tsujii. 2009. Overview of BioNLP'09 shared task on event extraction. In *BioNLP '09: Proc. of the Workshop on BioNLP*, pages 1–9, Morristown, NJ, USA. ACL.

Andrew K. McCallum. 2002. MALLET: A Machine Learning for Language Toolkit. `http://mallet.cs.umass.edu`.

Ben Medlock and Ted Briscoe. 2007. Weakly supervised learning for hedge classification in scientific literature. In *Proc. of the 45th Annual Meeting of the Association of Computational Linguistics*, pages 992–999, Prague, Czech Republic, June. ACL.

Arzucan Özgür and Dragomir R. Radev. 2009. Detecting speculations and their scopes in scientific text. In *EMNLP '09: Proc. of Conf. on Empirical Methods in Natural Language Processing*, pages 1398–1407, Morristown, NJ, USA. ACL.

György Szarvas. 2008. Hedge Classification in Biomedical Texts with a Weakly Supervised Selection of Keywords. In *Proceedings of ACL-08: HLT*, pages 281–289, Columbus, Ohio, June. ACL.

Özlem Uzuner, Xiaoran Zhang, and Tawanda Sibanda. 2009. Machine Learning and Rule-based Approaches to Assertion Classification. *Journal of the American Medical Informatics Association*, 16(1):109–115.

Özlem Uzuner. 2008. Second i2b2 workshop on natural language processing challenges for clinical records. In *AMIA Annual Symposium Proceedings*, pages 1252–3.

Veronika Vincze, György Szarvas, Richárd Farkas, György Móra, and János Csirik. 2008. The BioScope corpus: biomedical texts annotated for uncertainty, negation and their scopes. *BMC Bioinformatics*, 9(Suppl 11):S9.

A Baseline Approach for Detecting Sentences Containing Uncertainty

Erik Tjong Kim Sang
University of Groningen
erikt@xs4all.nl

Abstract

We apply a baseline approach to the CoNLL-2010 shared task data sets on hedge detection. Weights have been assigned to cue words marked in the training data based on their occurrences in certain and uncertain sentences. New sentences received scores that correspond with those of their best scoring cue word, if present. The best acceptance scores for uncertain sentences were determined using 10-fold cross validation on the training data. This approach performed reasonably on the shared task's biological (F=82.0) and Wikipedia (F=62.8) data sets.

1 Introduction

CoNLL-2010 offered two shared tasks which involve finding text parts which express uncertainty or unreliability (Farkas et al., 2010). We focus on Task 1, identifying sentences which contain statements which can be considered uncertain or unreliable. We train a basic statistical model on the training data supplied for the task, apply the trained model to the test data and discuss the results. The next section describes the format of the data and introduces the model that was used. Section three discusses the experiments with the model and their results. Section four concludes the paper.

2 Data and model

The CoNLL-2010 shared task training data sets contain sentences which are classified as either *certain* or *uncertain*. Sentences of the uncertain class contain one or more words which have been marked as indicator of uncertainty, the so-called hedge cues. Here is an example of such a sentence with the hedge cues written in **bold** font:

> These results **indicate that** in monocytic cell lineage, HIV-1 **could** mimic some differentiation/activation stimuli allowing nuclear NF-KB expression.

CoNLL-2010 offers two shared tasks: classifying sentences in running text as either *certain* or *uncertain* (Task 1) and finding hedge cues in sentences classified as *uncertain* together with their scopes (Task 2). We have only participated in Task 1.

We built a basic model for the training data, taking advantage of the fact that the hedge cues were marked explicitly. We estimated the probability of each training data word appearing in a hedge cue with unigram statistics:

$$P(w\ in\ cue) = \frac{f(w\ in\ cue)}{f(w)}$$

where $P(w\ in\ cue)$ is the probability that word w appears in a hedge cue, $f(w)$ is frequency of the word w in the data and $f(w\ in\ c)$ is the frequency of the word inside hedge cues. We performed only little text preprocessing, converting all words to lower case and separating six common punctuation signs from the words.

In the classification stage, we assigned to each word the estimated hedge cue probability according to the training data. Next, we assigned a score to each sentence that was equal to one minus the highest individual score of its words:

$$P(s\ is\ certain) = 1 - \underset{w\ in\ s}{\text{argmax}}\, P(w\ in\ cue)$$

$P(s\ is\ certain)$ is the estimated probability that the sentence s is certain, and it is equal to one minus the highest probability of any of its words being part of a hedge cue. So a sentence containing only words that never appeared as a hedge cue would receive score 1.0. Meanwhile a sentence

Proceedings of the Fourteenth Conference on Computational Natural Language Learning: Shared Task, pages 148–150,
Uppsala, Sweden, 15-16 July 2010.

with a single word that had appeared in a hedge cue in the training data would receive one minus the probability associated with that word. This model ignores any relations between the words of the sentence. We experimented with combining the scores of the different words but found the minimum word score to perform best.

3 Experiments

Apart from the word probabilities, we needed to obtain a good threshold score for deciding whether to classify a sentence as *certain* or *uncertain*. For this purpose, we performed a 10-fold cross-validation experiment on each of the two training data files (biological and Wikipedia) and measured the effect of different threshold values. The results can be found in Figure 1.

The model performed well on the biological training data, with F scores above 80 for a large range of threshold values (0.15–0.85). It performed less well on the Wikipedia training data, with a maximum F score of less than 60 and 50+ scores being limited to the threshold range 0.45–0.85. The maximum F scores were reached for threshold values 0.55 and 0.65 for biological data (F=88.8) and Wikipedia data (F=59.4), respectively. We selected the threshold value 0.55 for our further work because the associated precision and recall values were closer to each other than for value 0.65.

We build domain-specific models with the biological data (14,541 sentences) and the Wikipedia data (11,111 sentences) and applied the models to the related training data. We obtained an F score of 80.2 on the biological data (13th of 20 participants) and a score of 54.4 on the Wikipedia data (9th of 15 participants). The balance between precision and recall scores that we strived for when processing the training data, was not visible in the test results. On the biological test data the system's recall score was 13 points higher than the precision score while on the Wikipedia test data precision outperformed recall by 31 points (see Table 1).

Next, we tested the effect of increasing the data sets with data from another domain. We repeated the cross-validation experiments with the training data, this time adding the available data of the other domain to each of the sets of nine folds used as training data. Unfortunately, this did not result in a performance improvement. The best performance for the biological data dropped to F = 84.2 (threshold 0.60) while the top score for the Wikipedia data dropped to F = 56.5 (0.70).

train-test	thre.	Precis.	Recall	$F_{\beta=1}$
bio-bio	.55	74.3%	87.1%	80.2±1.0
wik-wik	.55	74.0%	43.0%	54.4±0.9
all-bio	.55	69.3%	74.6%	71.8±1.2
all-wik	.55	69.0%	44.6%	54.2±1.0

Table 1: Performances of the models for different combinations of training and test data sets with the associated acceptance threshold values. Training and testing with data from the same domain produces the best scores. Higher recall scores were obtained for biological data than for Wikipedia data. Standard deviations for F scores were estimated with bootstrap resampling (Yeh, 2000).

We kept the threshold value of 0.55, built a model from all available training data and tested its performance on the two test sets. In both cases the performances were lower than the ones obtained with domain dependent training data: F = 71.8 for biological data and F = 54.2 for Wikipedia data (see Table 1).

As post-deadline work, we added statistics for word bigrams to the model, following up work by Medlock (2008), who showed that considering word bigrams had a positive effect on hedge detection. We changed the probability estimation score of words appearing in a hedge cue to

$$P(w_{i-1}w_i\ in\ cue) = \frac{f(w_{i-1}w_i\ in\ cue)}{f(w_{i-1}w_i)}$$

where $w_{i-1}w_i$ is a bigram of successive words in a sentence. Bigrams were considered to be part of a hedge cue when either or both words were inside the hedge cue. Unigram probabilities were used as backoff for known words that appeared outside known bigrams while unknown words received the most common score for known words (0). Sentences received a score which is equal to one minus the highest score of their word bigrams:

$$P(s\ is\ certain) = 1 - \underset{w_{i-1}w_i\ in\ s}{\text{argmax}}\ P(w_{i-1}w_i\ in\ cue)$$

We repeated the threshold estimation experiments and found that new bigram scores enabled the models to perform slightly better on the training

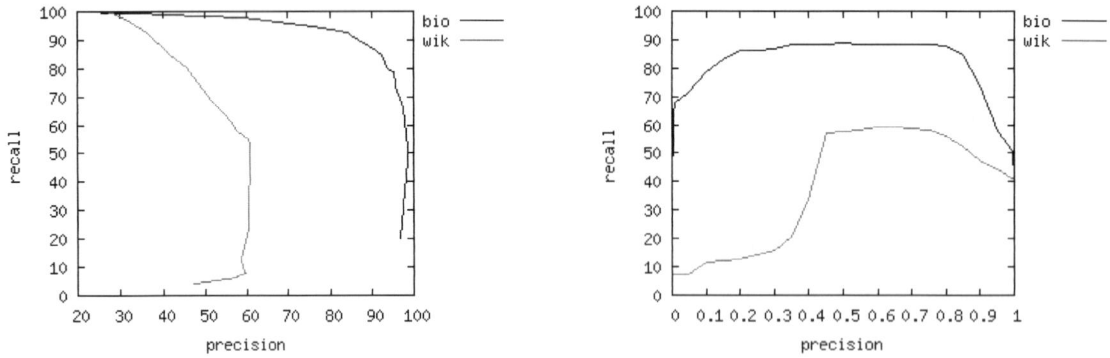

Figure 1: Precision-recall plot (left) and F plot (right) for different values of the certainty acceptance thresholds measured by 10-fold cross-validation experiments on the two shared task training data sets (biological and Wikipedia). The best attained F scores were 88.8 for biological data (threshold 0.55) and 59.4 for Wikipedia data (0.65).

data. The maximum F score for biological training data improved from 88.8 to 90.1 (threshold value 0.35) while the best F score for the Wikipedia training data moved up slightly to 59.8 (0.65).

We applied the bigram models with the two optimal threshold values for the training data to the test data sets. For the biological data, we obtained an F score of 82.0, a borderline significant improvement over the unigram model score. The performance on the Wikipedia data improved significantly, by eight points, to F = 62.8 (see Table 2). This is also an improvement of the official best score for this data set (60.2). We believe that the improvement originates from using the bigram model as well as applying a threshold value that is better suitable for the Wikipedia data set (note that in our unigram experiments we used the same threshold value for all data sets).

train-test	thre.	Precis.	Recall	$F_{\beta=1}$
bio-bio	.35	79.8%	84.4%	82.0±1.1
wik-wik	.65	62.2%	63.5%	62.8±0.8
all-bio	.50	73.2%	77.7%	75.4±1.2
all-wik	.60	63.5%	57.9%	60.6±0.9

Table 2: Performances of bigram models for different combinations of training and test data sets. The bigram models performed better than the unigram models (compare with Table 1).

4 Concluding remarks

We applied a baseline model to the sentence classification part of the CoNLL-2010 shared task on hedge detection. The model performed reasonably on biological data (F=82.0) but less well on Wikipedia data (F=62.8). The model performed best when trained and tested on data of the same domain. Including additional training data from another domain had a negative effect. Adding bigram statistics to the model, improved its performance on Wikipedia data, especially for recall.

Although the model presented in this paper performs reasonably on the hedge detection tasks, it is probably too simple to outperform more complex models. However, we hope to have shown its usefulness as baseline and as possible feature for more advanced models. We were surprised about the large difference in performance of the model on the two data sets. However, similar performance differences were reported by other participants in the shared task, so they seem data-related rather than being an effect of the chosen model. Finding the origin of the performance differences would be an interesting goal for future work.

References

Richárd Farkas, Veronika Vincze, György Móra, János Csirik, and György Szarvas. 2010. The CoNLL-2010 Shared Task: Learning to Detect Hedges and their Scope in Natural Language Text. In *Proc. of the Computational Natural Language Learning (CoNLL-2010): Shared Task*, pages 1–12.

Ben Medlock. 2008. Exploring hedge identification in biomedical literature. *Journal of Biomedical Informatics*, 41:636–654.

Alexander Yeh. 2000. More accurate tests for the statistical significance of result differences. In *Proceedings of the 18th International Conference on Computational Linguistics*, pages 947–953.

Hedge Classification with Syntactic Dependency Features based on an Ensemble Classifier

Yi Zheng, Qifeng Dai, Qiming Luo, Enhong Chen
Department of Computer Science,
University of Science and Technology of China, Hefei, China.
{xiaoe, dqf2008}@mail.ustc.edu.cn
{luoq, cheneh}@ustc.edu.cn

Abstract

We present our CoNLL-2010 Shared Task system in the paper. The system operates in three steps: sequence labeling, syntactic dependency parsing, and classification. We have participated in the Shared Task 1. Our experimental results measured by the in-domain and cross-domain F-scores on the biological domain are 81.11% and 67.99%, and on the Wikipedia domain 55.48% and 55.41%.

1 Introduction

The goals of the Shared Task (Farkas et al., 2010) are: (1) learning to detect sentences containing uncertainty and (2) learning to resolve the in-sentence scope of hedge cues. We have participated in the in-domain and cross-domain challenges of Task 1. Specifically, the aim of Task 1 is to identify sentences in texts that contain unreliable or uncertain information, and it is formulated as a binary classification problem.

Similar to Morante et al. (2009), we use the BIO-cue labels for all tokens in a sentence to predict whether a token is the first one of a hedge cue (B-cue), inside a hedge cue (I-cue), or outside of a hedge cue (O-cue). Thus we formulate the problem at the token level, and our task is to label tokens in every sentence with BIO-cue. Finally, sentences that contain at least one B-cue or I-cue are considered as uncertain.

Our system operates in three steps: sequence labeling, syntactic dependency parsing, and classification. Sequence labeling is a preprocessing step for splitting sentence into tokens and obtaining features of tokens. Then a syntactic dependency parser is applied to obtain the dependency information of tokens. Finally, we employ an ensemble classifier based on combining CRF (conditional random field) and MaxEnt (maximum entropy) classifiers to label each token with the BIO-cue.

Our experiments are conducted on two training data sets: one is the abstracts and full articles from BioScope (biomedical domain) corpus (Vincze et al., 2008)[1], the other one is paragraphs from Wikipedia possibly containing weasel information. Both training data sets have been annotated manually for hedge/weasel cues. The annotation of weasel/hedge cues is carried out at the phrase level. Sentences containing at least one hedge/weasel cue are considered as uncertain, while sentences with no hedge/weasel cues are considered as factual. The results show that employing the ensemble classifier outperforms the single classifier system on the Wikipedia data set, and using the syntactic dependency information in the feature set outperform the system without syntactic dependency information on the biological data set (in-domain).

In related work, Szarvas (2008) extended the methodology of Medlock and Briscoe (2007), and presented a hedge detection method in biomedical texts with a weakly supervised selection of keywords. Ganter and Strube (2009) proposed an approach for automatic detection of sentences containing linguistic hedges using Wikipedia weasel tags and syntactic patterns.

The remainder of this paper is organized as follows. Section 2 presents the technical details of our system. Section 3 presents experimental results and performance analysis. Section 4 presents our discussion of the experiments. Section 5 concludes the paper and proposes future work.

2 System Description

This section describes the implementation of our system.

2.1 Information Flow of Our System

Common classification systems consist of two steps: feature set construction and classification. The feature set construction process of our sys-

[1] http://www.inf.u-szeged.hu/rgai/bioscope

Proceedings of the Fourteenth Conference on Computational Natural Language Learning: Shared Task, pages 151–156,
Uppsala, Sweden, 15-16 July 2010. ©2010 Association for Computational Linguistics

tem consists of sequence labeling and syntactic dependency parsing. Figure 1 shows the main information flow of our system.

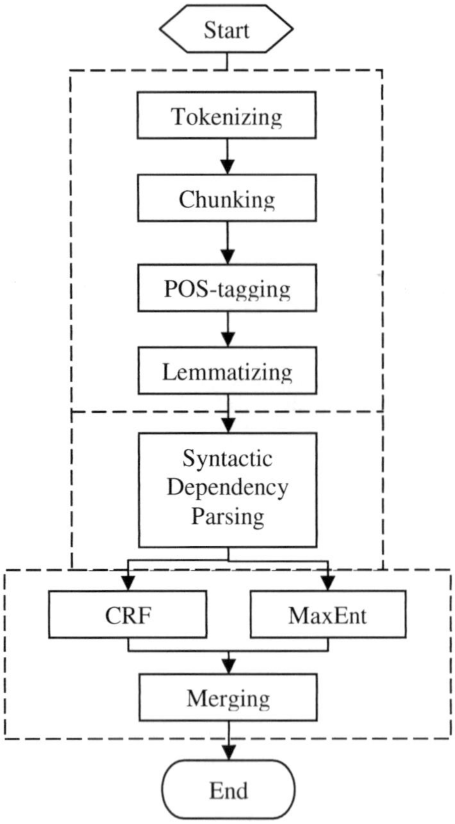

Figure 1: The main information flow of our system

2.2 Sequence labeling

The sequence labeling step consists of the following consecutive stages: (1) tokenizing, (2) chunking, (3) POS-tagging, (4) lemmatizing. Firstly, the PTBTokenizer[2] is employed to split sentence into tokens. Then, tokens are labeled with BIO-tags by the OpenNLP[3] chunker. Finally, Stanford Parser[4] is used to obtain the POS and lemma of tokens.

2.3 Syntactic Dependency Parsing

In the syntactic dependency parsing stage, we use the Stanford Parser again to obtain dependency information of tokens. Based on the Stanford typed dependencies manual (Marneffe and Manning 2008), we have decided to obtain the tree dependencies structure. During the process of parsing, we found that the parser may fail due to either empty sentences or very long sentences. To deal with very long sentences, we decided to allocate more memory. To deal with empty sentences, we decided to simply label them as certain ones because there are only a few empty sentences in the training and test data sets and we could ignore their influence.

2.4 Features

After sequence labeling and syntactic dependency parsing, we obtain candidate features. In our system, all the features belong to the following five categories: (1) token features, (2) dependency features, (3) neighbor features, (4) data features, (5) bigram and trigram features.

Token features of the current token are listed below:

- token: the current token.
- index: index of the current token in the sentence
- pos: POS of the current token.
- lemma: lemma of the current token.
- chunk: BIO-chunk tags of the current token.

Dependency features of the current token are listed below:

- parent_index: the index of the parent token of the current token.
- parent_token: the parent token of the current token.
- parent_lemma: the lemma of the parent token of the current token.
- parent_pos: the POS of the parent token of the current token.
- parent_relation: the dependency relation of the current token and its parent token.

Neighbor features of the current token include token, lemma, pos, chunk tag of three tokens to the right and three to the left.

Data features of current token are listed below:

- type: indicating documentPart[5] type of the sentence which contains the current token, such as Text, SectionTitle and so on.
- domain: distinguishing the Wikipedia and biological domain.
- abstract_article: indicating document type of the sentence which contains the current token, abstract or article.

[2] a tokenizer from Stanford Parser.

[3] http://www.opennlp.org/

[4] http://nlp.stanford.edu/software/lex-parser.shtml

[5] documentPart, SectionTitle, Text and so on are tags in the training and test data sets.

We empirically selected some bigram features and trigram features as listed below:

- left_token_2+left_token_1
- left_token_1+token
- token+right_token_1
- right_token_1+right_token_2
- left_token_2+left_token_1+token
- left_token_1+token+right_token_1
- token+right_token_1+right_token_2

These are the complete set of features for our system. If the value of a feature is empty, we set it to a default value. In the ensemble classifier, we have selected different features for each individual classifier. Details of this are described in the next subsection.

2.5 Classification

In our system, we have combined CRF++[6] and OpenNLP MaxEnt[7] classifiers into an ensemble classifier. The set of features for each classifier are shown in the column named "system" of Table 6. And the two classifiers are used in training and prediction separately, based on their individual set of features. Then we merge the results in this way: for each token, if the two predictions for it are both O-cue, then we label the token with an O-cue; otherwise, we label the token with a B-cue (one of the predictions is B-cue) or an I-cue (no B-cue in the predictions). The motivation of the ensemble classifier approach is based on the observation of our internal experiments using 10-fold cross validation, which we describe in Section 3. In addition, the parameters of OpenNLP MaxEnt classifier are all set to default values (number of iterations is 100, cutoff is 0 and without smoothing). For CRF++, we only set the option "-f" as 3 and the option "-c" as 1.5, and the others are set to default values.

3 Experimental Results

We have participated in four subtasks, biological in-domain challenge (Bio-in-domain), biological cross-domain challenge (Bio-cross-domain), Wikipedia in-domain challenge (Wiki-in-domain) and Wikipedia cross-domain challenge (Wiki-cross-domain). In all the experiments, TP, FP, FN and F-Score for the uncertainty class are used as the performance measures. We have tested our system with the test data set and obtained official results as shown in Table 1. In addition, we have performed several internal experiments on the training data set and several experiments on the test data set, which we describe in the next two subsections. The feature sets used for each subtask in our system are shown in Table 6, where each column denotes a feature set named after the title of the column ("System", "dep", ...). Actually, for different subtasks, we make use of the same feature set named "system".

SubTask	TP	FP	FN	F-Score
Bio-in-domain	717	261	73	81.11
Bio-cross-domain	566	309	224	67.99
Wiki-in-domain	974	303	1260	55.48
Wiki-cross-domain	991	352	1243	55.41

Table 1: Official results of our system.

3.1 Internal Experiments

Initially we only used a single classifier instead of an ensemble classifier. We performed 10-fold cross validation experiments on the training data set at the sentence level with different feature sets. The results of these experiments are shown in Table 2 and Table 3.

In internal experiments, we mainly focus on the results of different models and different feature sets. In Table 2 and Table 3, CRF and ME (MaxEnt) indicate the two classifiers; ENSMB stands for the ensemble classifier obtained by combining CRF and MaxEnt classifiers; the three words "dep", "neighbor" and "together" indicate the feature sets for different experiments shown in Table 6, and "together" is the union set of "dep" and "neighbor".

The results of ME and CRF experiments (third column of Table 2 and Table 3) show that the individual classifier wrongly predicts many uncertain sentences as certain ones. The number of such errors is much greater than the number of errors of predicting certain ones as uncertain. In other words, FN is greater than FP in our experiments and the recall ratio is very low, especially for the Wikipedia data set.

[6] http://crfpp.sourceforge.net/
[7] http://maxent.sourceforge.net/

Experiment	Biological in-domain				Biological cross-domain			
	TP	FP	FN	F-Score	TP	FP	FN	F-Score
ME-dep	244	28	34	88.73	220	24	58	84.29
CRF-dep	244	20	34	90.04	230	19	48	87.29
ENSMB-dep	248	32	30	88.89	235	28	43	86.88
ME-neighbor	229	14	49	87.91	211	12	67	84.23
CRF-neighbor	244	16	34	90.71	228	21	50	86.53
ENSMB-neighbor	247	22	31	90.31	241	26	37	88.44
ME-together	234	11	44	89.48	205	12	73	82.83
CRF-together	247	13	31	91.82	234	21	44	87.80
ENSMB-together	253	17	25	**92.36**	242	26	36	**88.64**

Table 2: Results of internal experiments on the biological training data set.

Experiment	Wikipedia in-domain				Wikipedia cross-domain			
	TP	FP	FN	F-Score	TP	FP	FN	F-Score
ME-dep	131	91	117	55.74	145	108	103	57.88
CRF-dep	108	51	140	53.07	115	60	133	54.37
ENSMB-dep	148	103	100	59.32	153	119	95	58.85
ME-neighbor	106	52	142	52.22	130	77	118	57.14
CRF-neighbor	123	44	125	59.28	123	72	125	55.53
ENSMB-neighbor	145	71	103	**62.50**	154	116	94	**59.46**
ME-together	100	57	148	49.38	117	69	131	53.92
CRF-together	125	54	123	58.55	127	67	121	57.47
ENSMB-together	141	83	107	59.75	146	104	102	58.63

Table 3: Results of internal experiments on the Wikipedia training data set.

Experiment	Biological in-domain				Biological cross-domain			
	TP	FP	FN	F-Score	TP	FP	FN	F-Score
System-ME	650	159	140	81.30	518	265	272	65.86
System-CRF	700	197	90	**82.99**	464	97	326	**68.69**
System-ENSMB	717	261	73	81.11	566	309	224	67.99

Table 4: Results of additional experiment of biological test data set.

Experiment	Wikipedia in-domain				Wikipedia cross-domain			
	TP	FP	FN	F-Score	TP	FP	FN	F-Score
System-ME	794	235	1440	48.67	798	284	1436	48.13
System-CRF	721	112	1513	47.02	747	153	1487	47.67
System-ENSMB	974	303	1260	**55.48**	991	352	1243	**55.41**

Table 5: Results of additional experiment of Wikipedia test data set.

Based on this analysis, we propose an ensemble classifier approach to decrease FN in order to improve the recall ratio. The results of the ensemble classifier show that: along with the decreasing of FN, FP and TP are both increasing. Although the recall ratio increases, the precision ratio decreases at the same time. Therefore, the ensemble classifier approach is a trade-off between precision and recall. For data sets with low recall ratio, such as Wikipedia, the ensemble classifier outperforms each single classifier in terms of F-score, just as the ME, CRF and ENSMB experiments show in Table 2 and Table 3.

In addition, we have performed simple feature selection in the internal experiments. The comparison of "dep", "neighbor" and "together" experiments shown in Table 2 demonstrates that the dependency and neighbor features are both beneficial only for the biological in-domain experiment. This may be because that sentences of the biological data are more regular than those of the Wikipedia data.

3.2 Additional experiments on test data set

We have also performed experiments on the test data set, and the results are shown in Table 4 and Table 5. With the same set of features of our system as shown in Table 6, we have performed three experiments: System-ME (ME denotes MaxEnt classifier), System-CRF (CRF denotes CRF classifier) and System-ENSMB (ENSMB denotes ensemble classifier), where "System" denotes the feature set in Table 6. The meanings of these words are similar to internal experiments.

As Table 4 and Table 5 show, for the Wikipedia test data set, the ensemble classifier outperforms each single classifier in terms of F-score by improving the recall ratio with a larger extent than the extent of the decreasing of the precision ratio. For the biological test data set, the ensemble classifier outperforms System-ME but underperforms System-CRF. This may be due to the relatively high values of the precision and recall ratios already obtained by each single classifier.

4 Discussion

The features in our experiments are selected empirically, and the performance of our system could be improved with more elaborate feature selection. From the experimental results, we observe that there are still many uncertain sentences predicted as certain ones. This indicates that the ability of learning uncertain information with the current classifiers and feature sets needs to be improved. We had the plan of exploring the ensemble classifier by combining CRF, MaxEnt and SVM (Support Vector Machine), but it was given up due to limited time. In addition, we were not able to complete experiments with MaxEnt classifier based on bigram and trigram features due to limited time. Actually only two labels I and O are needed for Task 1. We have not done the experiments with only I and O labels, and we plan to do it in the future.

According to our observation, the low F-score on the Wikipedia data set is due to many uncertain phrases. By contrast, for the biological data set, the uncertain information consists of mostly single words rather than phrases. It is difficult for a classifier to learn uncertain information consisting of 3 words or more. As we have observed, these uncertain phrases follow several patterns. A hybrid approach based on rule-based and statistical approaches to recognize them seems to be a promising.

5 Conclusion and Future Work

Our CoNLL-2010 Shared Task system operates in three steps: sequence labeling, syntactic dependency parsing, and classification. The results show that employing the ensemble classifier outperforms each single classifier for the Wikipedia data set, and using the syntactic dependency information in the feature set outperform the system without syntactic dependency information for the biological data set (in-domain). Our final system achieves promising results. Due to limited time, we have only performed simple feature selection empirically. In the future, we plan to explore more elaborate feature selection and explore ensemble classifier by combining more classifiers.

Acknowledgments

The work was supported by the National Natural Science Foundation of China (No.60775037), the National High Technology Research and Development Program of China (863 Program, No.2009 AA01Z123), and Specialized Research Fund for the Doctoral Program of Higher Education (No.20093402110017).

References

Richárd Farkas, Veronika Vincze, György Móra, János Csirik, and György Szarvas. 2010. The CoNLL-2010 Shared Task: Learning to Detect Hedges and their Scope in Natural Language Text. In *Proceedings of CoNLL-2010: Shared Task*, pages 1–12.

Viola Ganter, and Michael Strube. 2009. Finding hedges by chasing weasels: Hedge detection using Wikipedia tags and shallow linguistic features. In *Proceedings of the ACL-IJCNLP 2009 Conference Short Papers*, pages 173–176.

Marie-Catherine de Marneffe, and Christopher D. Manning. 2008. *Stanford typed dependencies manual*, September 2008.

Ben Medlock, and Ted Briscoe. 2007. Weakly supervised learning for hedge classification in scientific literature. In *Proc. of ACL 2007*, pages 992–999.

Roser Morante, and Walter Daelemans. 2009. Learning the scope of hedge cues in biomedical texts. In *Proc. of the BioNLP 2009 Workshop*, pages 28–36.

György Szarvas. 2008. Hedge classification in biomedical texts with a weakly supervised selection of keywords. In *Proc. of ACL 2008*, pages 281–289.

Veronika Vincze, György Szarvas, Richárd Farkas, György Móra, and János Csirik. 2008. The BioScope corpus: biomedical texts annotated for uncertainty, negation and their scopes. *BMC Bioinformatics*, 9(Suppl 11):S9.

Feature	System	Dep	Neighbor	Together
token	mc	mc	mc	mc
index	m	m	m	m
pos	mc	mc	mc	mc
lemma	mc	mc	mc	mc
chunk		mc	mc	mc
parent_index	mc	mc		mc
parent_token		mc		mc
parent_lemma	mc	mc		mc
parent_relation	mc	mc		mc
parent_pos	mc	mc		mc
left_token_1	c		c	c
left_lemma_1	mc		mc	mc
left_pos_1	mc		mc	mc
left_chunk_1			mc	mc
left_token_2	c		c	c
left_lemma_2	c		mc	mc
left_pos_2	mc		mc	mc
left_chunk_2			mc	mc
left_token_3				
left_lemma_3	mc		m	m
left_pos_3	mc		m	m
left_chunk_3			m	m
right_token_1	c		c	c
right_lemma_1	mc		mc	mc
right _pos_1	mc		mc	mc
right _chunk_1			mc	mc
right_token_2	c		c	c
right _lemma_2	mc		mc	mc
right _pos_2	c		mc	mc
right _chunk_2			mc	mc
right_token_3				
right _lemma_3	c		m	m
right _pos_3	mc		m	m
right _chunk_3			m	m
type	m	mc	mc	mc
domain	m	mc	mc	mc
abstract_article	m	mc	mc	mc
left_token_2+left_token_1	c		c	c
left_token_1+token	c		c	c
token+right_token_1	c		c	c
right_token_1+right_token_2	c		c	c
left_token_2+left_token_1+token	c		c	c
left_token_1+token+right_token_1	c		c	c
token+right_token_1+right_token_2	c		c	c

Table 6: Features selected for different experiments. The symbol m indicates MaxEnt classifier and c indicates CRF classifier.

Author Index